Australian

Signpost MATHS

5

Mentals

Alan McSeveny

Rachel McSeveny

Pearson Australia
(a division of Pearson Australia Group Pty Ltd)
459–471 Church Street, Level 1, Building B, Richmond, Victoria 3121
PO Box 23360, Melbourne, Victoria 8012
www.pearson.com.au

First published 2018 by Pearson Australia
2028 2027 2026 2025
10 9 8 7 6 5 4 3 2 1

Content and Learning Specialist: Sophie Matta
Project Manager: Shelly Wang
Production Manager: Elizabeth Gosman
Editor: Nicola Krogdahl
Designers: Anne Donald & Jennifer Johnston
Cover Designer: Jennifer Johnston
Rights & Permissions Editor: Samantha Russell-Tulip
Senior Publishing Services Analyst: Rob Currulli
Cover art: Michael Barter
Cover background: rf_vector/Shutterstock.com
Illustrators: Michael Barter, Wendy Gorton, John Winter

Printed in Australia by Pegasus Media and Logistics

ISBN 978 1 4886 2189 5

Pearson Australia Group Pty Ltd ABN 40 004 245 943

Some of the images used in *Australian Signpost Maths 5 Mentals* might have associations with deceased Indigenous Australians. Please be aware that these images might cause sadness or distress in Aboriginal or Torres Strait Islander communities.

Introduction

Using the Mentals Books

Each unit of the Mentals Book is programmed to review Student Book content for the previous two weeks (based on the Suggested Program in the Teacher's Book). For example, Unit 15 of the Mentals Book can be set as homework to review weeks 13 and 14 of the Student Book while week 15 is being taught.

Presentation

- The content of the strands Number and Algebra, Measurement and Geometry, and Statistics and Probability is covered thoroughly.
- Essential skills are explained.
- Language, problem solving, graphs and tables are given a high profile.
- Mathematics is applied to real-life situations wherever possible.
- The **Arithmetic Card** (page 5) is an exciting teaching tool for practising basic number skills.
- **ID Cards** (pages 6 to 9) review the terms essential to success in the course.
- **Measurement examples** and **tables** (page 84 and inside back cover) are provided so that students can estimate effectively.

Mixed-topic Questions

The units present questions in a mixed-topic format.

- This is essential for thorough understanding and continuous review.
- In real life, similar questions don't often occur together.
- It allows the teacher to discover weaknesses that could otherwise pass unnoticed.
- It provides a real test of understanding.

Graded Questions

- Column 1: easier
- Columns 2 and 3: harder
- Column 4: Extension and Challenge

Motivation

- Cartoons make mathematics more appealing.
- There are two lizards hidden on each page for students to find.

Extra Activities

- Problem solving **strategies** are introduced in a carefully planned sequence throughout the series.

- Important concepts from **Number and Algebra** and **Measurement and Geometry** are explored.

- **Measurement** concepts and activities are introduced and investigated.

- **Statistics and Probability** concepts (Data and Chance) are presented for revision and extension.

- A **tables** program for each of the four operations is included.
- It is important for students to try to learn addition and multiplication tables by heart.

 • *AUSTRALIAN SIGNPOST MATHS 5 MENTALS* • ISBN 978 1 4886 2189 5

5 Contents

Unit Activities

Unit	Content	Extra Activity	Unit	Content	Extra Activity
1:1/2 **1:3/4**	× 2, × 4 Personal measures	× tables Measure	**20:1/2** **20:3/4**	÷ 3, ÷ 6 Compass directions	÷ tables Concept
2:1/2 **2:3/4**	× 10, × 5 – 3, – 7	× tables – tables	**21:1/2** **21:3/4**	2D Space Problem Solving	Concept Strategy time
3:1/2 **3:3/4**	× 3, × 4 Problem Solving	× tables Strategy time	**22:1/2** **22:3/4**	Area and perimeter Language	Strategy time ID Card C
4:1/2 **4:3/4**	× 3, × 6 Problem Solving	× tables Strategy time	**23:1/2** **23:3/4**	÷ 7, ÷ 8 Roman numerals	÷ tables Concept
5:1/2 **5:3/4**	× 7 Division	× tables ÷ tables	**24:1/2** **24:3/4**	– 3, – 5, – 9 Division	– tables ÷ tables
6:1/2 **6:3/4**	× 8 Division	× tables ÷ tables	**25:1/2** **25:3/4**	× 3, × 6 Problem Solving	× tables Strategy time
7:1/2 **7:3/4**	× 9 Language	× tables ID Card A	**26:1/2** **26:3/4**	× 9, × 7 Problem Solving	× tables Strategy time
8:1/2 **8:3/4**	– 6, – 8 Problem Solving	– tables Strategy time	**27:1/2** **27:3/4**	Perimeter Language	Measure ID Card A
9:1/2 **9:3/4**	Problem Solving Rounding off	Strategy time Concept	**28:1/2** **28:3/4**	Perimeter Number patterns	Measure Concept
10:1/2 **10:3/4**	Factors × 2, × 5, × 4, × 10, × 0, × 1	Concept × tables	**29:1/2** **29:3/4**	Perimeter × 6, × 7, × 8	Measure × tables
11:1/2 **11:3/4**	Problem Solving × 10, × 5	Strategy time × tables	**30:1/2** **30:3/4**	Is this game fair? Language	Chance ID Card D
12:1/2 **12:3/4**	Dot plots Language	Data ID Card D	**31:1/2** **31:3/4**	× 3, × 5, × 9 Codes	× tables Concept
13:1/2 **13:3/4**	Dot plots Area	Data Measure	**32:1/2** **32:3/4**	÷ 2, ÷ 4 Magic squares	÷ tables Concept
14:1/2 **14:3/4**	Division with remainders × 3, × 6	Concept × tables	**33:1/2** **33:3/4**	Language Roman numerals	ID Card B Concept
15:1/2 **15:3/4**	Division with remainders – 9, – 5	Concept – tables	**34:1/2** **34:3/4**	Comparing chance × 9, ÷ 9	Chance ×, ÷ tables
16:1/2 **16:3/4**	Chance as a fraction 15 -, 16 -	Chance – tables	**35:1/2** **35:3/4**	Rounding money Mass	Concept Strategy time
17:1/2 **17:3/4**	Using a graph Language	Concept ID Card B	**36:1/2** **36:3/4**	× 4, × 9 Problem solving	× tables Strategy time
18:1/2 **18:3/4**	The jump strategy × 7, × 8	Strategy time × tables	**37:1/2** **37:3/4**	Language Personal measures	ID Card C Measure
19:1/2 **19:3/4**	Compass points × 8, × 6	Concept × tables	**Answers**	These can be found in the middle of this book on pages A1 to A12.	

Arithmetic Card

	A	B	C	D	E	F	G	H	I	J	K	L	M
1	20	9	110	20	6	11	$100	$\frac{67}{100}$	0·52	97%	$\frac{56}{100}$	0·68	67
2	16	1	170	50	14	21	$32	$\frac{3}{100}$	0·2	52%	$\frac{8}{100}$	0·7	62
3	12	6	200	10	2	27	$48	$\frac{75}{100}$	0·75	39%	$\frac{27}{100}$	0·8	50
4	18	2	130	70	18	25	$90	$\frac{46}{100}$	0·39	74%	$\frac{15}{100}$	0·4	41
5	13	8	160	100	10	13	$117	$\frac{5}{100}$	0·4	63%	$\frac{88}{100}$	0·75	33
6	15	5	180	30	16	17	$150	$\frac{9}{100}$	0·98	6%	$\frac{42}{100}$	1	26
7	19	3	150	80	4	29	$76	$\frac{14}{100}$	0·67	18%	$\frac{74}{100}$	0·69	19
8	14	7	190	60	12	15	$28	$\frac{83}{100}$	0·5	45%	$\frac{66}{100}$	1·2	14
9	11	4	140	90	20	23	$55	$\frac{6}{100}$	0·13	87%	$\frac{39}{100}$	0·13	7
10	17	10	120	40	8	19	$85	$\frac{1}{100}$	0·8	21%	$\frac{95}{100}$	0·88	3

How to Use this Card

If students were told to "subtract B from C", they would write:

1. 110 – 9 = 101
2. 170 – 1 = 169
3. 200 – 6 = 194
4. 130 – 2 = 128
5. 160 – 8 = 152
6. 180 – 5 = 175
7. 150 – 3 = 147
8. 190 – 7 = 183
9. 140 – 4 = 136
10. 120 – 10 = 110

Other instructions might be:

- **What is left from $200 if I spend the amount in column G?**
- **What multiplied by 10 gives column C?**
- **Write column J as a decimal.**
- **Add column B to column F.**
- **Multiply column B by 4.**
- **Add columns A and C.**
- **Add columns H and K.**
- **Subtract column B from column A.**
- **Halve column E.**

The applications of this card are endless.

ID Card A

Do not write on this card.

1 **m** stands for m______.	**2** **mm** stands for m______.	**3** **cm** stands for c______.	**4** **km** stands for k______.	**5** **L** stands for l______.
6 **mL** stands for m______.	**7** **g** stands for g______.	**8** **kg** stands for k______.	**9** **s** stands for s______.	**10** **min** stands for m______.
11 **h** stands for h______.	**12** **cm^2** stands for s______ c______.	**13** **m^2** stands for s______ m______.	**14** **ha** stands for h______.	**15** **cm^3** stands for c______ c______.
16 **m^3** stands for c______ m______.	**17** **°C** stands for d______ C______.	**18** **5 groups of 7** means 5 ____ 7	**19** **4 rows of 10** means 4 ____ 10	**20** **Share 20 among 5** means 20 ____ 5
21 **How many groups of 6 in 42?** means 42 ____ 6	**22** **1, 2, 3, …** are the c ______ numbers.	**23** **2, 4, 6, …** are the e ______ numbers.	**24** **1, 3, 5, …** are the o ______ numbers	**25** **1st, 2nd, …** are the o ______ numbers
26 **72 086** has 5 d______.	**27** **The factors of 8** are 1, 8, ______ and ______.	**28** **7, 14, 21, …** are multiples of ______.	**29** **35, 40 and 45** are all divisible by ______.	**30** **$5\overline{)47}$ = 9 r 2** 'r' means r______.

See page A1 for answers.

ID Card B

Do not write on this card.

1

A ray is part of a l________.

2

straight l________

3

c________ line

4

w________ line

5

z________ line

6
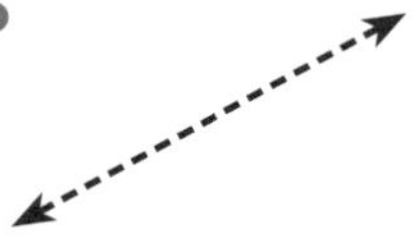
d________ line

7

p________ lines

8

p________ lines

9

h________ line

10

v________ line

11
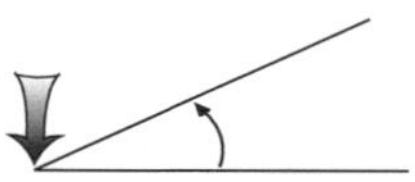
c________ (or vertex) of an angle

12
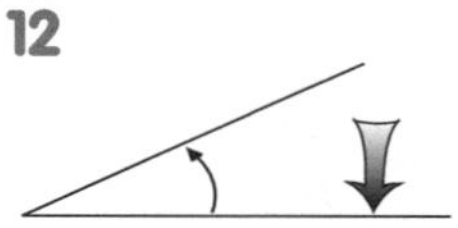
a________ of an angle

13
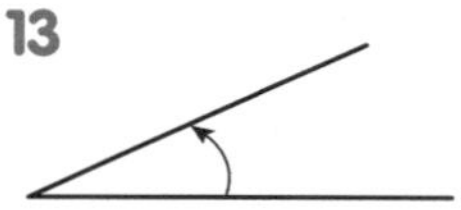
a________ angle

14
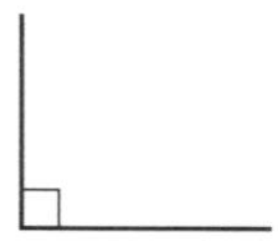
r________ angle

15
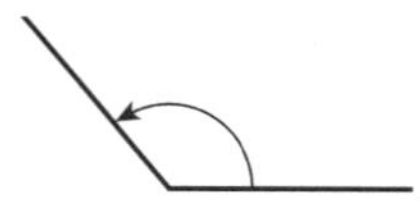
o________ angle

16

s________ angle

17
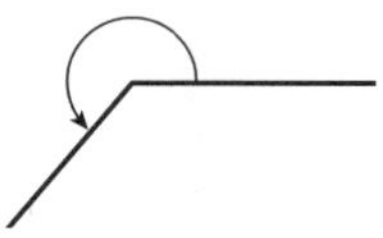
r________ angle

18
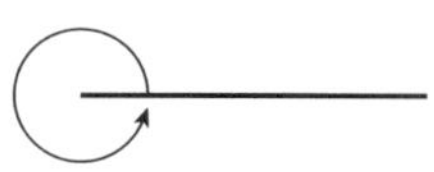
r________

19
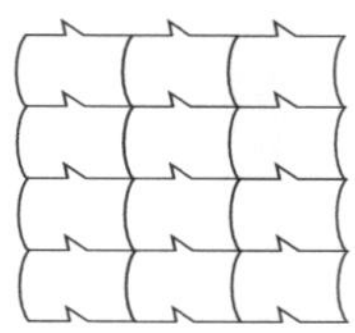
t________

20
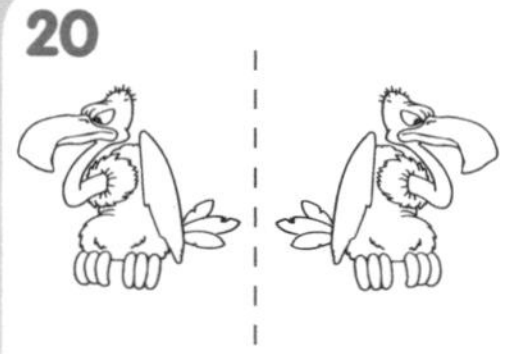
f________

21

s________

22
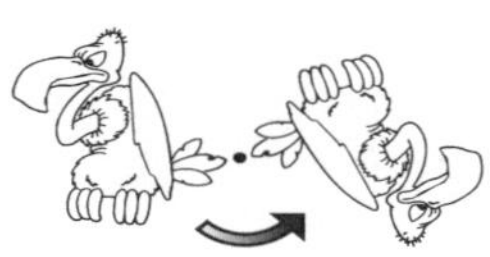
t________

23
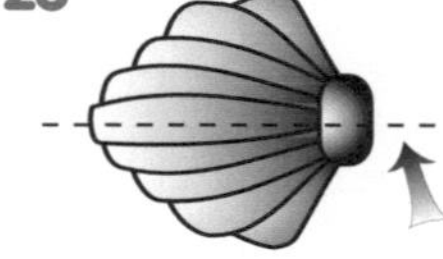
axis of s________

24
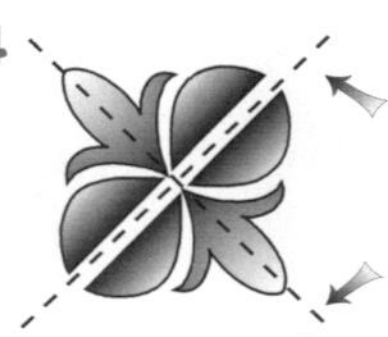
a________ of symmetry

25
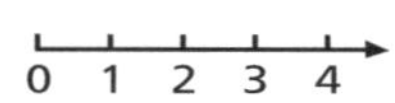

n________ line

26
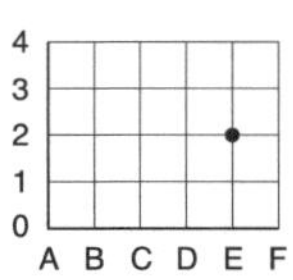

The c________ of the dot are **E2**.

27

p________ graph

28
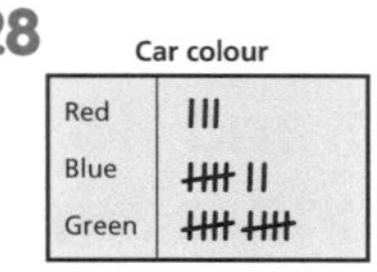

This is a t________.

29
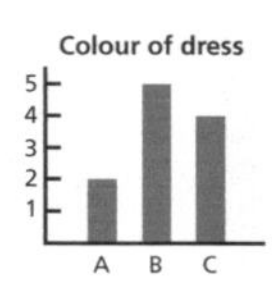

c________ graph

30

l________ graph

See page A1 for answers.

ID Card C

Do not write on this card.

1

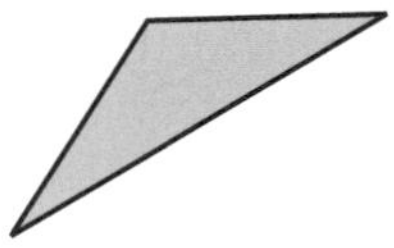

t ________

2

s ________

3

r ________

4

p ________

5

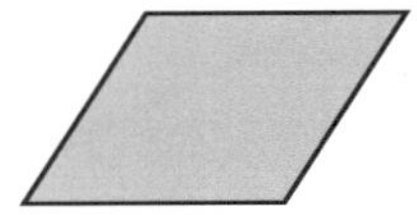

r ________

6

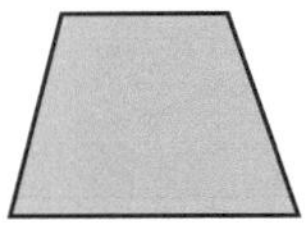

t ________

7

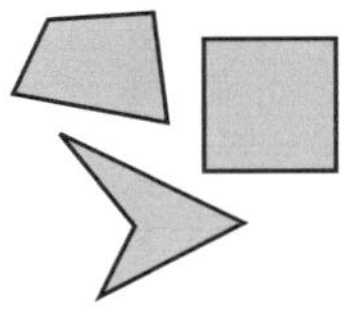

q ________

8

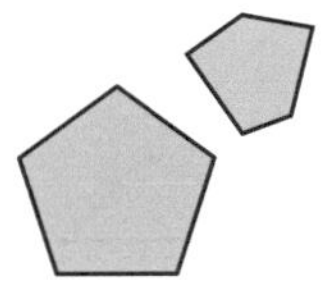

p ________

9

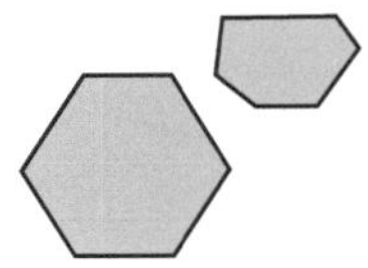

h ________

10

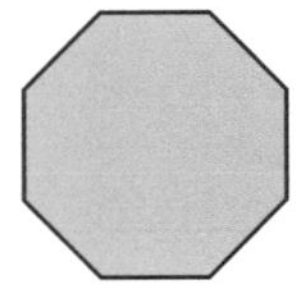

o ________

11

c ________

12

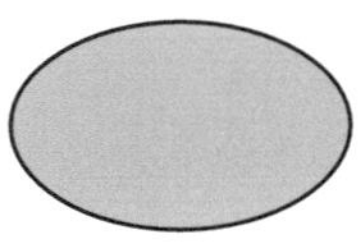

o ________

13

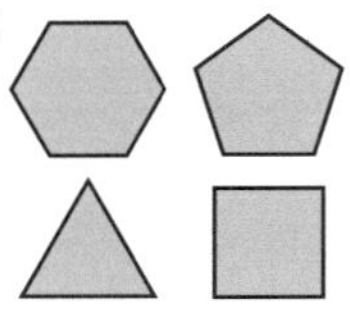

r ________ shapes

14

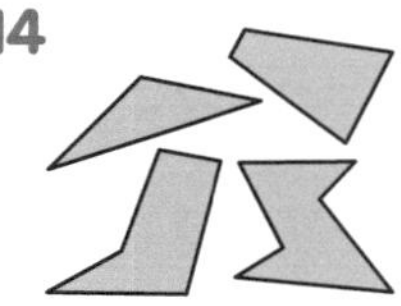

i ________ shapes

15

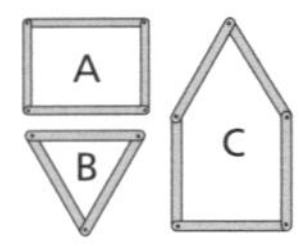

Shape ______ is rigid.

16

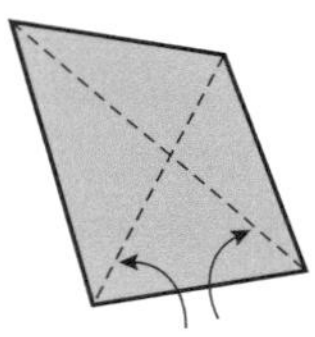

d ________

17

3

1 square

m ________

18

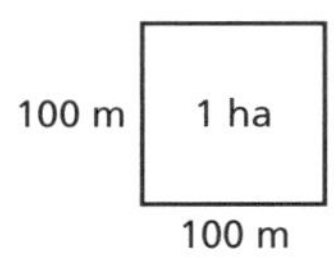

This area is

1 h________.

19

$$\frac{3}{8}$$

means

3 out of ______.

20

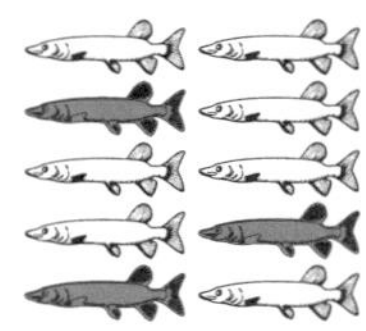

$\frac{\quad}{10}$ shaded

21

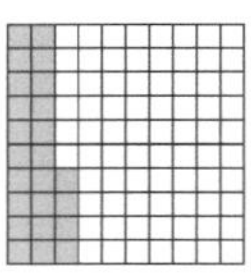

$\frac{\quad}{100}$ shaded

22

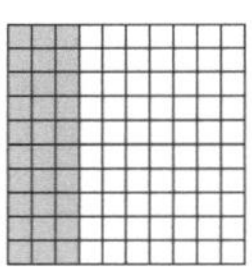

$\frac{\quad}{10}$ shaded

23

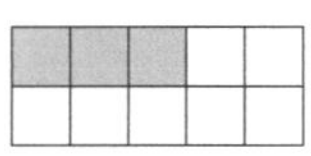

0·___ shaded

24

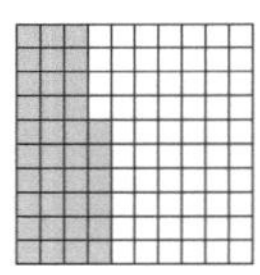

0·___ shaded

25

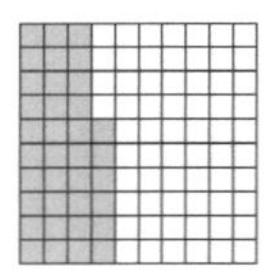

___ tenths and

___ hundredths

26

19%

means

19 out of ____.

27

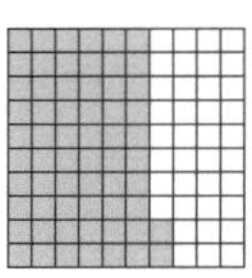

________ %

shaded

28

1 and 36 hundredths

is

____·____

29

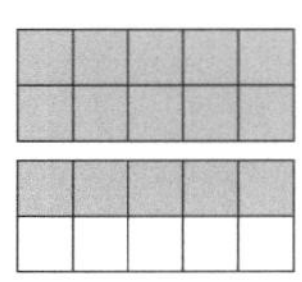

is

____·____

30

Complete:

$0{\cdot}3 = \frac{\quad}{10}$

$0{\cdot}30 = \frac{\quad}{10}$

See page A1 for answers.

ID Card D

Do not write on this card.

1

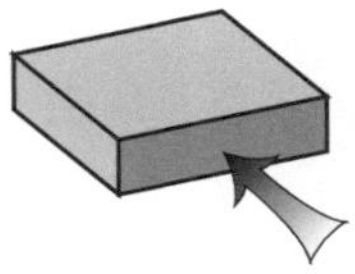

f ________

2

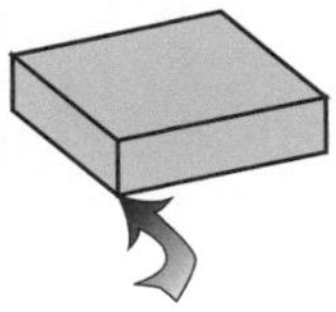

v ________
or c ________

3

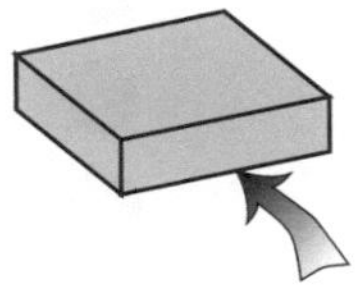

e ________

4

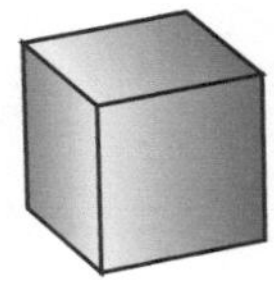

c ________

5

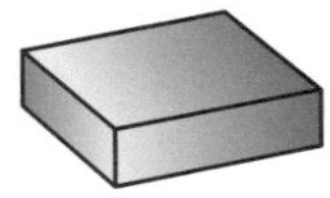

r ________
p ________

6

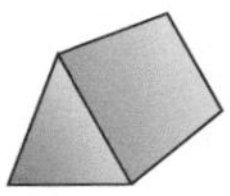

t ________
p ________

7

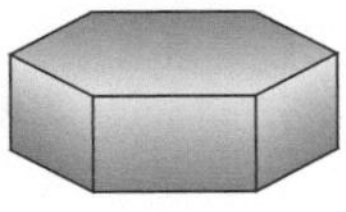

h ________
p ________

8

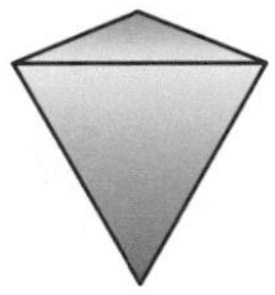

t ________
p ________

9

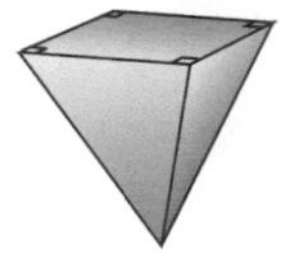

s ________
p ________

10

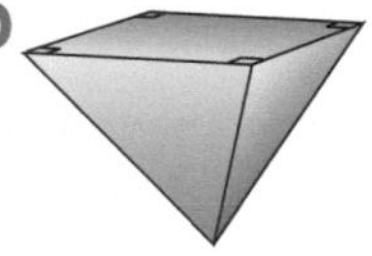

r ________
p ________

11

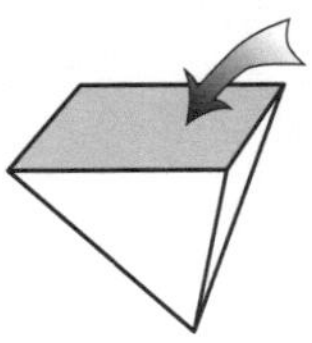

b ________

12

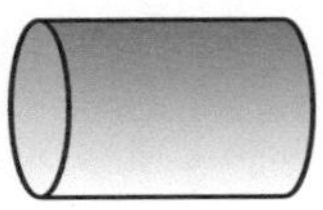

c ________

13

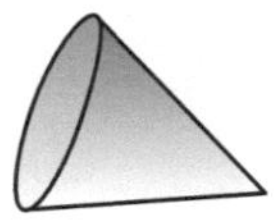

c ________

14

s ________

15

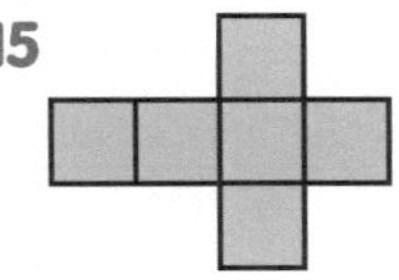

net of a
c ________

16

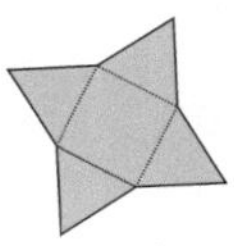

net of a
s ________
p ________

17

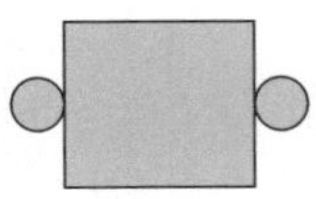

net of a
c ________

18

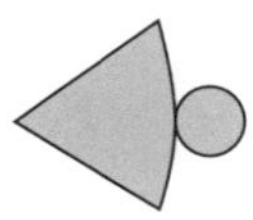

net of a
c ________

19

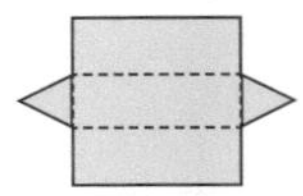

net of a
t ________
p ________

20

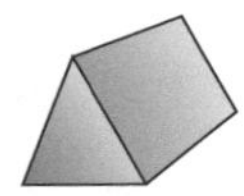

Side view is:

21

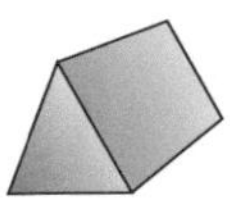

Front view is:

22

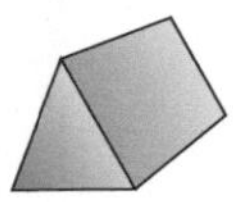

Top view is:

23

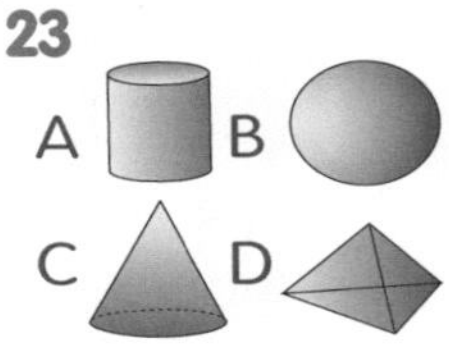

________ will not roll.

24

7:30 pm

in 24-hour time
is
____:____

25

05:40

in digital time
is
____:____ am

26

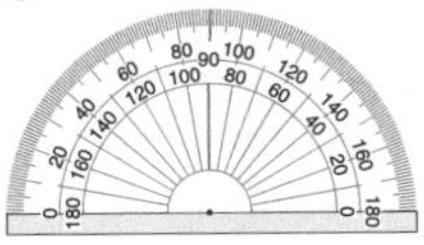

p ________

27

pair of
c ________

28

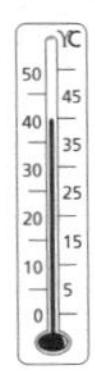

t ________

29

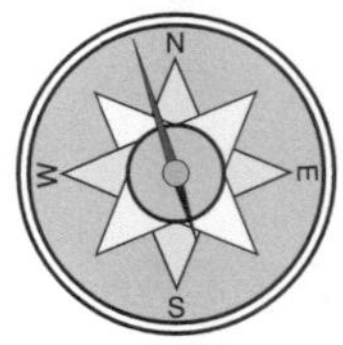

c ________

30

t ________
m ________

See page A1 for answers.

1:1 ☐ out of 15

❶ 7 + 8 ______

❷ 12 – 9 ______

❸ 4 × 2 ______

❹ 8 + 6 ______

❺
```
  18
+ 11
────
```

❻ 13 – 4 ______

❼ 3 × 3 ______

❽ 9 plus 5. ______

❾ 4 groups of 5. ______

❿
```
  15
–  4
────
```

⓫ Write these numbers on the place value chart.

a 4280 b 2893 c 724

	Thousands	Hundreds	Tens	Units
a				
b				
c				

⓬ 34 6 9 12 13

a Which of these are odd? ______

b Which of these are even? ______

⓭ Write the numeral for nine hundred and forty-two. ______

⓮ Write 65c in decimal form. ______

⓯ Seth made 20 cakes.

He gave 2 to his Nan, 1 to his Dad, and 3 to friends. How many cakes did he have left?

______

1:2 ☐ out of 17

❶ 12 + 7 ______

❷ 16 + 4 ______

❸ 10 – 7 ______

❹ 11 – 6 ______

❺
```
  67
+ 22
────
```

❻ 9 × 2 ______

❼ 7 × 4 ______

❽ 17 subtract 7. ______

❾ 20 minus 12. ______

❿
```
  79
– 43
────
```

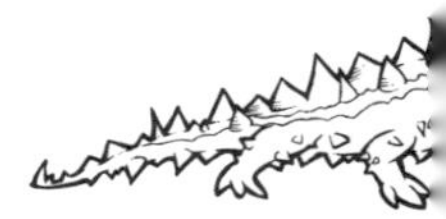

⓫ Change from $2 if I spend:

a $1.15 ______ b $0.85 ______

⓬ Of 38 biscuits, 28 were eaten.

How many were left?

______

⓭ Name 2 coins that together make 30 cents.

______ ______

⓮ What fraction is shaded?

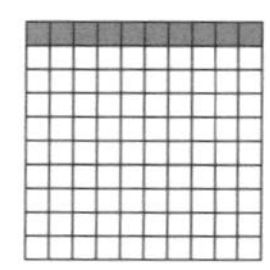

______ out of ______

⓯ 6 photos fill a page. How many pages can be filled by 24 photos? ______

⓰ Which is smaller, 3632 or 3622? ______

⓱
a

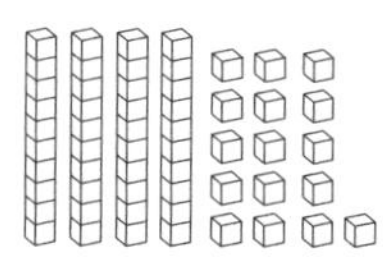

56 – 29 = ______

b

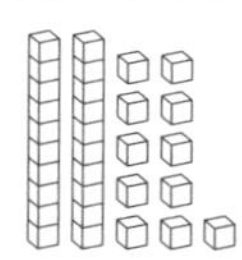

31 – 16 = ______

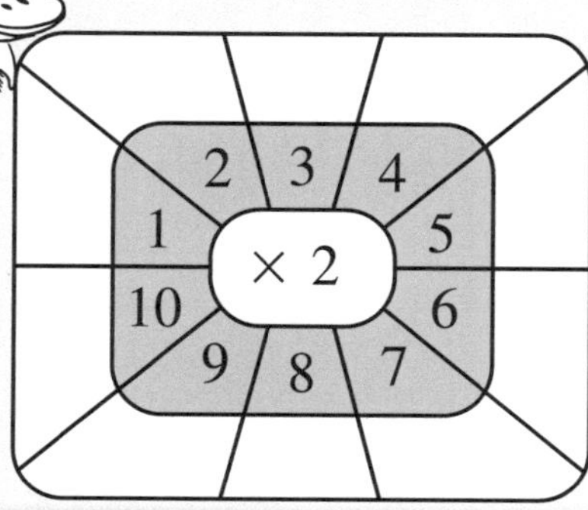

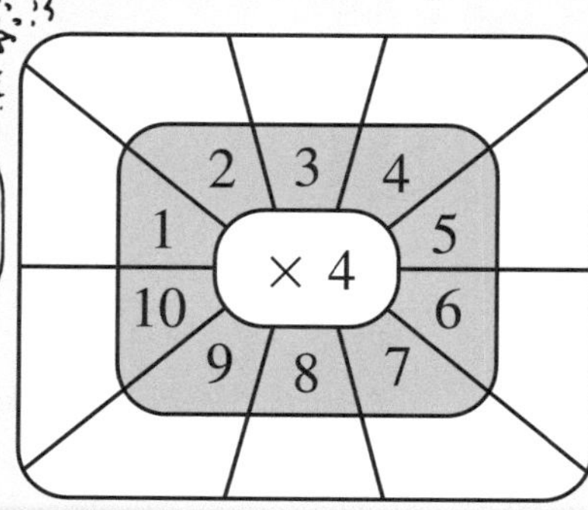

1:3 ☐ out of 14

1. $\begin{array}{r} 79 \\ +213 \\ \hline \end{array}$

2. $\begin{array}{r} 172 \\ +\ \ 56 \\ \hline \end{array}$

3. $\begin{array}{r} 421 \\ +\ \ 99 \\ \hline \end{array}$

4. $9\overline{)27}$

5. $7\overline{)42}$

6. $9\overline{)72}$

7. Write the numeral modelled here. ______

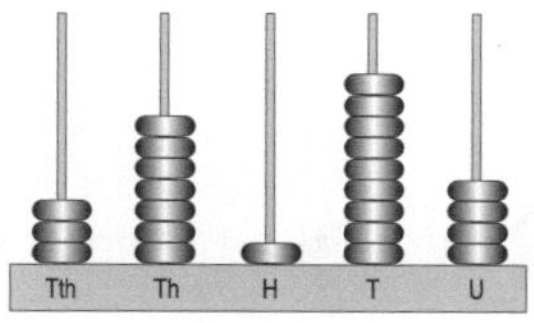

8. A farmer had 87 sheep and sold 52. How many did she have left? ______

9. What fraction is shown? ______

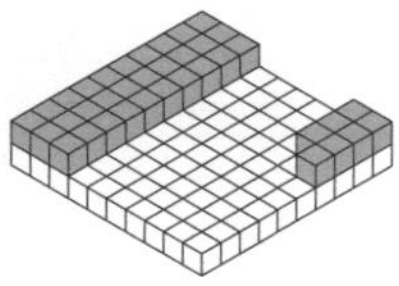

10. Add 20 each time.

14, ______, ______, ______, ______

11. The next odd number after 31. ______

12. How many sides has a quadrilateral? ______

13. **a** Subtract 5 from 9. ______

b The product of 5 and 9.

14. 4 girls shared 44 grapes. How many grapes was each girl given? ______

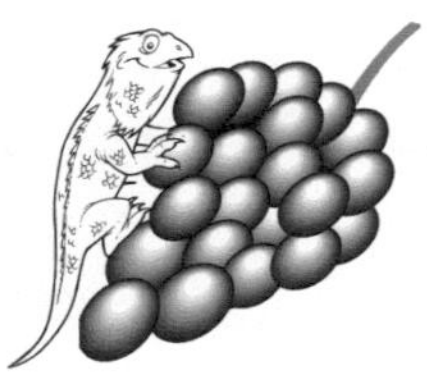

1:4 Extension ☐ out of 6

1. 349 + 34 ______

2. **a** 111 more than 1 232. ______

b 212 more than 3 400. ______

3. Alex had 4 ice-cream containers with 4 000 mL of ice-cream in each. How many litres did she have? ______

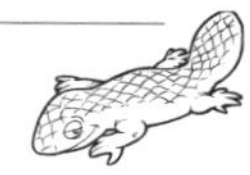

4. **a** $\frac{1}{2}$ of 20 ______

b $\frac{1}{4}$ of 20 ______

c $\frac{1}{5}$ of 20 ______

d $\frac{1}{10}$ of 20 ______

5. The smallest number of coins that will total exactly $10.75. ______

6. How many different outfits can you make from 2 shirts and 5 pants? ______

Challenge

Draw a prism and describe it.

______

______

______

______

______

Fill out this table about yourself, a relative or a friend.

Name: ______ **Date:** ______

Age: ______	Mass: ______ kg	Shoe size: ______
Height: ______ cm	Waist: ______ cm	Neck size: ______ cm

2:1 ☐ out of 17

1. 9 + 6 ______
2. 7 × 3 ______
3. 8 − 7 ______
4. 5 × 4 ______
5. $\begin{array}{r} 38 \\ -26 \\ \hline \end{array}$
6. 8 × 2 ______
7. 11 + 7 ______
8. 12 minus 5. ______
9. Add 6 and 4. ______
10. $\begin{array}{r} 28 \\ +31 \\ \hline \end{array}$
11. Subtract 7 from 15. ______
12. Jill's skipping rope was 90 cm long. She cut 10 cm off. How long is the rope now? ______
13. 

    Write the total value of these coins in decimal form. ______
14. 7 rows of 4. ______
15. Does a spoon weigh more than 1 kilogram? ______
16. How many minutes before 5 o'clock?

    a  ______

    b  ______

17. Give the unit of measure for the length:

    a of a table 1·5 ______

    b of a mobile phone 10·5 ______

2:2 ☐ out of 15

1. 14 − 6 ______
2. 6 × 5 ______
3. 9 − 4 ______
4. 19 + 3 ______
5. $\begin{array}{r} 4 \\ \times 8 \\ \hline \end{array}$
6. 3 × 7 ______
7. 4 + 9 ______
8. 4 groups of 4. ______
9. 3 plus 8. ______
10. $\begin{array}{r} 58 \\ -26 \\ \hline \end{array}$
11. Write the numeral shown. ______

    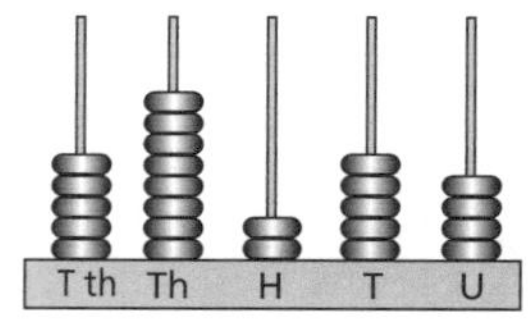

12. Each Monday for 4 weeks, Lien picked 6 flowers.

    How many flowers did she pick altogether? ______
13. a 21 days = ______ weeks

    b 70 days = ______ weeks
14. 1 m, 2 m, 3 m, 6 m, 20 m, 2 cm, 20 cm, 2 mm, 5 mm, 2 km, 20 km

    Choose the best answer above for the:

    a height of a door ______

    b length of a new pencil ______

    c width of a classroom ______

    d height of your desk ______
15. How many groups of:

    a 8? ______

    b 12? ______

 • *AUSTRALIAN SIGNPOST MATHS 5 MENTALS* • ISBN 978 1 4886 2189 5

2:3 out of 15

❶ 334 + 159

❷ 249 + 178

❸ 198 + 37

❹ 7)35

❺ 9)36

❻ 8)72

❼ Shade one third of the snakes.

❽ How many hours from:

a 4 am to 7 am? ______

b 12 noon to 3 pm? ______

❾ In which season is January? ______

❿ There are 35 sweets and 23 are eaten. How many sweets are left? ______

⓫ In this hundred square:

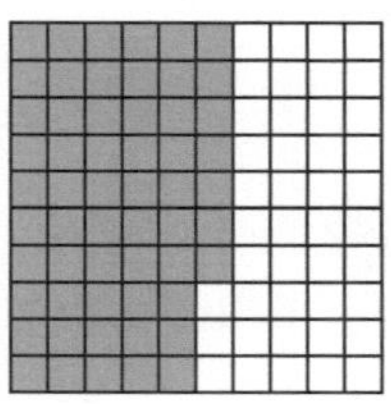

a part shaded is ______ hundredths.

b part not shaded is ______ out of ______.

⓬ $0.40 + $0.15 + $0.20 ______

⓭ Stuart made 17 Anzac biscuits and Samantha made 6. How many biscuits altogether? ______

⓮ Minutes in 2 hours. ______

⓯ Days in 6 weeks. ______

2:4 Extension out of 7

❶ a 25 + 25 + 25 + 25 ______

b 25 × 3 ______

c 25 × 5 ______

❷ How many legs on 3 cats, 8 birds and 5 snakes? ______

❸ After losing $18 and finding only $12, I had $16 left. How much did I start with? ______

❹ What must we add to $5.75 to make $10.50? ______

❺ In two dozen eggs, there were 10 more duck eggs than chicken eggs. How many duck eggs? ______

❻ a How many sides on 11 octagons? ______

b (7 × 8) + (7 × 8) ______

❼ 6 × 10 × 9 ______

Challenge

Draw horizontal lines and record the length of each.

3:1 [ ] out of 16

1. 7 − 5 ____
2. 8 + 4 ____
3. 2 × 7 ____
4. 12 + 6 ____
5. $\begin{array}{r} 57 \\ -\ 31 \\ \hline \end{array}$
6. 6 × 4 ____
7. 10 − 2 ____
8. Double 6. ____
9. 5 more than 7. ____
10. $\begin{array}{r} 13 \\ +\ \ 8 \\ \hline \end{array}$

11. This shape is a p________________ .

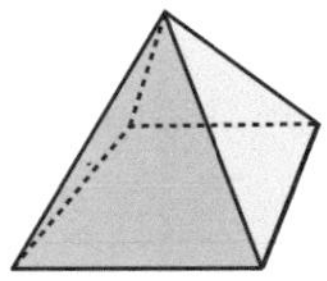

12. What change from \$4 would be given if Natalie spent \$1.40? ____

13. Name these shapes.

a  ____

b 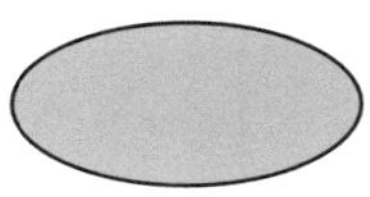 ____

c 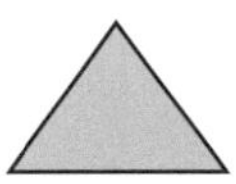 ____

d 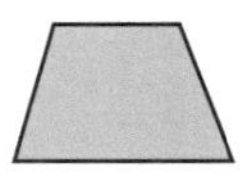 ____

14. Take away 3 from 15. ____

15. Round 56 to the nearest ten. ____

16. How many digits are in the numeral 2 361? ____

3:2 [ ] out of 16

1. 7 + 12 ____
2. 6 × 6 ____
3. 10 + 11 ____
4. 7 × 5 ____
5. $\begin{array}{r} 66 \\ -\ 24 \\ \hline \end{array}$
6. 2 × 8 ____
7. 6 − 5 ____
8. Take 3 from 8. ____
9. 2 rows of 5. ____
10. $\begin{array}{r} 4 \\ \times\ 9 \\ \hline \end{array}$

11. John had 32 coins. 14 of these were Australian. How many were not Australian coins? ____

12. Is this a net of a cube? ____

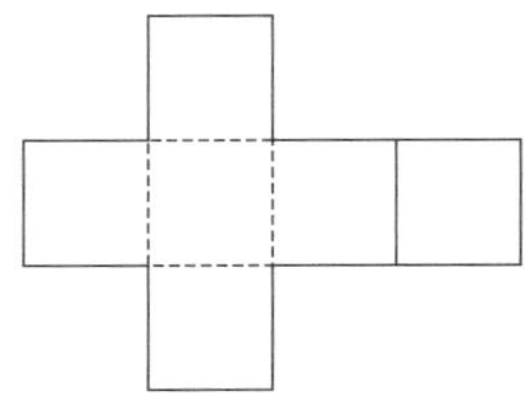

13. Is the area of a door more or less than one square metre? ____

14. On a cube, how many:

a faces? ____ **b** edges? ____

15. Complete this pattern if the dotted lines are lines of symmetry.

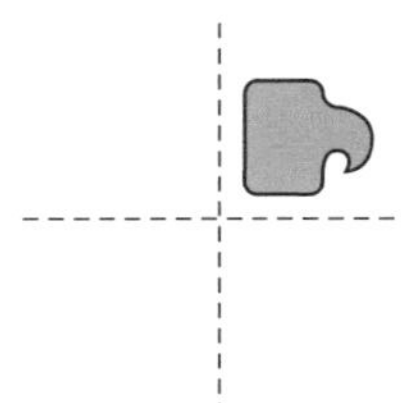

16. 'Consecutive' means following on one after the other. Name 2 consecutive months that have the same number of days.

____ ____

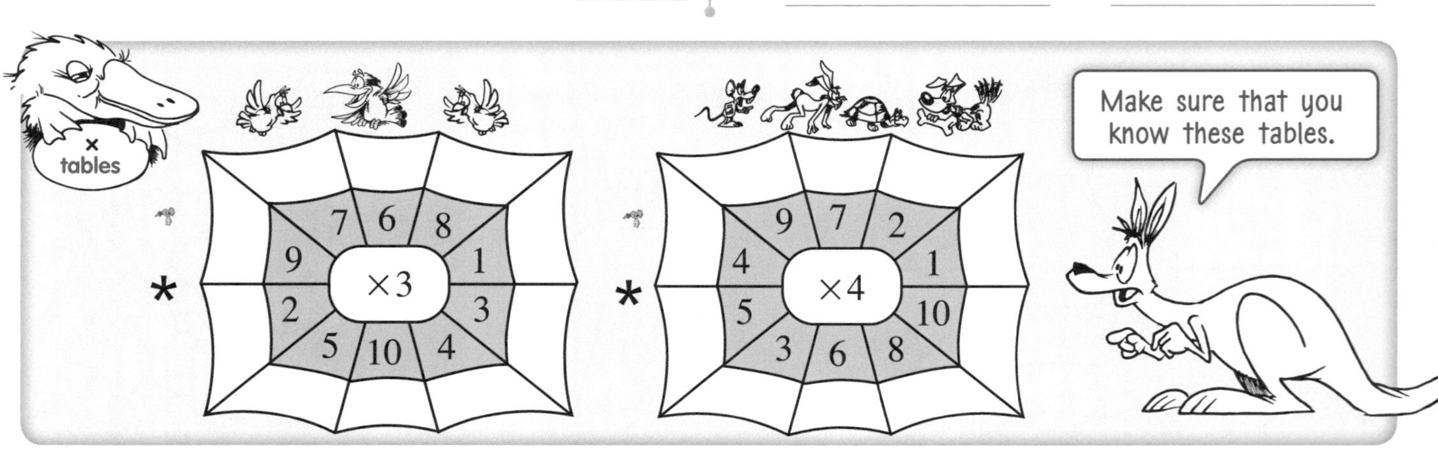

 ISBN 978 1 4886 2189 5

3:3 out of 15

1. 76 + 51 =

$$\begin{array}{r} 76 \\ +\ 51 \\ \hline \end{array}$$

2. $$\begin{array}{r} 65 \\ +\ 176 \\ \hline \end{array}$$

3. $$\begin{array}{r} 112 \\ +\ 274 \\ \hline \end{array}$$

4. $8\overline{)48}$

5. $8\overline{)64}$

6. $8\overline{)24}$

7. The change from $50 if I buy a watch for $37.

8. Could this shape be folded to make a cube?

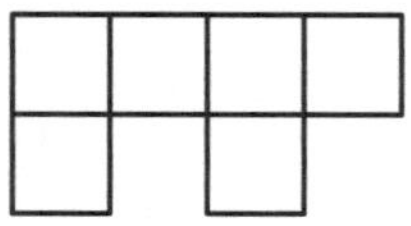

9. Greg had ten 20c coins. How much money did he have?

10. Would an eggcup hold more water than a teacup?

11. The sixth month of the year?

12. What is the total of 40c, 20c and 5c?

13. Groups of 2 in 10.

14. 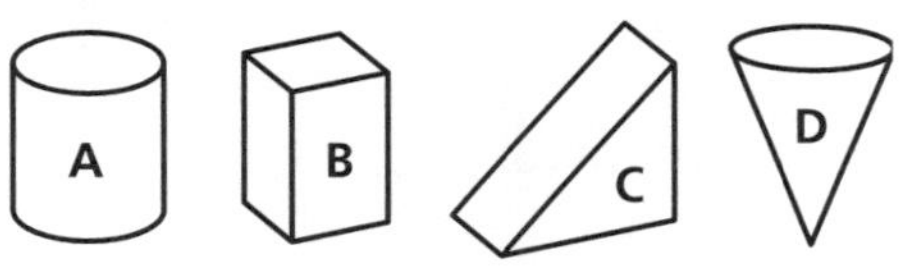

Which of these 3D objects is a:

a prism?

b cone?

15. What am I, if my 4 faces are all triangles?

3:4 out of 6

Extension

1. How many legs on 5 cows, 3 horses and 8 chickens?

2. Boxes of 4 globes are packed in this container which has 2 levels. How many globes are there?

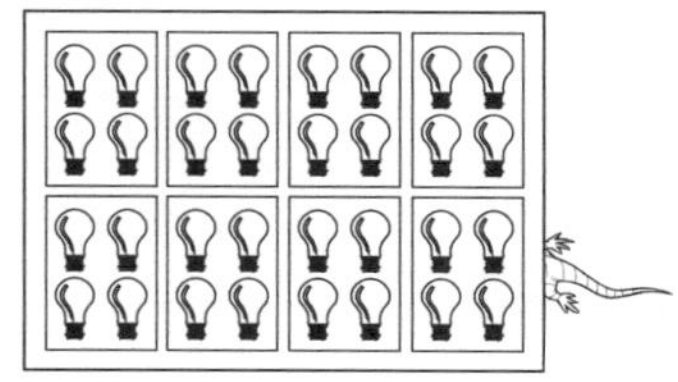

3. If 2 cups of flour make 10 little cakes, how many cups of flour are needed to make 25 little cakes?

4. **a** To half of $1, add 65 cents.

   b From a quarter of $1, take away 20 cents.

5. In our class, there are 26 students. If half of the class have pets, how many students own pets?

6. $4 \times 4 \times 20$

Challenge

Draw a pyramid and describe it.

a From Blue, Shark, Danger, Deep and Water, two different words must be chosen to name a movie. How many different names can be made?

b List all 3-digit numbers smaller than 500 that can be made using the digits 0, 3, 6 and 9, if digits can only be used once in each number.

4:1 ☐ out of 16

1. 2 × 10 ____
2. 15 + 6 ____
3. 6 ÷ 2 ____
4. 20 − 10 ____
5. $\begin{array}{r} 46 \\ +\ 23 \\ \hline \end{array}$
6. 8 − 6 ____
7. 4 × 7 ____
8. 3 lots of 4. ____
9. 13 plus 6. ____
10. $\begin{array}{r} 74 \\ -\ 52 \\ \hline \end{array}$
11. This is the net of a ________.

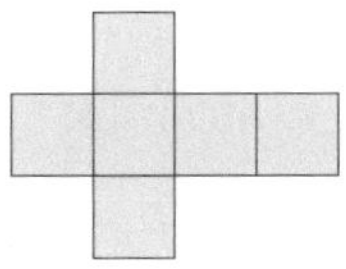

12. Write the numeral shown.

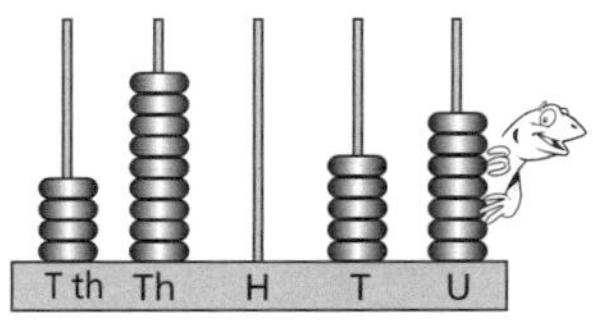

____

13. **a** The value of the 7 in 7412. ____
    b The value of the 6 in 5763. ____
14. 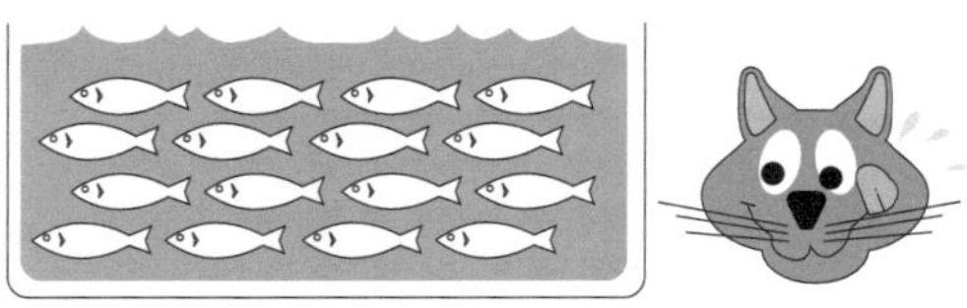

    Find a fair share if the fish were shared among 4 cats. ________ each
15. Weeks in a fortnight. ____
16. Write the value of 5 in:
    a 5302 ____
    b 6051 ____

4:2 ☐ out of 17

1. 7 + 3 ____
2. 40 ÷ 10 ____
3. 3 × 8 ____
4. 9 − 6 ____
5. $\begin{array}{r} 20 \\ \times\ \ 4 \\ \hline \end{array}$
6. 5 × 6 ____
7. 20 ÷ 5 ____
8. 5 × 7 ____
9. 13 minus 7. ____
10. $\begin{array}{r} 49 \\ -\ 20 \\ \hline \end{array}$
11. 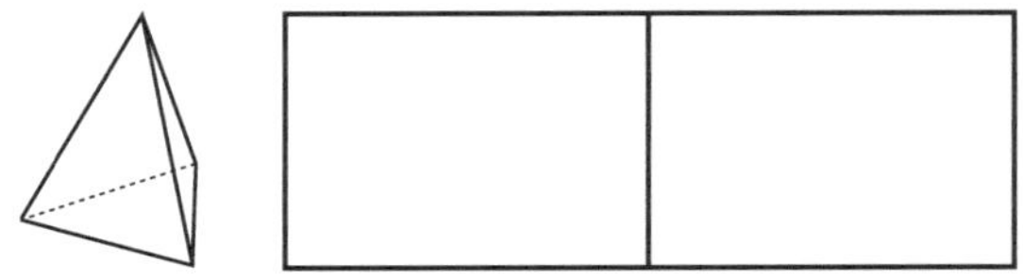

    Draw the top and side view of the pyramid above.
12. Write 4093 in words.

    ____
13. What is the value of the 6 in 697 243? ________
14. Share 24 gifts between 6 people.

    ________ each.
15. Write the numeral for:

    90 000 + 700 + 40 + 5 ________
16. What months are in spring?

    ____
17. Write the number two hundred and thirty-one thousand five hundred and eight. ________

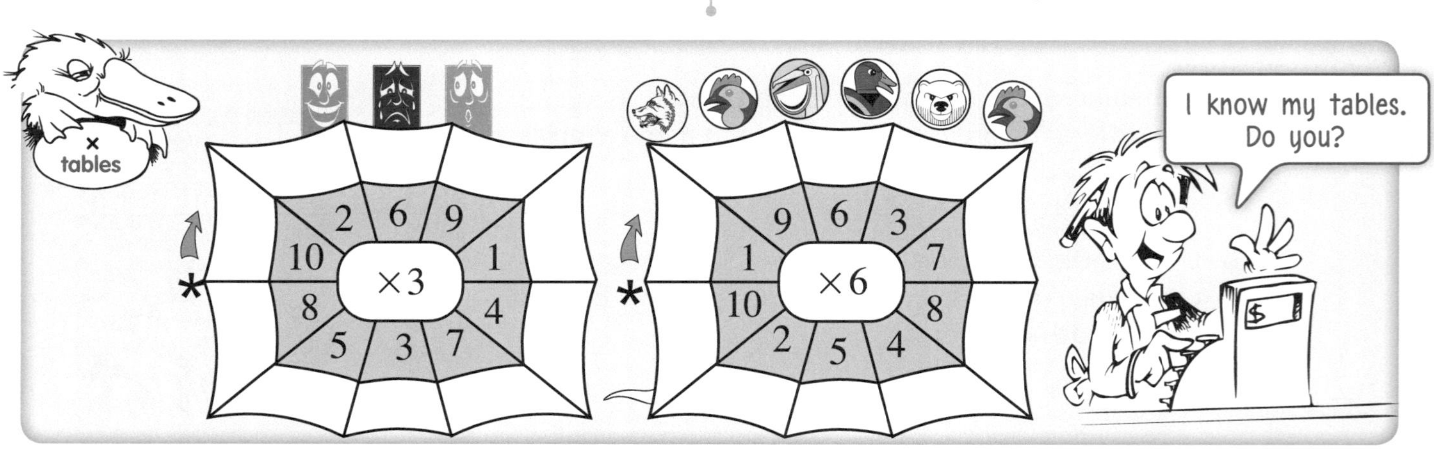

4:3 [ ] out of 12

❶
```
  425
+ 284
```

❷
```
  597
+ 352
```

❸
```
  778
+ 456
```

❹ 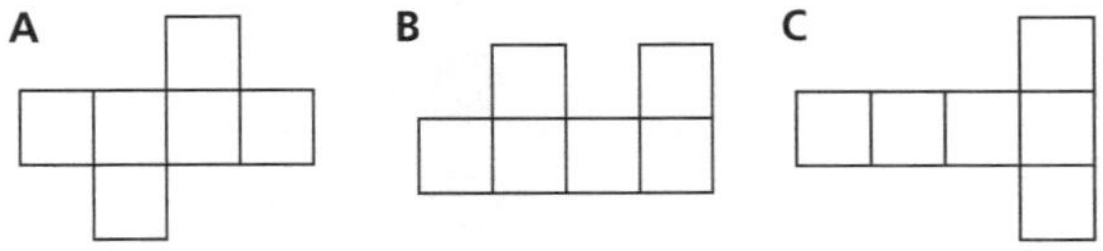

Which of these nets will not make a cube? ______

❺ Write the numeral for 700 000 + 20 000 + 1 000 + 500 + 20 + 3. ______

❻ Today is Friday. What day will it be in 12 days time? ______

❼ Minutes in:

a three quarters of an hour ______

b one and a half hours ______

❽ Circle the largest number.

2 197 642 4 698 557 4 313 126

❾ **a** 72 more than 105. ______

b 57 more than 28. ______

❿ 1 200, 1 300, ______, ______, ______

⓫ Use < or > in:

a 5 972 ______ 4 891

b 9 013 ______ 6 721

⓬ Name this solid.

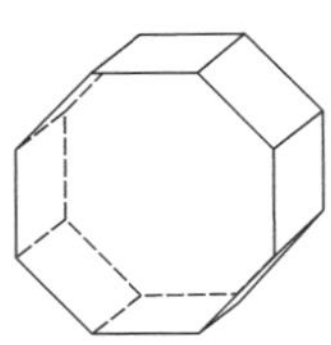

______

4:4 Extension [ ] out of 6

❶ Seven cubes of side length 1 cm are glued as shown. How many faces has the shape?

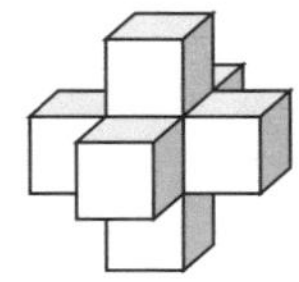

______

❷ 8 pens fill a packet. How many packets can be filled with 94 pens? ______

❸ **a** $10\frac{1}{2} - 7$ ______

b $8\frac{1}{2} - 2$ ______

❹ **a** 12 minutes after 9:25. ______

b 30 minutes before 9:25. ______

❺ **a** 938 + 402 ______

b 919 + 121 ______

❻ How long would it take Mrs Foster to pay for a washing machine that costs $450 if she pays $50 each week?

______

Challenge

Write as much as you can about the number 6 534 108.

______

______

______

______

______

For each pattern, give the number of circles that would be used in the 4th and 10th pictures.

	1st picture	2nd picture	3rd picture	4th	10th
a	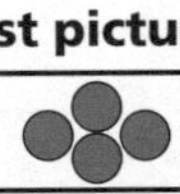	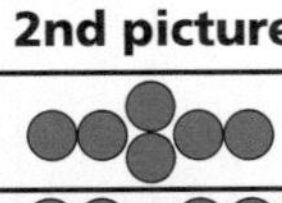			
b	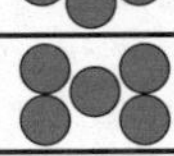	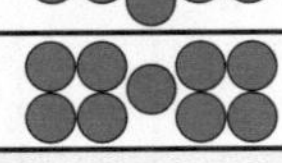	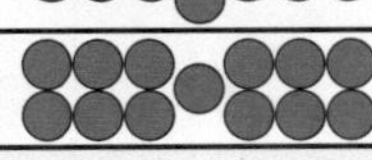		

 AUSTRALIAN SIGNPOST MATHS 5 MENTALS • ISBN 978 1 4886 2189 5

5:1 ☐ out of 16

1. 5 × 2 ______
2. 11 − 6 ______
3. 7 × 4 ______
4. 18 ÷ 9 ______
5. $\begin{array}{r} 9 \\ +\,10 \\ \hline \end{array}$
6. 2 × 5 ______
7. 3 × 4 ______
8. Add 5 and 8. ______
9. Take 4 from 9. ______
10. $\begin{array}{r} 41 \\ \times\;\;2 \\ \hline \end{array}$

11. Write the numeral for:
    a 50 000 + 3 000 + 200 + 5 ______
    b 20 000 + 300 + 80 + 1 ______
12. One hour later than 6:35 am. ______
13. a Is 173 closer to 100 or 200? ______
    b Is $1.49 closer to $1 or $2? ______
14. Metres in one kilometre. ______
15. 400 000 + 300 + 50 + 2 ______
16. 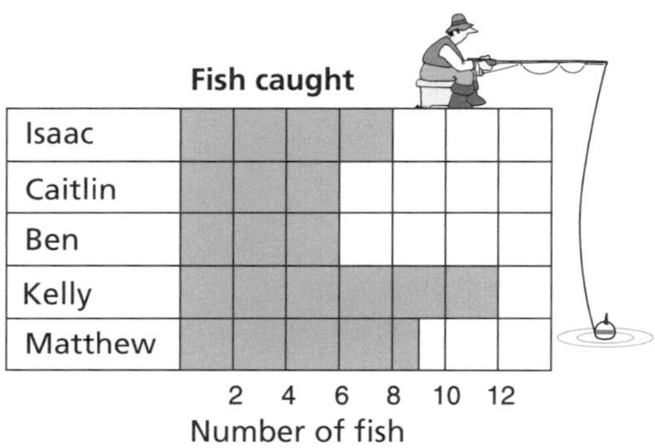

    a What is the difference between the number of fish caught by Kelly and the number caught by Caitlin? ______
    b Who caught 9 fish? ______

5:2 ☐ out of 20

1. 7 + 9 ______
2. 24 ÷ 6 ______
3. 20 − 14 ______
4. 4 × 8 ______
5. $\begin{array}{r} 43 \\ +\,15 \\ \hline \end{array}$
6. 6 × 9 ______
7. 18 + 6 ______
8. 49 ÷ 7 ______
9. 8 × 5 ______
10. $\begin{array}{r} 96 \\ -\,50 \\ \hline \end{array}$

11. What is the value of the 9 in 197 273? ______
12. Write the numeral for 300 000 + 90 000 + 5 000 + 300 + 90 + 2. ______
13. Share 20 between 4. ______ each
14. Kilometres in 7 000 m. ______
15. Write the numeral one million, nine hundred thousand two hundred and forty-seven. ______
16. Circle the larger number:
    2 951 623 2 951 633
17. 4 297 m = ______ km ______ m
18. Is 3 289 closer to 3 200 or 3 300? ______
19. a Hours from 2 pm to 6 pm. ______
    b Hours from 9 am to 3 pm. ______
20. This is a: ______

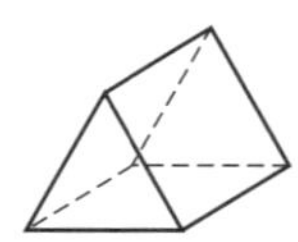

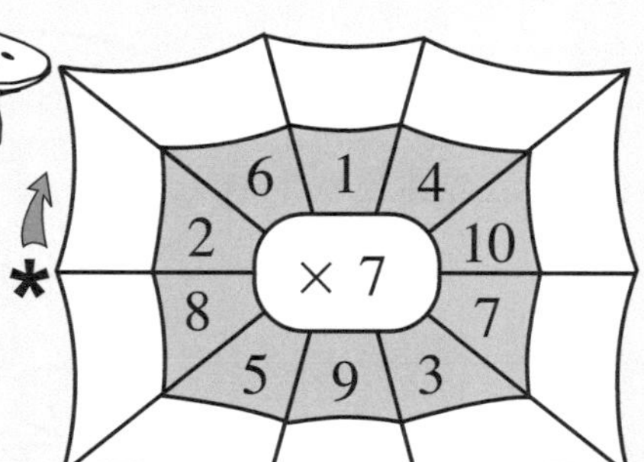

5 × 7	
3 × 7	
7 × 7	
9 × 7	

 ISBN 978 1 4886 2189 5

5:3 ☐ out of 12

1.
```
  312
  231
+  15
```

2.
```
   27
  150
+ 212
```

3.
```
  341
   25
+ 112
```

4. Write in order from largest to smallest.
3 359 574, 3 395 637, 3 392 035

____

5. Share 28 books among 4 girls.
One share = ______

6. Days in one leap year. ______

7. **a** Round off 437, correct to the nearest hundred. ______

   b If a number is rounded off to 500, what could it have been? ______

8. Metres in one kilometre. ______

9. What is the time 29 minutes after 4:12? ______

10. In which season is February? ______

11. Round 2 457 372 to the nearest million. ______

12. On a square pyramid, how many:

   a faces? ______

   b edges? ______

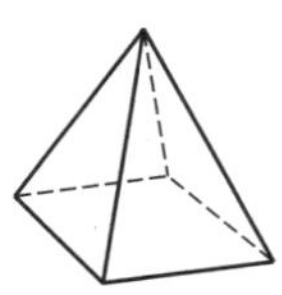

5:4 Extension ☐ out of 6

1. Months in $7\frac{1}{4}$ years? ______

2. 'am' means: ______

3. How many days in summer? ______

4. **a** 3×28 ______

   b 4×28 ______

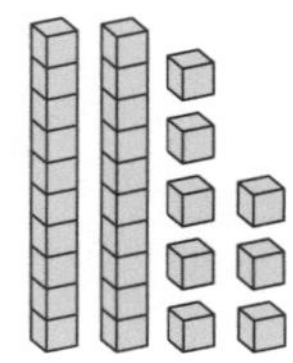

5. If this pattern continued, what would the 35th shape look like?

▲, ●, ■, △, ○, □, ▲, ●, ______

6.

Every 4 minutes a dove flies away. How long would it take the doves to leave? ______

Challenge

Represent and label at least two mixed numbers.

	÷ 2	÷ 4	÷ 1
8			

	÷ 2	÷ 12	÷ 6	÷ 3
12				

	÷ 6	÷ 9	÷ 3
18			

	÷ 2	÷ 6	÷ 4	÷ 8
24				

 • *AUSTRALIAN SIGNPOST MATHS 5 MENTALS* • ISBN 978 1 4886 2189 5

6:1

out of 19

1. 9 + 6 ______
2. 4 × 3 ______
3. 6 + 8 ______
4. 7 – 2 ______
5. $\begin{array}{r} 51 \\ +\ \ 8 \\ \hline \end{array}$
6. 12 minus 8. ______
7. Double 4. ______
8. Half of 16. ______
9. 8 ÷ 2 ______
10. $\begin{array}{r} 7 \\ +32 \\ \hline \end{array}$
11. Make the smallest number you can using all of the digits:

    5 2 8 7 ______
12. 10 000 + 2 000 + 50 + 9 ______
13. Days in 1 year. ______
14. Share 8 cakes among 4 people.
    One share = ______
15. Days in 1 fortnight. ______
16. Is the length of a cricket bat closer to 30 cm, 1 m or 1 km?

______

17. 4 bags of 20 balls. ______ balls
18. Use < or > in:
    - **a** 19 704 ______ 19 695
    - **b** 38 431 ______ 38 507
19. Write the numeral six million twenty-three thousand four hundred and three. ______

6:2

out of 16

1. 11 – 3 ______
2. 4 × 6 ______
3. 2 + 13 ______
4. 2 × 3 ______
5. $\begin{array}{r} 4 \\ \times\ 2 \\ \hline \end{array}$
6. Half of 20. ______
7. 48 + 3 ______
8. 9 + 4 + 2 ______
9. Add 7 and 6. ______
10. $\begin{array}{r} 96c \\ -\ 13c \\ \hline \end{array}$
11. Write in order from largest to smallest.
    8 781 344, 8 768 367, 8 780 033

    ______
12. Share 15 books among 3 people.
    One share = ______
13. The winter months. ______

    ______
14. Round off 888 to the nearest hundred. ______
15. 500 metres is ______ of a kilometre.
16.

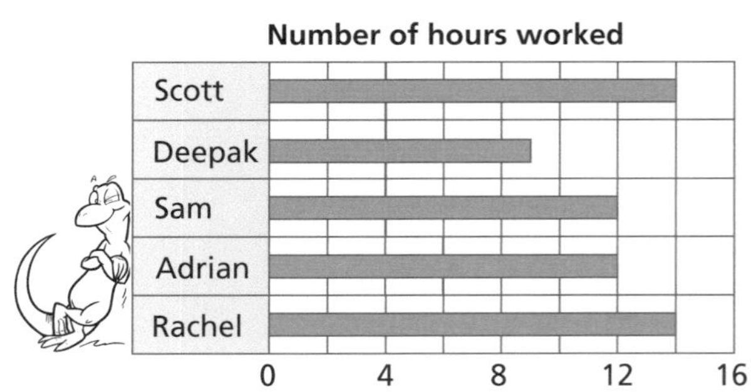

   - **a** For how long did Adrian work? ______
   - **b** How many hours were worked altogether? ______

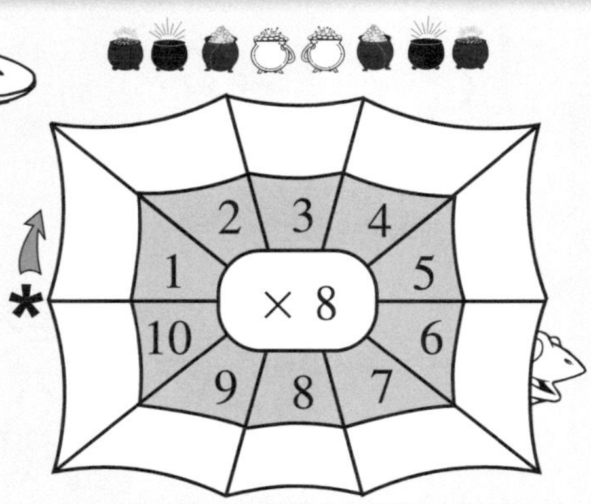

a Greg had 7 sheets of stickers. 8 were on each sheet. How many stickers were there? ______

b Each of the 6 pictures on our ties come in 8 colours. How many different ties do we have? ______

6:3 — out of 10

1.
 HTU

 569
+133

2.
 HTU

 167
+243

3. Share 21 toys among 3 children. One share = ______

4. 9072 m = ______ km ______ m

5. Write 2 km 87 m as metres. ______ m

6. a 5 minutes before 1:05? ______

b 10 minutes before 1:05? ______

7. 2 m, 10 cm, 20 cm, 45 cm
Which of these would be about the width of your head? ______

8. Estimate your height. ______

9. My trip took 34 minutes. When did I arrive if I left home at 8:30 am? ______

10. Round 5 687 940 to the nearest million. ______

6:4 — out of 7 — Extension

1. I bought 6 pens for $24. How much would it cost for:
a one? ______ b two? ______

2. Mum swam 1 kilometre. Evan swam a quarter of this distance. How far did Evan swim? ______

3. □ + 32 = 81 □ = ______

4. Four lots of $1\frac{1}{2}$. ______

5. a 265 + 145 ______
b 265 − 145 ______

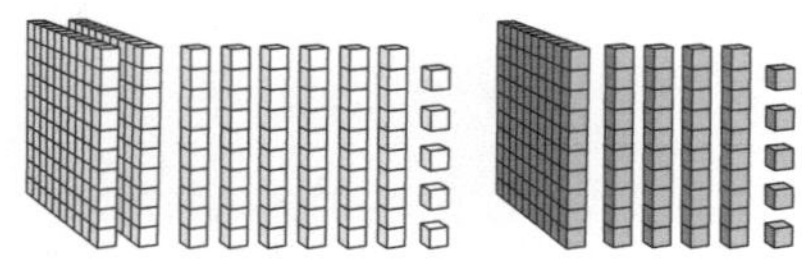

6. In every space made by a row of 6 trees, we planted 8 flowers. How many flowers did we plant? ______

7. a Centuries in 2 000 years. ______
b Decades in 700 years. ______

Challenge

Draw a 2D shape and describe it.

______

______

______

______

______

	÷ 5	÷ 10	÷ 2
10			

	÷ 3	÷ 1	÷ 9
27			

	÷ 6	÷ 5	÷ 2
30			

	÷ 2	÷ 6	÷ 7
42			

7:1

out of 19

1. 11 − 9 ____
2. 9 × 2 ____
3. 30 ÷ 10 ____
4. 29 + 2 ____
5. $\begin{array}{r} 63 \\ +25 \\ \hline \end{array}$
6. 8 + 1 + 6 ____
7. 3 ÷ 3 ____
8. 2 rows of 7. ____
9. 13 take away 3. ____
10. $\begin{array}{r} 89 \\ +35 \\ \hline \end{array}$
11. 90 000 + 300 + 70 + 2 ____
12. Metres in 9 km. ____
13. a 'km' is the abbreviation for: ____________.

    b 'cm' is the abbreviation for: ____________.
14. What is the perimeter of this rectangle? ____

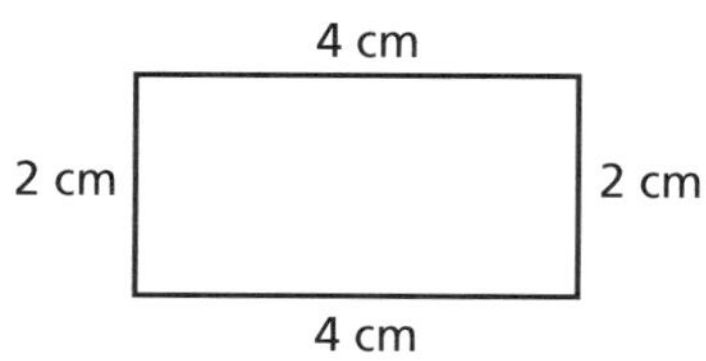

15. '6 lots of 3' means: ____
16. The product of 5 and 6. ____
17. Round off 73 to the nearest ten. ____
18. Write the decimal shown by this model. ____

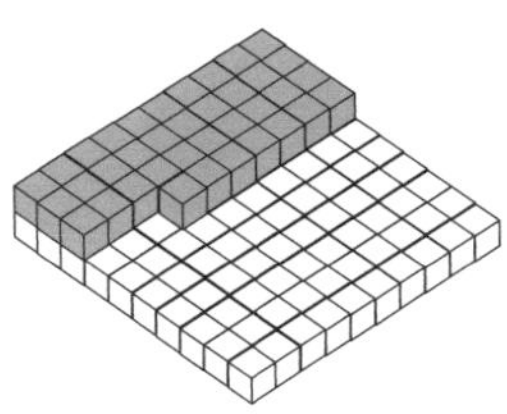

19. Write the numeral for four thousand and seven. ____

7:2

out of 17

1. 1 × 9 ____
2. 6 + 7 ____
3. 10 ÷ 2 ____
4. 6 × 3 ____
5. $\begin{array}{r} 94 \\ -24 \\ \hline \end{array}$
6. 10 − 1 ____
7. 5 + 4 ____
8. 4 × 9 ____
9. 3 lots of 7. ____
10. $\begin{array}{r} 76 \\ +13 \\ \hline \end{array}$
11. Share 36 cards among 4 girls. One share = ____
12. a Hours from 1 am to 7 am. ____

    b Hours from 3 am to 11 pm. ____
13. a Round off 7 624 correct to the nearest thousand. ____

    b Round off 9 654 correct to the nearest hundred. ____
14. Metres in 1 kilometre. ____
15. Which is larger, 3 000 or 800? ____
16. Write the numeral for $(3 \times 10^3) + (6 \times 10^2) + (5 \times 10) + 6$. ____
17. Jessica has 4 dolls, 12 games and 8 spinning tops. Complete the column graph to show the number of each toy.

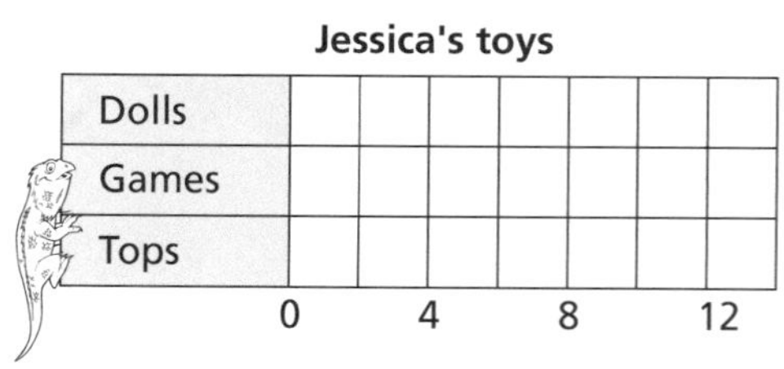

1 × 9	
2 × 9	
3 × 9	
4 × 9	
5 × 9	

6 × 9	
7 × 9	
8 × 9	
9 × 9	
10 × 9	

 • *AUSTRALIAN SIGNPOST MATHS 5 MENTALS* • ISBN 978 1 4886 2189 5

7:3 ☐ out of 10

1
$$\begin{array}{r} 419 \\ +\ 23 \\ \hline \end{array}$$

2
$$\begin{array}{r} 234 \\ +258 \\ \hline \end{array}$$

3
$$\begin{array}{r} 55 \\ +356 \\ \hline \end{array}$$

4

	Tens	Ones
	3	8
−	2	7

5

	Hund	Tens	Ones
	6	3	5
+	2	0	4

6 Write the value of the 7 in 6780 using a power of ten. ________

7 What number is halfway between 7 and 15? ________

8

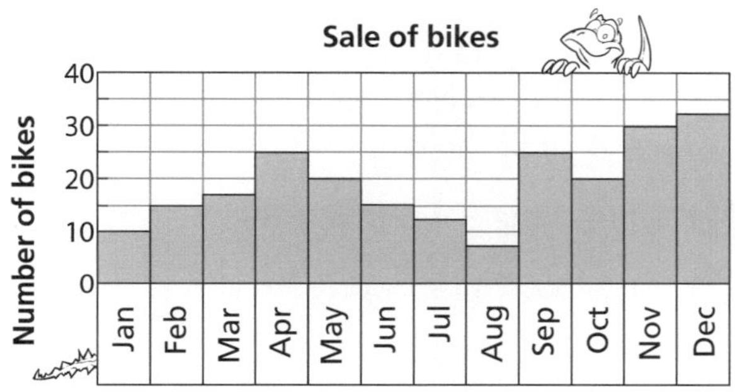

a Which month had the most sales? ________

b Why would this month have the most sales?

____

c How many sales in spring? ________

9 Kilometres in 2000 m. ________

10 **a** The abbreviation for 'minutes'. ________

b The abbreviation for 'hours'. ________

7:4 Extension ☐ out of 5

1 Estimate each perimeter to the nearest centimetre.

a 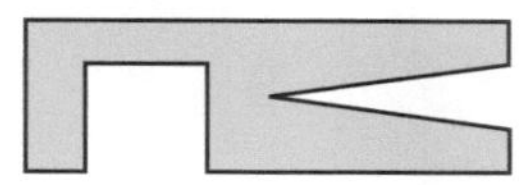

b 

A circle's perimeter is called the circumference.

________ ________

2 How many days in summer? ________

3 **a** (5 × 3) + (4 × 4) ________

b (7 × 5) + (5 × 5) ________

4 Fill in the boxes.

a
$$\begin{array}{r} \square\square \\ \times\ \ 3 \\ \hline \square\ 9\ 2 \end{array}$$

b
$$\begin{array}{r} 1\ 2\ 9 \\ 3\overline{)\square\square\square} \end{array}$$

5 3 × 3 × 90 ________

Challenge

Draw and label different shapes that have a perimeter of 12 cm.

Turn to ID Card A on page 6.
Give the answer for these numbers.

(1) ________ (2) ________ (3) ________
(4) ________ (5) ________ (6) ________
(7) ________ (8) ________ (10) ________
(15) ________

8:1 ☐ out of 16

1. 6 + 5 ______
2. 5 × 7 ______
3. 20 – 12 ______
4. 10 ÷ 5 ______
5.
   7
   × 2
   ___
6. 3 groups of 6. ______
7. Add 2 and 9. ______
8. 6 × 8 ______
9. Double 11. ______
10.
    53
    + 31
    ___

11. What fraction is shaded?

______

12. Make a tally for the animals in this farmyard.

Chickens	
Pigs	
Cows	

13. Use < or > in:

a 791 ________ 2473

b 4021 ________ 3037

14. The even numbers between 9 and 16. ________

15. The value of the 6 in 3671. ________

16. Shade 20 out of 100. What fraction would not be shaded?

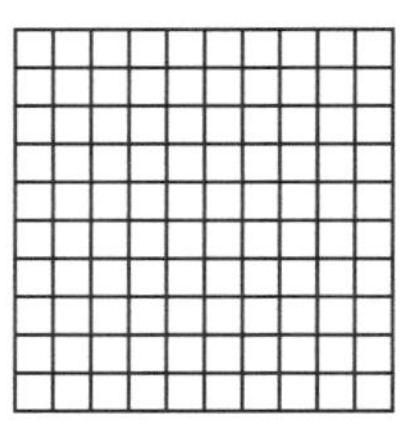

____

8:2 ☐ out of 17

1. 7 × 2 ______
2. 10 + 6 ______
3. 17 – 6 ______
4. 6 × 3 ______
5.
   15
   + 35
   ___
6. 9 × 4 ______
7. 5 rows of 2. ______
8. 8 – 6 ______
9. 5 more than 6. ______
10.
    15
    – 8
    ___

11. Write the numeral for $(8 \times 10^3) + (3 \times 10^2) + (8 \times 10) + 1$. ______

12. The perimeter of this rectangle.

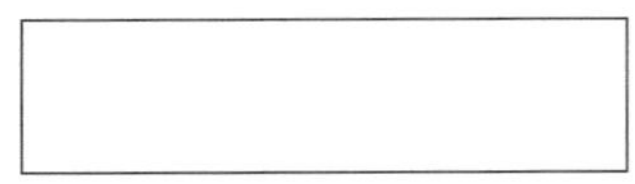

______

13. Make the smallest number you can using all of the digits 9, 5, 1 and 7. ______

14. What is the 8 worth in 6895? ______

15. Write 603211 in words.

____

____

16. **a** The fraction shaded is:

    ______ tenths and

    ______ hundredths.

    b The decimal for this model is:

    ______

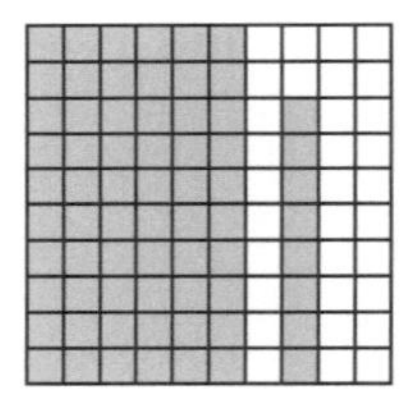

17. For 6789, which digit is in the thousands column? ______

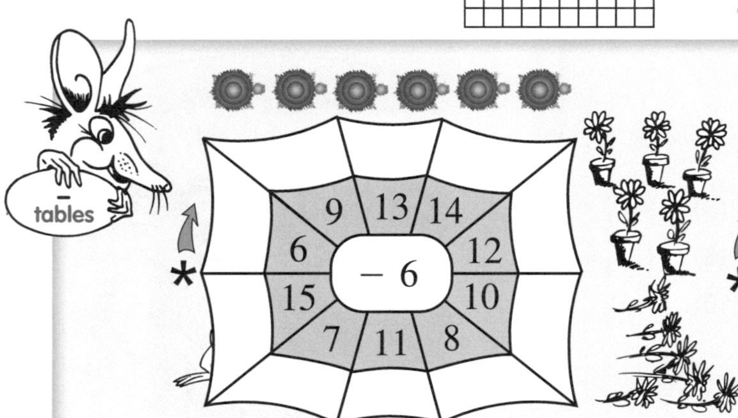

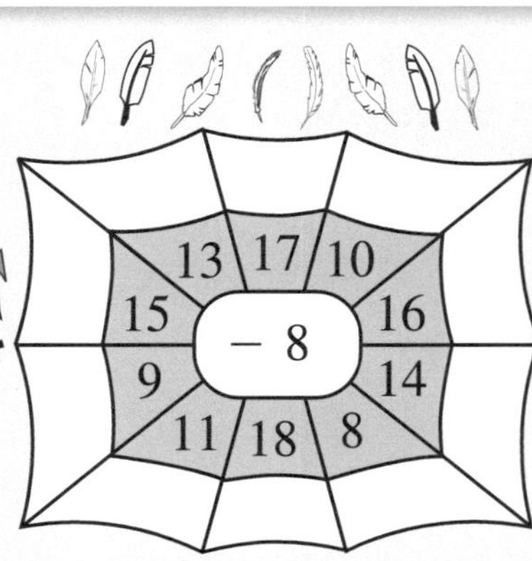

6 + ☐ = 15

8 + ☐ = 14

 ISBN 978 1 4886 2189 5

8:3 ☐ out of 9

1

	Hund	Tens	Ones
	5	9	2
–	3	2	0

2

	Hund	Tens	Ones
	7	6	5
–	5	2	0

3 Write the value of the 3 in 3940 using a power of ten. ________

4 The perimeter of this shape. ________

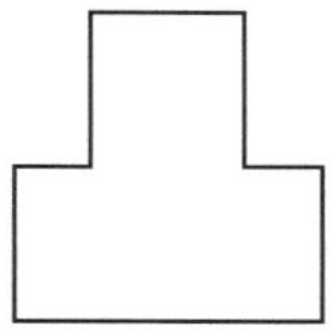

5 Groups of 8 apples in 24. ________

6 How many pictures are needed to represent:

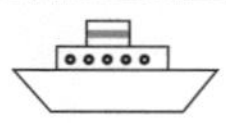

a 90 ships? ________ **b** 120 ships? ________

7 Complete this number pattern.

485, 490, 495, ________, ________, ________

8 **a** Fraction shaded = ☐/☐

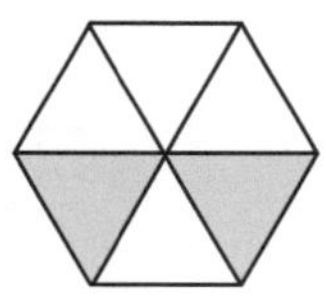

b Fraction not shaded = ☐/☐

c $\frac{2}{6}$ + ☐/6 make 1 whole.

9 Colour 6 tenths red and 3 tenths blue. What fraction have you coloured?

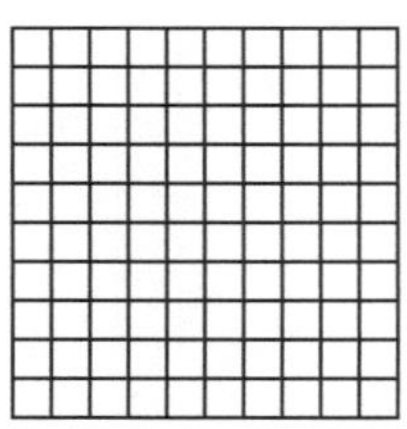

____

8:4 Extension ☐ out of 7

1 The product of 9 and 6, minus 7. ________

2 If the shaded part has the value given, find the value of the whole.

a

____

b

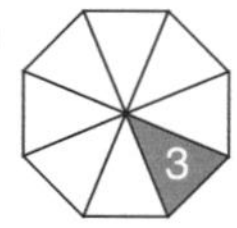

____

3 8 kg of bananas cost me $16.80. How much would 2 kg cost?

____

4 47+ ☐ = 82

5

Bananas in 15 groups of 6. ________

6 What fraction of one dollar is 10 cents? ________

7 (6 × 8) + (3 × 2) ________

Challenge

Draw and label fractions that add to make a whole.

Party time

Patrick's party started at 7 pm. In the first 5 minutes 3 friends came. In the next 5 minutes 8 friends came. In each 5 minute period until 7:30 pm 4 more friends came. How many friends had arrived by 7:30 pm?

____

9:1 ☐ out of 17

1. 5 + 5 ____
2. 3 × 2 ____
3. 11 − 5 ____
4. 6 ÷ 6 ____
5. $\begin{array}{r} 3 \\ \times 4 \\ \hline \end{array}$
6. 9 × 3 ____
7. 8 + 9 ____
8. 15 ÷ 3 ____
9. Take 4 from 22. ____
10. $\begin{array}{r} 63 \\ +34 \\ \hline \end{array}$
11. Write the first 6 multiples of 3.

    ____, ____, ____, ____, ____, ____
12. Write these numbers from smallest to largest.
    7684, 8147, 6879, 10000

    ____
13. Write down all of the factors of 12.

    ____
14. Flip, slide or turn?

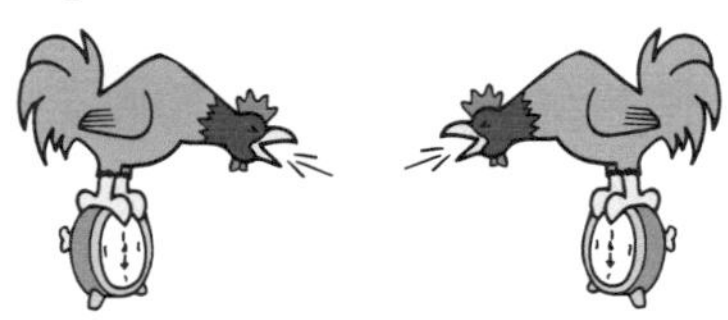

____

15. What is four lots of 50 cents? ____
16. What fraction is covered?

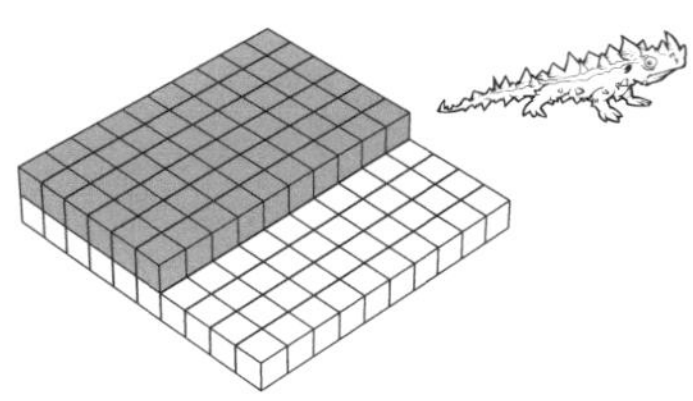

____ hundredths

17. Years in 1 century. ____

9:2 ☐ out of 15

1. 6 + 6 ____
2. 5 × 9 ____
3. 14 − 12 ____
4. 1 × 8 ____
5. $\begin{array}{r} 69 \\ -31 \\ \hline \end{array}$
6. 36 ÷ 4 ____
7. 19 − 8 ____
8. 6 groups of 7. ____
9. 9 × 3 ____
10. $\begin{array}{r} 3 \\ \times 3 \\ \hline \end{array}$
11. Match words with the same meaning.

flip	rotation
slide	translation
turn	reflection

12. Is 14 an even number? ____
13. Write in order from smallest to largest.

    $\frac{1}{2}$ $\frac{1}{8}$ $\frac{1}{4}$ ____________
14. Use the table to complete this column graph.

Team	Number
Kings	12
Eels	8
Rams	20

Number in each team

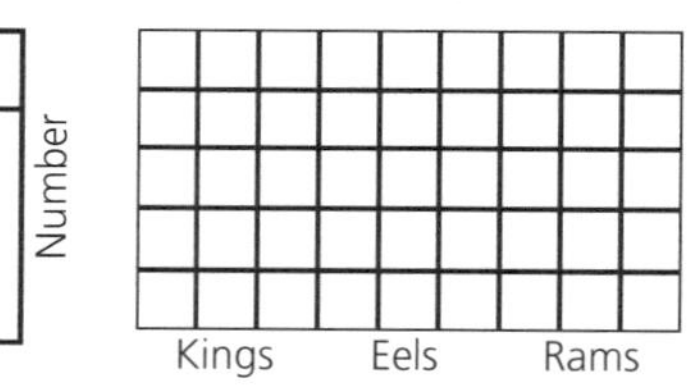

15.

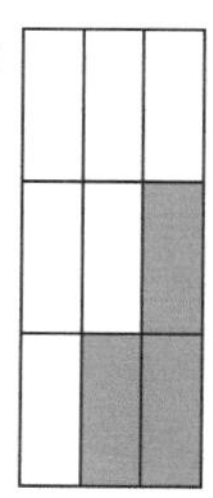

a Fraction shaded = $\frac{☐}{☐}$

b Fraction not shaded = $\frac{☐}{☐}$

c $\frac{3}{9} = \frac{☐}{9}$ make 1 whole.

Use a pencil to draw on this figure.

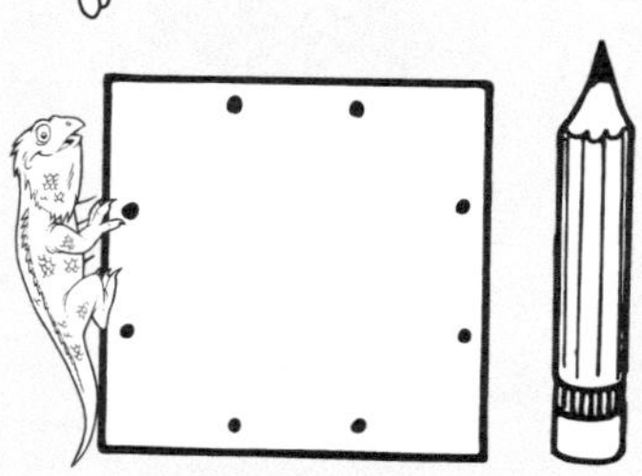

If only these dots are used:

a how many different squares can be drawn? ____

b how many rectangles can be drawn? ____

c Using the dots shown, how many octagons can be drawn? ____

Remember: A square is a special rectangle.

9:3 out of 6

❶

	Tens	Ones
	9	6
–	3	8

❷

	Hund	Tens	Ones
	2	9	3
–		3	8

❸ Write the first 6 multiples of 5.

_____, _____, _____, _____, _____, _____

❹ The factors of 9. __________

❺

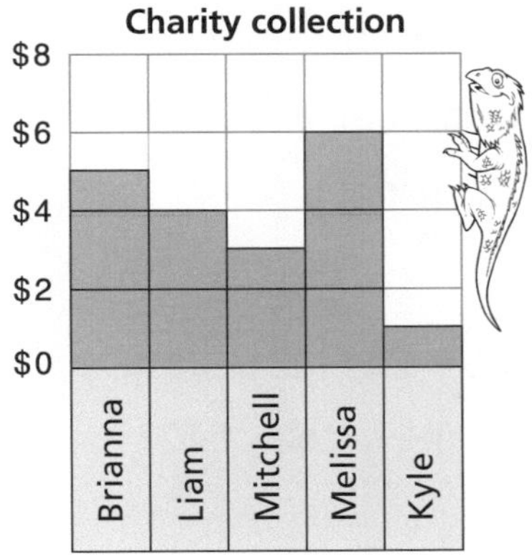

a How much money did Brianna give? _____

b What was the total amount of money given? _____

c How much more was needed to make a total of $30? _____

❻ **a** On this square, shade 49 hundredths.

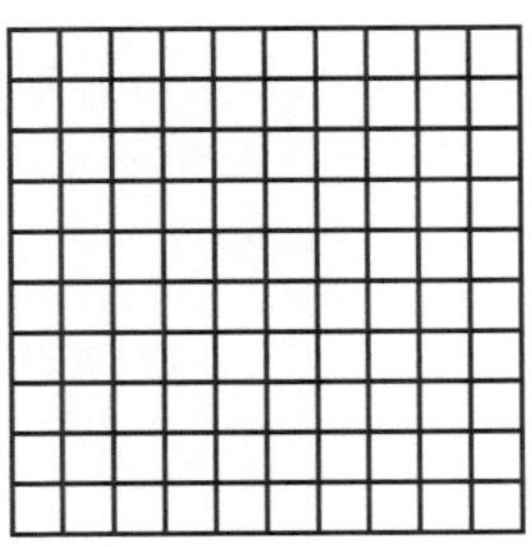

b A batsman has scored 49 runs. How many more for a century?

_____

9:4 out of 5

Extension

❶ If the fish facing right was reflected back and forth, which way would it be facing on the:

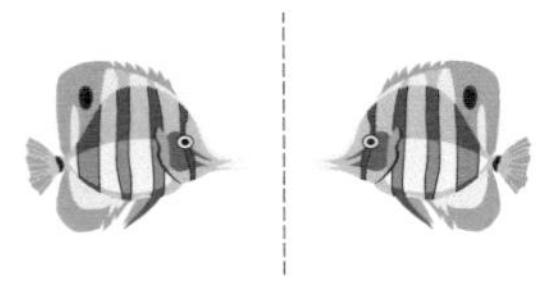

a 29th reflection? _____ **b** 106th reflection? _____

❷ How many three-digit numbers can you make using the digits 2, 3 and 4 if:

a the digits cannot be used more than once in each number? _____

b the digits can be used more than once in each number? _____

❸ **a** (27 – 17) × 10 _____

b (6 × 3) + (9 × 2) _____

❹

How many matches are needed to make a line of 30 triangles? _____

❺ 2 × 20 × 7 _____

Challenge

List multiples of:

a 2 __________

b 3 __________

c 4 __________

d 5 __________

e 6 __________

251, 351, 451

1 Find the total of the numbers above if they are:

a first rounded to the nearest 100 _____

b first rounded to the nearest 10 _____

c left unchanged _____

249, 349, 449

2 Find the total of the numbers above if they are:

a first rounded to the nearest 100 _____

b first rounded to the nearest 10 _____

c left unchanged _____

3 **a** (251+351+451)–(249+349+449) _____

b (300+400+500)–(200+300+400) _____

10:1   ☐ out of 17

1. 9 + 3 ______
2. 7 × 9 ______
3. 13 – 6 ______
4. 9 ÷ 3 ______
5. $\begin{array}{r} 5 \\ \times\ 2 \\ \hline \end{array}$
6. 4 × 6 ______
7. 5 rows of 6. ______
8. 15 subtract 7. ______
9. Half of 12. ______
10. $\begin{array}{r} 37 \\ -\ 17 \\ \hline \end{array}$

11. Is this a flip, a slide or a turn?

______

12. Another word for slide is: ______
13. The odd number between 15 and 19. ______
14. 

Write the total value of these coins. ______

15. Make the smallest possible number using: 1, 8, 6, 2. ______
16. What solid can be made from this net?

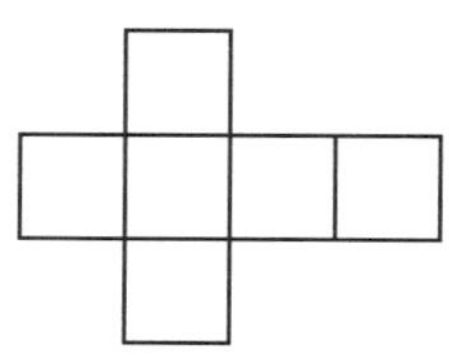

______

17. **Animals seen**

Dogs	卌 卌 卌 |||	Cats	卌 卌 卌 ||

a How many dogs were seen? ______

b How many cats were seen? ______

10:2   ☐ out of 16

1. 4 × 8 ______
2. 19 – 6 ______
3. 40 ÷ 5 ______
4. 3 × 3 ______
5. $\begin{array}{r} 89 \\ -\ \ 8 \\ \hline \end{array}$
6. 112 minus 10. ______
7. 8 + 5 ______
8. Double 7. ______
9. 2 groups of 12. ______
10. $\begin{array}{r} 416 \\ +\ \ 85 \\ \hline \end{array}$

11. List the first 6 multiples of 7.

______, ______, ______, ______, ______, ______

12. The ordinal number six before 23rd. ______
13. This is the net of a:

s ______

p ______

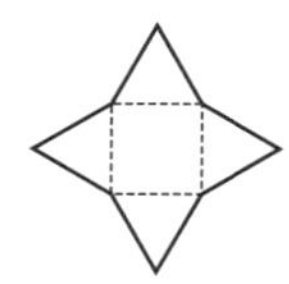

14. What are the factors of 12?

______, ______, ______, ______, ______, ______

15. Match each fraction with a part of the decagon.

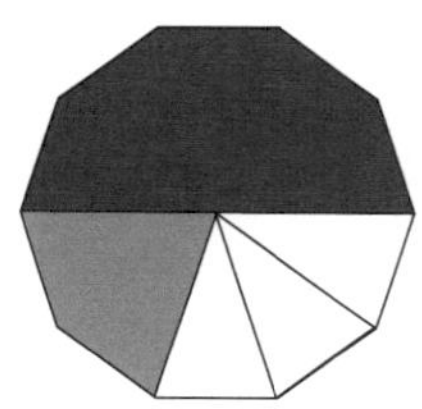

16. What fraction of this hundred square is shaded?

______ hundredths

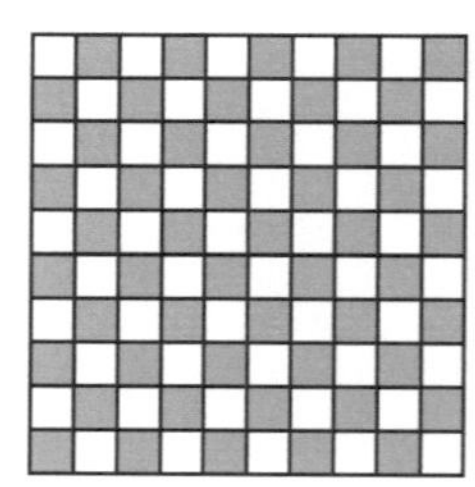

For each row, circle the factors of the given number.

Number	Possible factors						
16	1	2	3	4	6	8	16
25	1	2	3	5	10	25	50
18	1	2	3	4	6	9	18
9	1	2	3	4	5	6	9

Number	Possible factors						
12	1	2	3	4	6	12	24
28	1	2	4	6	7	14	28
81	1	3	9	18	27	40	81
121	1	3	7	9	11	22	121

10:3 out of 7

1. 490 − 223
2. 289 − 110
3. 317 − 284
4. Write in order from smallest to largest.

   $\frac{1}{5}$ $\frac{1}{10}$ $\frac{1}{3}$ ________

5. Complete this symmetrical design about the vertical line.

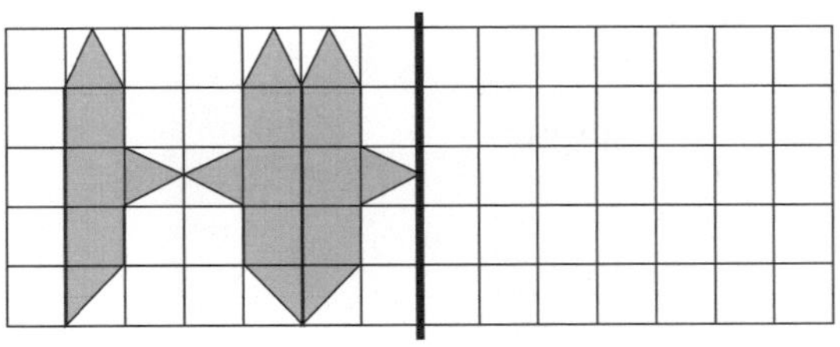

6. **a** The factors of 8. ________

   b The value of 7 in 1674. ________

7. 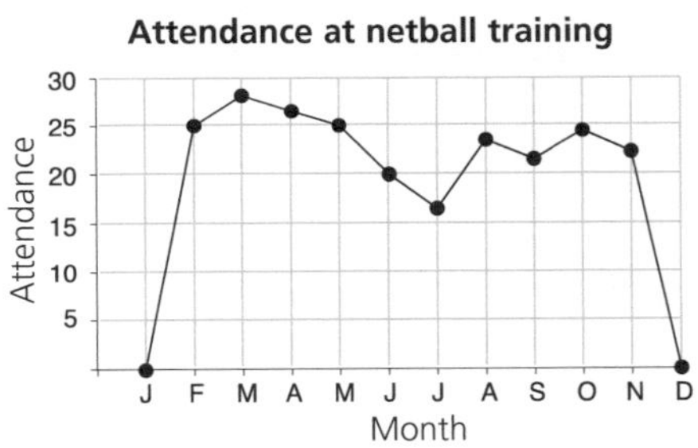

   a The attendance in August. ________

   b In which month did all 28 attend? ________

   c Give a possible explanation for the January and December attendances.

   ____

   ____

Extension

10:4 out of 5

1. The whole has a value of 20.
   Write the value of each shaded part.

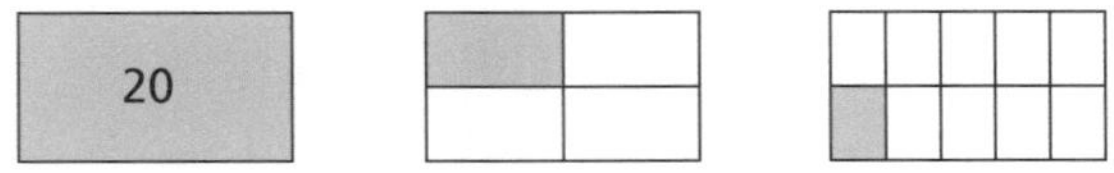

2. If 24 × 32 = 768,

   a 768 ÷ 24 ________

   b 768 ÷ 32 ________

3. Complete this pattern.

   1, 3, 7, 15, ______, ______

4. The cost of:

   HAMBURGERS
   $2.70 each, or
   2 for $5.00

   a 4 hamburgers ________

   b 12 hamburgers ________

5. **a** (4 × 9) + (5 × 5) ________

   b (24 − 18) × 5 ________

Challenge

Create a symmetrical design using transformations.

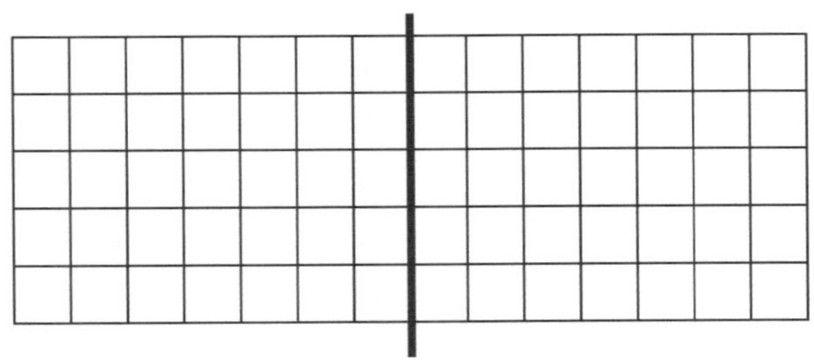

a

	2	4	6	8	10
× 2					

b

	2	4	6	8	10
× 5					

c

	1	2	3	4	5
× 4					

d

	1	2	3	4	5
× 10					

e

	6	3	8	7	9
× 0					

f

	4	7	3	9	6
× 1					

11:1 ☐ out of 16

1. 7 × 6 ______
2. 9 + 2 ______
3. 8 ÷ 2 ______
4. 9 – 6 ______
5.
```
  46
– 24
```
6. 4 + 7 ______
7. 2 × 10 ______
8. 5 rows of 7. ______
9. 20 take 16. ______
10.
```
  458
+  25
```
11. What object has position:

   a upper left? ______
   b lower right? ______
   c upper right? ______
12. 

   a Write the total value of these coins. ______
   b Sides on a fifty cent coin. ______
13. Arrange these numbers from smallest to largest.
   1 473 1 692 1 304 1 724
   ______
14. 13, 15 and 17 are o______ numbers.
15. Shade three quarters of this circle.
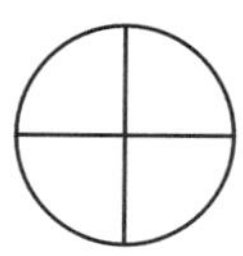
16. Write the numeral for:
   a 3 000 + 600 + 50 ______
   b 2 000 + 400 + 1 ______

11:2 ☐ out of 15

1. 16 ÷ 4 ______
2. 10 × 1 ______
3. 8 – 6 ______
4. 5 × 4 ______
5.
```
  8
× 2
```
6. 13 minus 9. ______
7. 6 × 7 ______
8. 18 ÷ 9 ______
9. 7 × 7 ______
10.
```
  $62
– $36
```

11. Which picture shows:
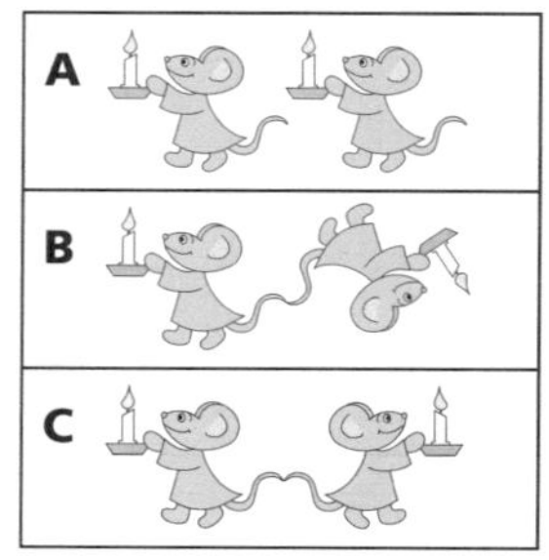

   a reflection? ______
   b a translation? ______
   c a rotation? ______
12. How many sides does an octagon have? ______
13. Write 2 053 in expanded form.
   ______
   ______
14. 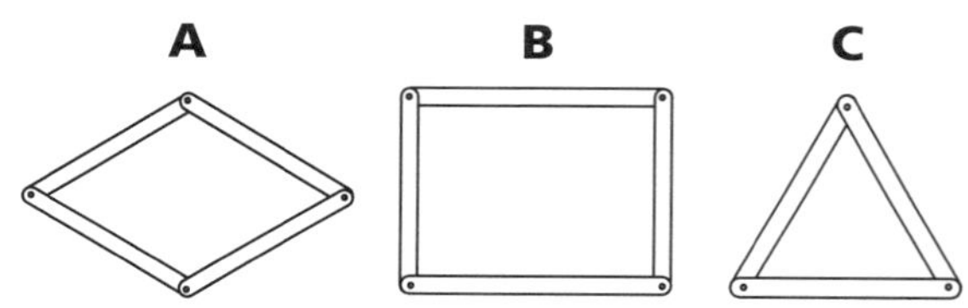

   Which shape is rigid? ______
15. Is this the net of a cube?
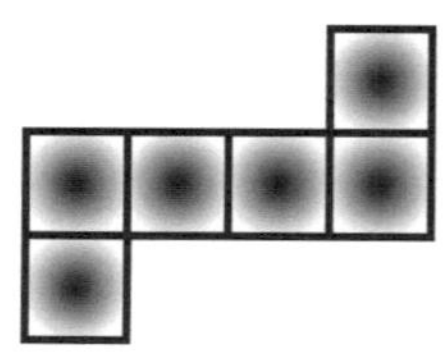
   ______

Each student traced a path on this grid.

1 Wayne started at C, moved 2 up, 6 right, 1 down, then 5 left. Where did he end up? ______

2 Chloe ended up at H after moving 3 up, 5 right, 3 down, 3 left then 2 up. Where did she start from? ______

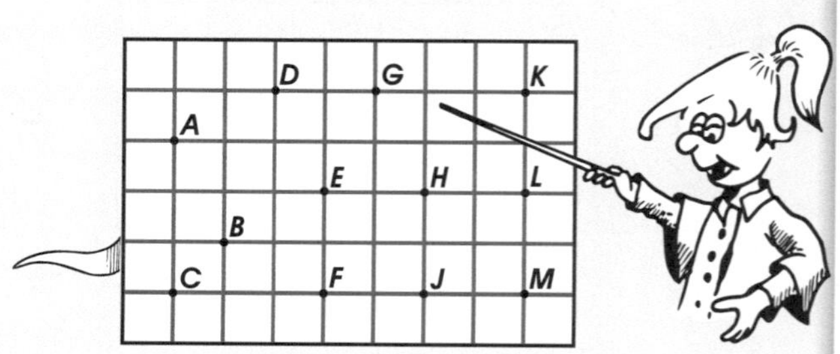

 • *AUSTRALIAN SIGNPOST MATHS 5 MENTALS* • ISBN 978 1 4886 2189 5

11:3 — out of 10

1. 649 + 231

2. \$4.50 \$1.25

3. \$9.99 \$2.35

4. 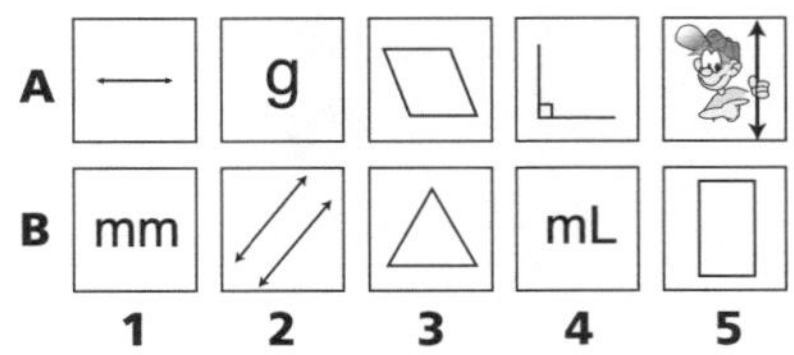

a What is shown at 5B? ______

Write the coordinates for the:

b parallelogram ______

c parallel lines ______

5. Write the size of this angle.

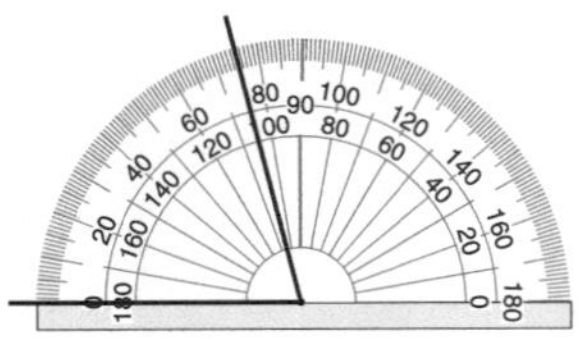

______

6. 1210, 1220, 1230, ______, ______, ______, ______, ______

7. How many right angles are in one straight angle? ______

8. This is the net of a ______.

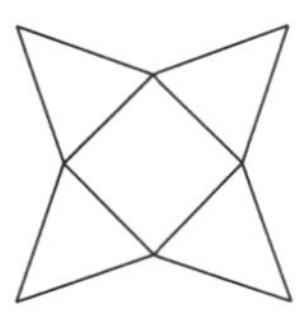

9. Is this a flip, a slide or a turn?

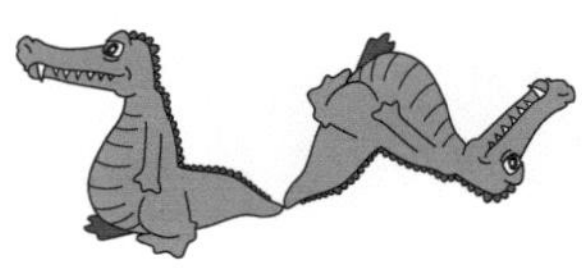

______

10. Another word for flip is ______.

11:4 — Extension — out of 5

1. What is the least number of matches needed to make 12 triangles?

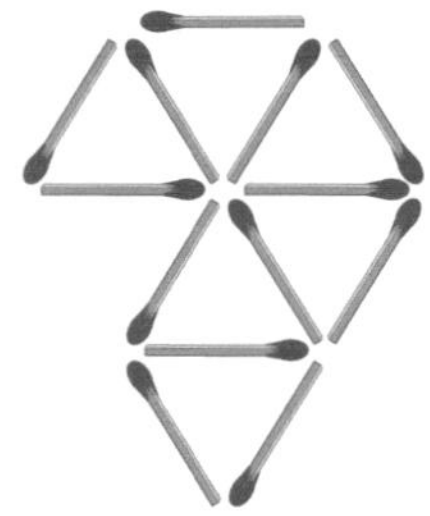

______

2. 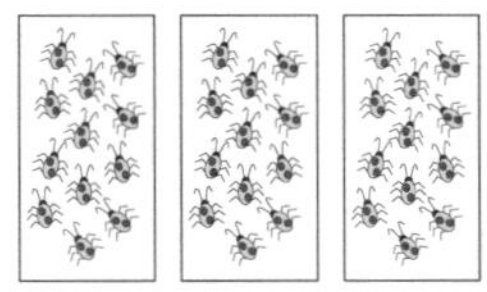

How many beetles in 3 groups of 12 beetles? ______

3. What number is halfway between:

a 87 and 99? ______

b 64 and 98? ______

4. Shade $\frac{6}{12}$ of this shape.

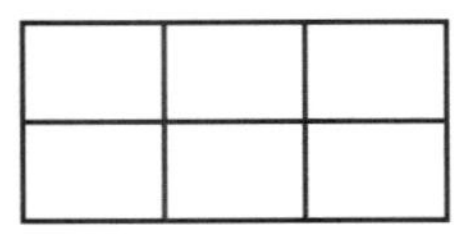

5. One share, if 28 toys are shared among:

a 2 boxes ______ b 4 boxes ______

Challenge

Draw a design that has rotational symmetry.

Time: ______ s

Time: ______ s

12:1 ☐ out of 15

1. 4 × 10 ______
2. 6 − 6 ______
3. 25 ÷ 5 ______
4. 4 + 5 ______
5. $\begin{array}{r} \$45 \\ +\ \$92 \\ \hline \end{array}$
6. 21 ÷ 3 ______
7. 8 × 8 ______
8. 4 × 5 ______
9. 12 take away 11. ______
10. $\begin{array}{r} 10 \\ \times\ \ 4 \\ \hline \end{array}$
11. Estimate and then measure the length of this pencil.

Estimate = ________ cm

Measure = ________ cm

12. I have 18 plants for sale. If I sell half of them today, how many are left? ______
13. **a** Cents in $6.50. ______

    b 375 cents in decimal form. ______
14. How many faces has a triangular pyramid? ______

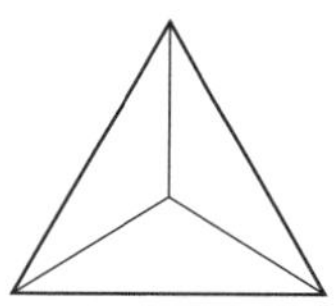

15. Draw the flip for this shape.

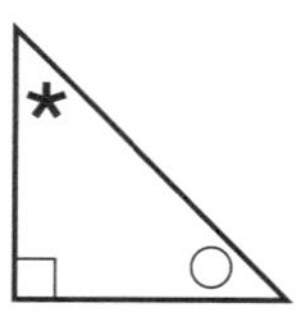

12:2 ☐ out of 15

1. 8 − 5 ______
2. 9 + 4 ______
3. 6 × 2 ______
4. 12 ÷ 4 ______
5. $\begin{array}{r} 62\text{c} \\ -\ \ 7\text{c} \\ \hline \end{array}$
6. 10 + 10 ______
7. 4 × 4 ______
8. 7 rows of 4. ______
9. 9 minus 5. ______
10. $\begin{array}{r} 29 \\ -\ \ 7 \\ \hline \end{array}$
11. Deduct $4.00 from $21.00. ______
12. Write the size of this angle. ______

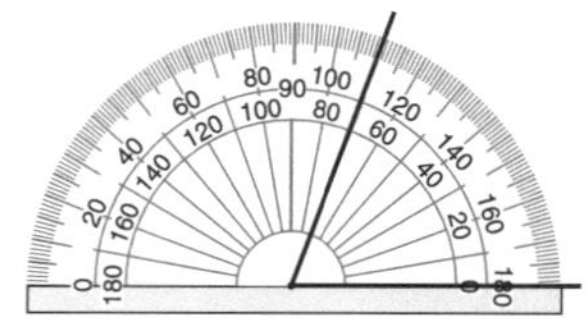

13. Write 109 703 in words.

    ____

    ____
14. **a** Round 4672 to the nearest thousand. ______

    b How many times can a ribbon 11 cm long be cut from a length of 60 cm? ______
15. 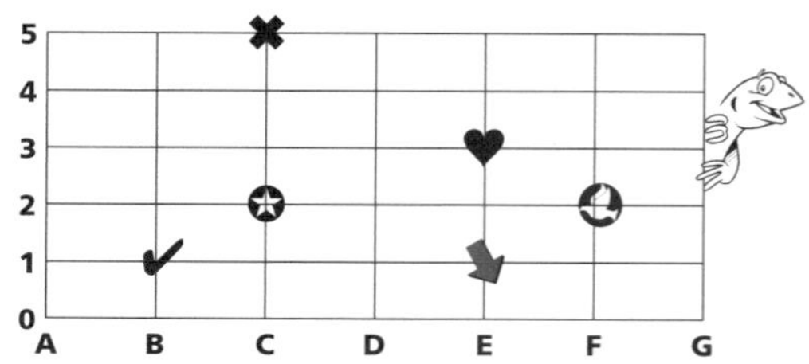

Draw the symbol found at:

a C2 ______ **b** E3 ______

c B1 ______ **d** E1 ______

Using a dot plot

Heather drew this dot plot of her days absent this year.

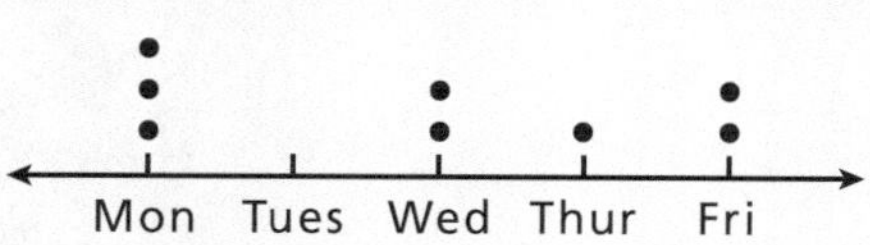

a On which day was she away most? ______

b On which day was she away least? ______

c How many days was she away? ______

d Draw a dot plot of these results.

1, 3, 2, 2, 1, 2, 2, 0, 1, 1, 2, 1, 3, 0, 2.

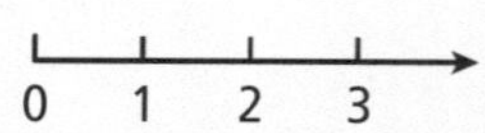

12:3 out of 10

1. $6.73 − $1.45

2. $3.85 − $2.37

3. Weeks in 56 days. ______

4. Draw a turn for this shape.

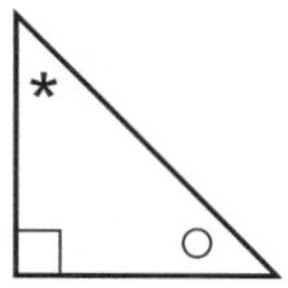

5. How many 5c coins make $2? ______

6. 4345, 4350, 4355, ______, ______

7. Name the type of angle if its size is 163°. ______

8. 2 kg of fish cost $8.00. What is the cost of 1 kg of fish?

______

9. 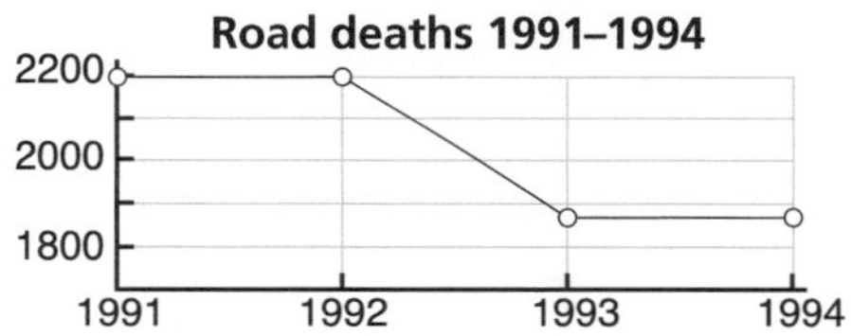

   a Estimate the total number of road deaths from 1991 to 1994. ______

   b In which year do you think breath tests for alcohol started? ______

10. 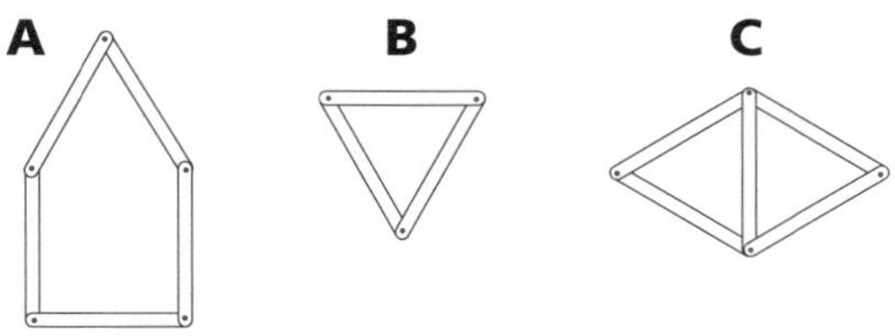

   Which shape is not rigid? ______

12:4 out of 6

Extension

1. I earned 10 times more than I spent. I earned $970. How much did I spend? ______

2. The whole has a value of 24. Write the value of each shaded part.

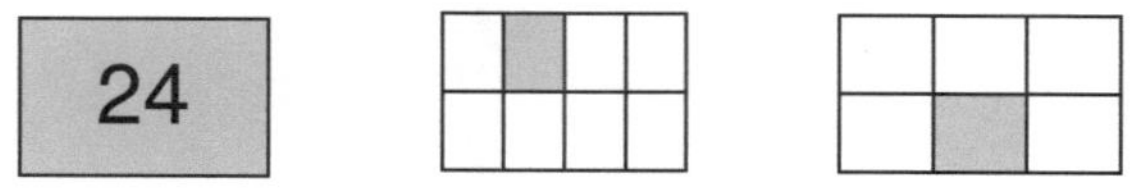

______ ______

3. 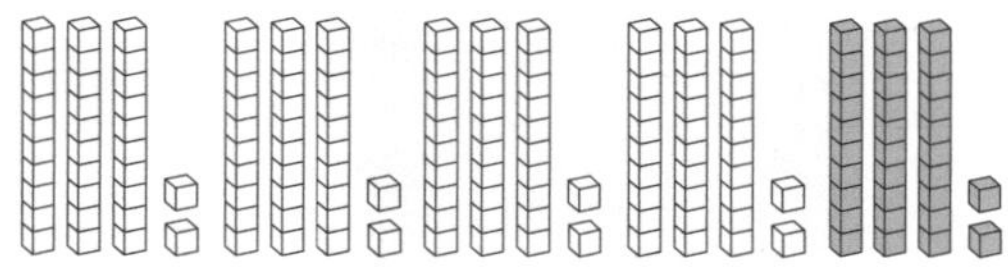

   a 4 × 32 ______ **b** 5 × 32 ______

4. How many days are in the last 6 months of a year? ______

5. (23 – 17) × 8 ______

6. (7 × 3) + (8 × 4) ______

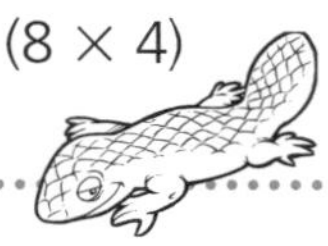

Challenge

Draw and label different types of angles.

Turn to ID Card D on page 9.

Give the answers for these numbers.

(4) ______	(5) ______ ______
(6) ______ ______	(7) ______ ______
(8) ______ ______	(9) ______ ______
(12) ______ ______	(13) ______

13:1 — out of 15

1. 10 × 3 ______
2. 17 – 6 ______
3. 35 + 7 ______
4. 4 × 7 ______
5. $\begin{array}{r} 733 \\ +\,163 \\ \hline \end{array}$
6. 20 ÷ 1 ______
7. Half of 22. ______
8. Double 17. ______
9. 24 ÷ 6 ______
10. $\begin{array}{r} 23 \\ +\,361 \\ \hline \end{array}$
11. How many groups of 5 stars?

Number of groups: ______

Number left over: ______

12. Name the shape that won't roll.

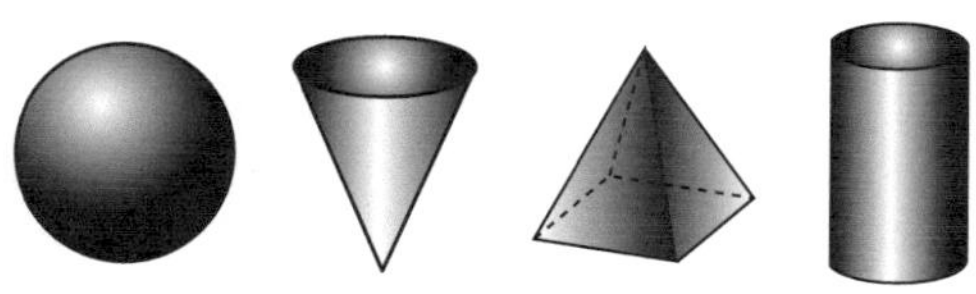

______

13. 4 groups of 7 cows.

______ cows

14. Use < or > in:

a 5902 ______ 5912

b 6714 ______ 6657

15. Write the fraction shown.

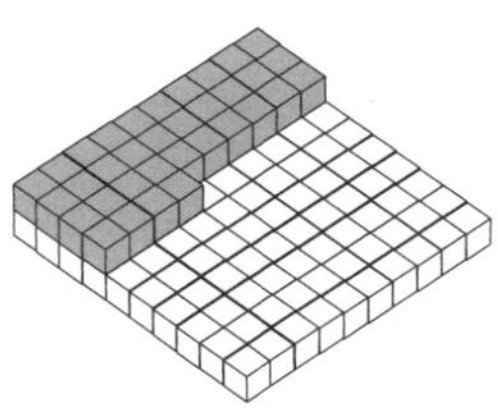

______

13:2 — out of 18

1. 39 – 7 ______
2. 5 × 20 ______
3. 9 × 50 ______
4. 8 ÷ 4 ______
5. $\begin{array}{r} 67 \\ -\,28 \\ \hline \end{array}$
6. 4 × 40 ______
7. 15 take 9. ______
8. 26 plus 7. ______
9. 16 ÷ 2 ______
10. $\begin{array}{r} 21 \\ -\,15 \\ \hline \end{array}$
11. 7000 + 60 + 9 ______
12. Half of $24. ______
13. Deduct $5 from $30. ______
14. Write the size of this angle.

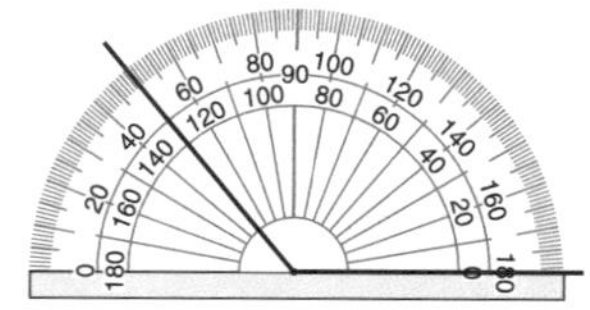

______

15. Name this shape.

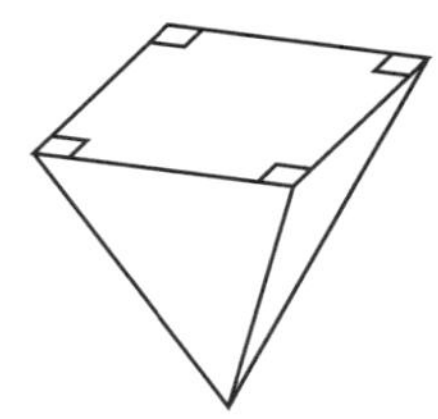

______

16. $3\frac{1}{2}$, 4, $4\frac{1}{2}$, ______, ______, ______
17. $1\frac{4}{10}$ as a decimal. ______
18. Complete:

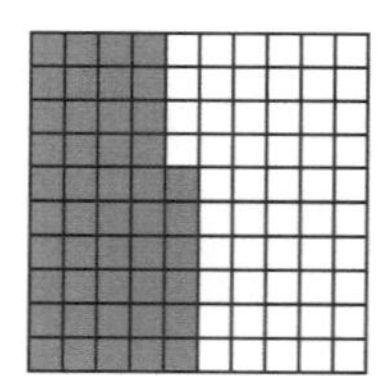

a ______ hundredths

b ______ out of ______

c 0·______

Using a dot plot

Luke drew this dot plot of the number of goals kicked in each game.

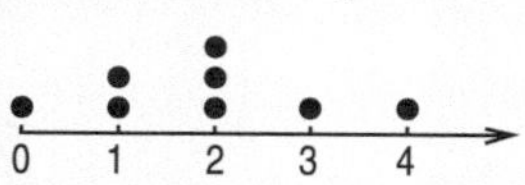

a What number was kicked most often? ______

b How many times was one goal kicked? ______

c How many goals were kicked altogether? ______

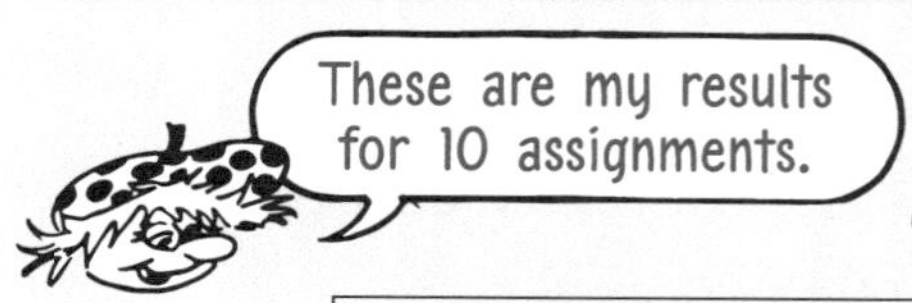

A, C, A, D, B, B, B, A, A, C

d Draw a dot plot of these results.

 ISBN 978 1 4886 2189 5

out of 11

1. $9.28 − $4.63

2. $7.53 − $5.38

3. a $5\overline{)34}$ r b $8\overline{)77}$ r

4.

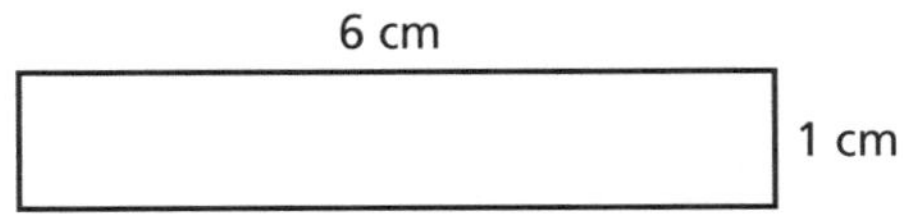

In this rectangle, find:

a the perimeter ______

b the area ______

5. Luke has 12 flowers in his garden. This is 4 times as many as Jan. How many has Jan? ______

6. Days in 3 weeks. ______

7. How many tens in 100? ______

8. What fraction of this shape is shaded? ______

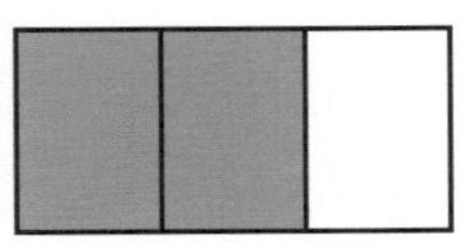

9. Name the type of angle if its size is 67°. ______

10. Bob planted plants in rows of 5. He planted 8 full rows and had 3 plants left. How many plants were there altogether? ______

11. Write the fraction for zero point seven. ______

Extension

out of 6

1. One quarter of $12.60. ______

2. Complete the pattern:

   0·16, 0·18, 0·2, ______, ______, ______

3. **a** ☐ ÷ 3 = 17 ☐ = ______

   b ☐ × 4 = 48 ☐ = ______

4. We shared 5 oranges among 10 players. How much did each player get? ______

5. What fraction is shaded?

   a

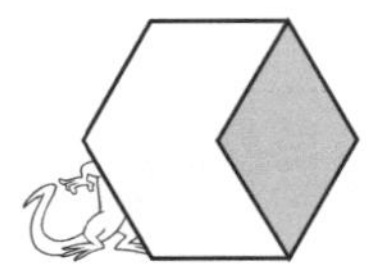

   ______

   b

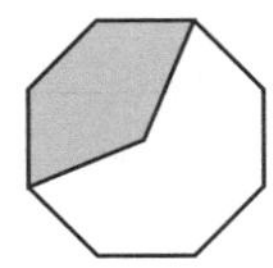

   ______

6. (21 – 11) × (14 – 8) ______

Challenge

Draw and label different shapes that have an area of 8 cm².

Measure

Find the area of each shape.

a

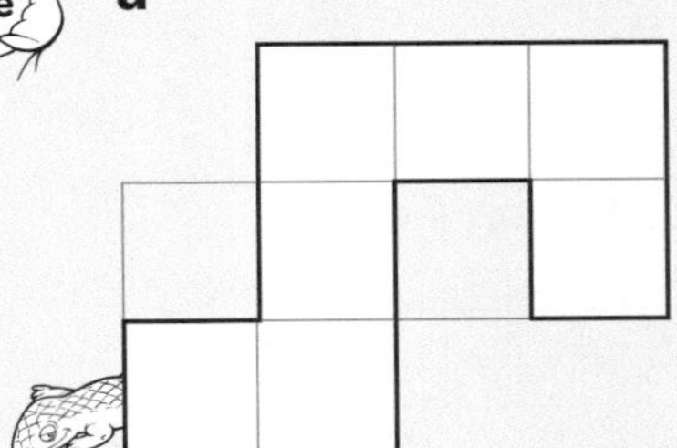

______ cm²

b

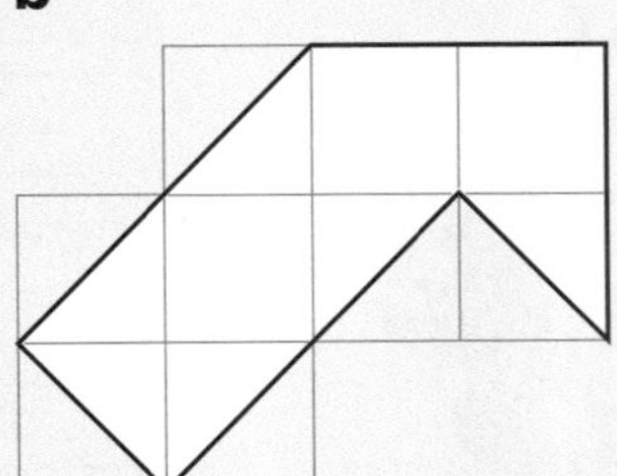

______ cm²

c

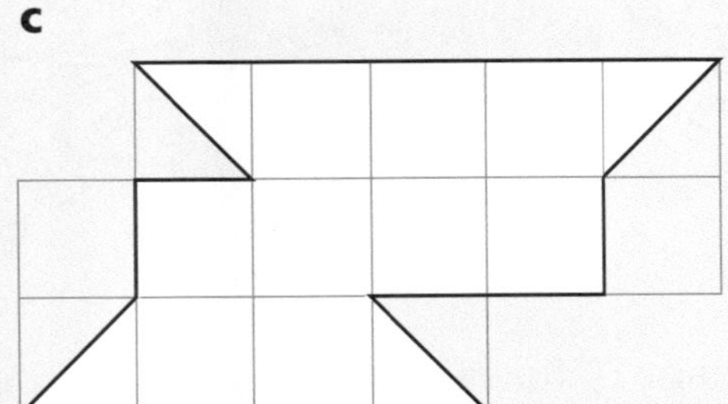

______ cm²

14:1 ☐ out of 17

1. 5 × 6 ____
2. 7 + 4 ____
3. 28 ÷ 2 ____
4. 7 × 6 ____
5. $\begin{array}{r} 436 \\ +\ 22 \\ \hline \end{array}$
6. 18 – 4 ____
7. 6 rows of 6. ____
8. 100 take away 7. ____
9. Half of 34. ____
10. $\begin{array}{r} 22 \\ -\ 4 \\ \hline \end{array}$
11. Write the fraction for zero point one. ____
12. 
    a What fraction is shaded? ____
    b What fraction is not shaded? ____
13. Share this number of stickers among 5 children.
    One share = ____
    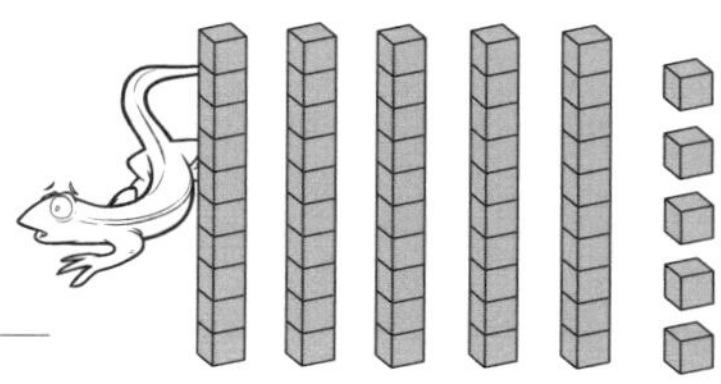
14. Write the even numbers between 10 and 20. ____
15. 33 hundredths as a decimal. ____
16. Write 4070 in words. ____
17. a 5 groups of 3 stars. ____
    b 4 rows of 7 beads. ____

14:2 ☐ out of 17

1. 18 ÷ 2 ____
2. 7 + 6 ____
3. 19 – 4 ____
4. 15 ÷ 3 ____
5. $\begin{array}{r} 96 \\ -24 \\ \hline \end{array}$
6. 7 × 40 ____
7. 13 – 5 ____
8. 6 rows of 3. ____
9. 10 ÷ 2 ____
10. $\begin{array}{r} 29 \\ +51 \\ \hline \end{array}$
11. Write as a decimal:

    a $\frac{3}{10}$ ____ b $\frac{7}{10}$ ____
    c $\frac{1}{2}$ ____ d $1\frac{1}{10}$ ____
12. a How many pairs of birds, if I have 12 males and 12 females? ____

    b How many pairs of gloves, if I have 18 gloves? ____
13. Complete this pattern.
    4, 7, 10, 13, ____, ____, ____
14. Find the area of a rectangle with 5 m and 6 m sides. ____
15. These are shared among four collectors.
    One share = ____
    Left over = ____

16. Write 0·63 as a fraction. ____
17. Write the fraction for 67 hundredths. ____

Share 14 flowers among 3 people.
Answer: 4 each with 2 left over.

a Share 20 coins among 3 students.

☐ coins each, with ☐ left over.

b Share 27 cards among 4 girls.

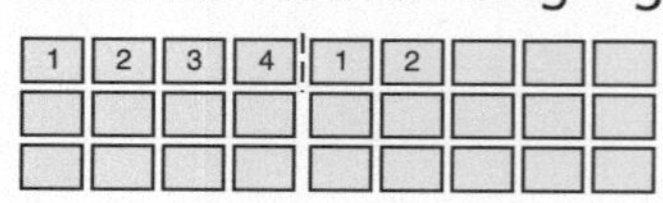

☐ cards each, with ☐ left over.

 • ISBN 978 1 4886 2189 5

14:3 ☐ out of 14

1
```
  165
+ 124
```

2
```
  137
+ 293
```

3
```
  229
+  37
```

4 5)29 r

5 7)67 r

6 Complete:

0·08, 0·09, 0·10, ________, ________, ________

7 Share 19 helmets among 4 Vikings.

One share = ________

Left over = ________

8 For this rectangle, find:

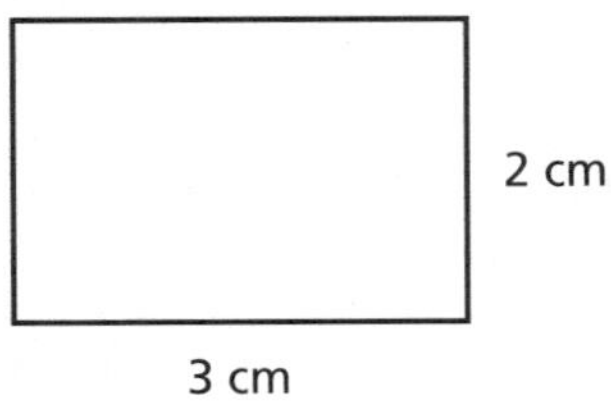

a the perimeter ________

b the area ________

9 Half of $3. ________

10 How many digits in 6 543? ________

11 How many faces has a triangular prism? ________

12 18, 24, 30, 36, ______, ______, ______

13 Continue the pattern below.

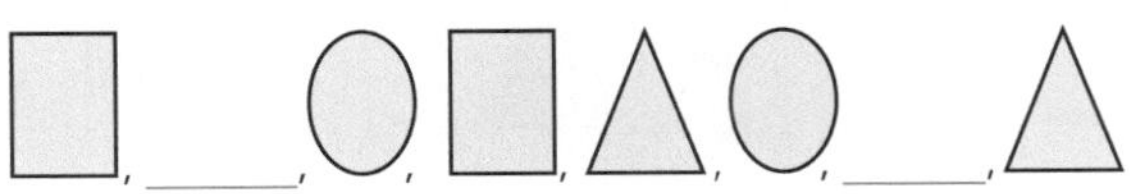

14 **a** Fraction shaded. ________

b Fraction not shaded. ________

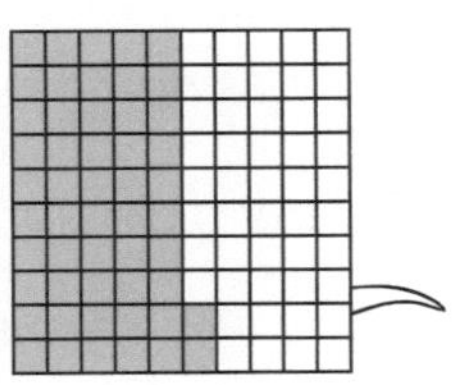

14:4 Extension ☐ out of 4

1 Why is $\frac{1}{8}$ less than $\frac{1}{4}$?

____

____

2 4, 11, 17, 25, 32, 39

a Which number is incorrect in the pattern above? ________

b If the pattern continued correctly, what would the 10th number be? ________

3 If the shaded part has the value given, find the value of the whole.

a

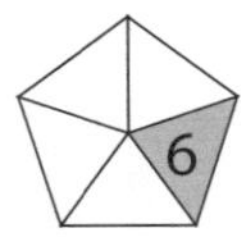

____

b

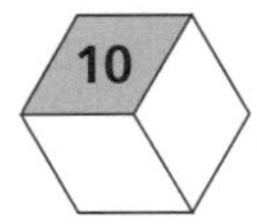

____

4 Four aeroplanes, all the same, have 32 lights altogether. How many lights are on each plane?

____

Challenge

List areas that would be measured in m^2 (eg a tennis court).

____

____

____

____

____

____

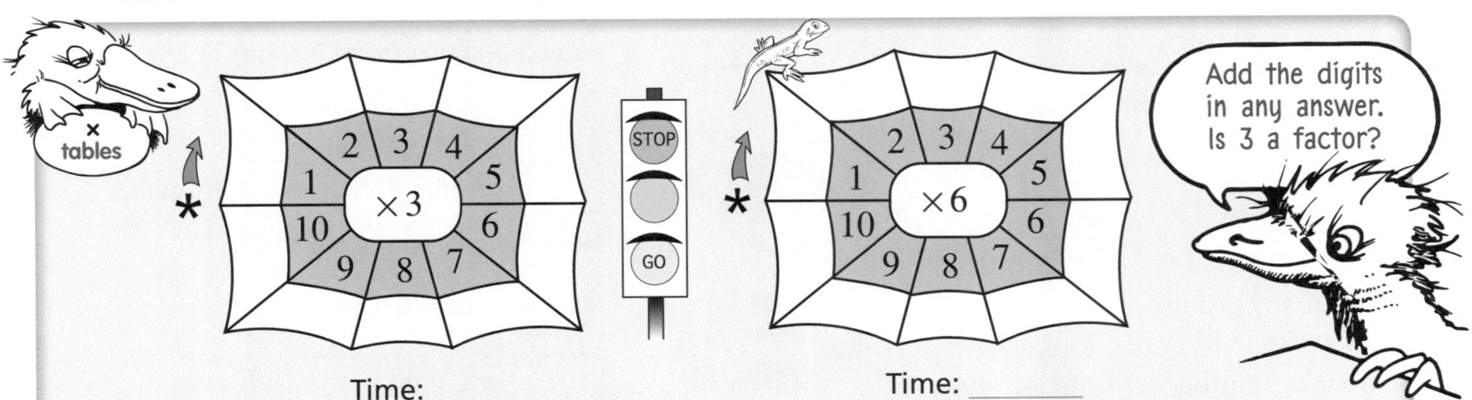

Time: ________ Time: ________

15:1 ☐ out of 15

1. 18 + 3 ____
2. 71 – 71 ____
3. 8 × 5 ____
4. 24 ÷ 4 ____
5. $\begin{array}{r} 42 \\ \times\ \ 3 \\ \hline \end{array}$
6. 19 – 2 ____
7. 5 × 5 ____
8. 32 ÷ 8 ____
9. Double 14. ____
10. $\begin{array}{r} 67 \\ -\,19 \\ \hline \end{array}$

11. How many right angles has a square? ____
12. **a** Fraction shaded ____

    b Fraction not shaded. ____

13. **a** This is a ________ note.

(purple)

    b The value of 3 of these notes. ____

14.

Find four equal shares of the birds.

One share = ________ left over = ________

15. Name the solid modelled.

a

b

________ ________

15:2 ☐ out of 18

1. 4 × 4 ____
2. 13 – 3 ____
3. 40 ÷ 5 ____
4. 3 × 7 ____
5. $\begin{array}{r} 44 \\ +\,37 \\ \hline \end{array}$
6. 10 ÷ 10 ____
7. 100 – 7 ____
8. Half of 22. ____
9. 6 rows of 2. ____
10. $\begin{array}{r} 600 \\ -\ \ 25 \\ \hline \end{array}$

11. Write the size of this angle. ________

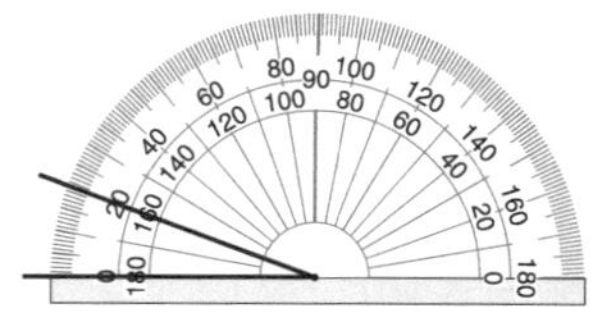

12. These shapes are called i________ shapes.

13. 4 days after Wednesday. ________
14. 10 minutes + 25 minutes ________
15. Write $2\frac{63}{100}$ as a decimal. ________
16. Complete the pattern below.

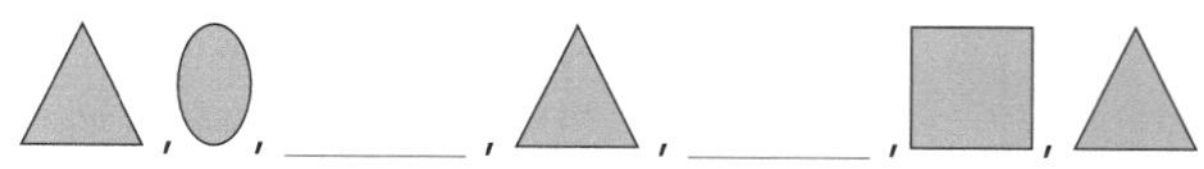

17. If I have 12 pairs, how many shoes do I have? ________
18. How many groups of 5 in 23?

    ________ groups and ________ left over.

Division as repeated subtraction

How many groups of 5 notes in 22?

Answer: 4 groups with 2 left over.

a How many groups of 3 cubes in 28?

☐ groups, with ☐ left over.

b How many lots of 4 stars in 51?

☐ lots, with ☐ left over.

15:3 ☐ out of 13

❶
$$\begin{array}{r} 397 \\ -213 \\ \hline \end{array}$$

❷
$$\begin{array}{r} 635 \\ -432 \\ \hline \end{array}$$

❸
$$\begin{array}{r} 842 \\ -735 \\ \hline \end{array}$$

❹ 7)26 r

❺ 9)76 r

❻ **a** Draw a right angle. **b** Draw a reflex angle.

❼ How many groups of 4?

_______ groups

How many left over? _______ left over

❽ What colour is a $1 coin? _______

❾ True or false?
21 + 4 = 12 + 12 _______

❿ Cody is twice as old as Bill.
If Cody is 30, how old is Bill? _______

⓫ Is an obtuse angle greater than an acute angle? _______

⓬ Find the area of a rectangle with 4 m and 9 m sides. _______

⓭ Complete the pattern below.

a 8, 12, _____, _____, 24, 28

b 7, 12, _____, 22, _____, 32

15:4 ☐ out of 5 Extension

❶ Complete the pattern below.

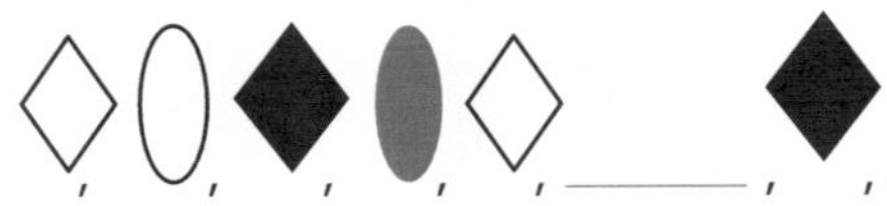

❷ If the pattern above continued, what would the 56th shape be? _______

❸ How many angles, out of A to H, are:

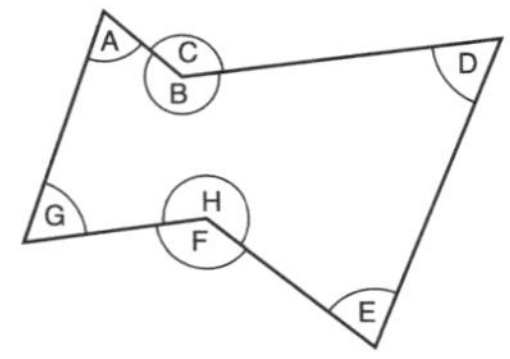

a acute? _______

b reflex? _______

❹ If the shaded part has the value given, find the value of the whole.

a

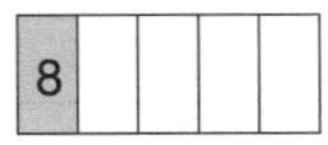

b

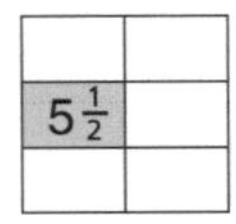

_______ _______

❺ ☐ and △ are counting numbers less than 10 and ☐ + △ +7 = 24.

So ☐ and △ are: _______ and _______.

Challenge

Make up your own number patterns and write the rule for each.

 • *AUSTRALIAN SIGNPOST MATHS 5 MENTALS* • ISBN 978 1 4886 2189 5

16:1 ☐ out of 17

1. 16 – 2 ____
2. 4 ÷ 4 ____
3. 9 × 5 ____
4. 27 – 3 ____
5. $\begin{array}{r} 360 \\ +230 \\ \hline \end{array}$
6. 7 × 4 ____
7. 4 + 38 ____
8. 3 rows of 5. ____
9. 103 take away 10. ____
10. $\begin{array}{r} 300 \\ -128 \\ \hline \end{array}$
11. 4, 8, 12, ____, ____, ____, ____, ____
12. How many digits in 6 709? ____
13. Write the numeral for the number shown. ____

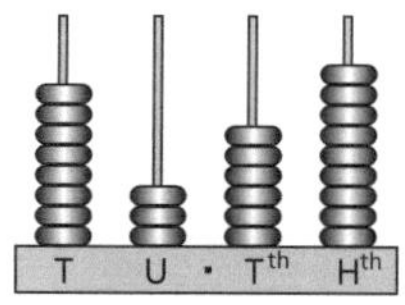

14. a This is a ____ note.
    b The value of 3 of these notes. ____

(red)

15. Half of $18. ____
16. How much more than 13 is 21? ____
17.

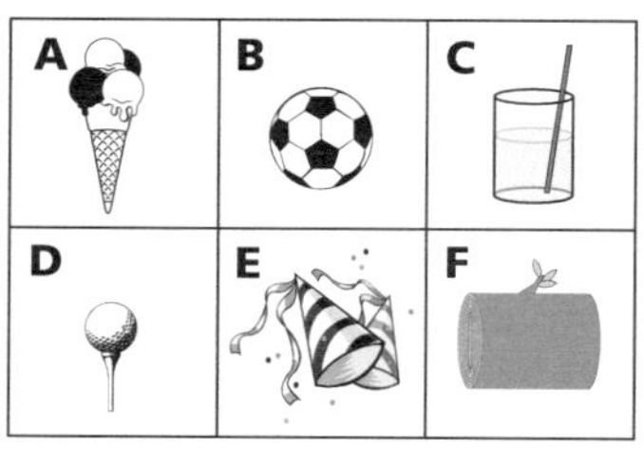

Which pictures show:
    a cones? ____
    b cylinders? ____

16:2 ☐ out of 15

1. 20 + 10 ____
2. 38 + 12 ____
3. 4 × 3 ____
4. 101 – 5 ____
5. $\begin{array}{r} 23 \\ +17 \\ \hline \end{array}$
6. Add 12 and 58. ____
7. 16 take away 9. ____
8. 5 + ____ = 11
9. Half of 70. ____
10. $\begin{array}{r} 64\,\text{mL} \\ -12\,\text{mL} \\ \hline \end{array}$
11. Give the type of angle if its size is:
    a 62° ____
    b 177° ____
12. Of which solid is this a net? ____

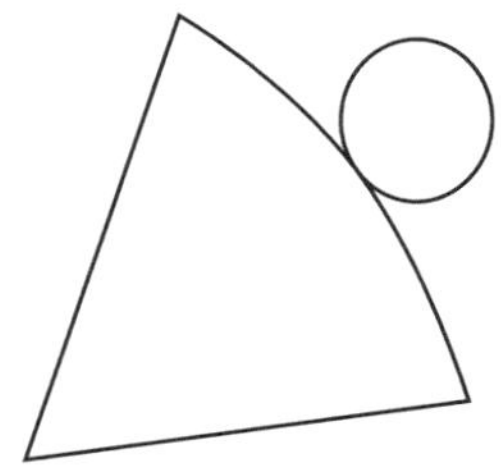

13.

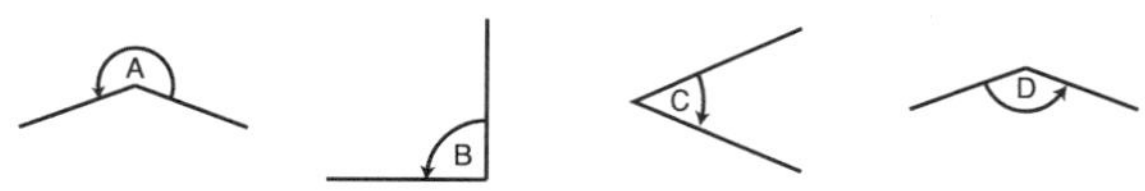

    a Put these angles in order, with the smallest first. ____
    What type of angle (above) is:
    b A? ____ c B? ____
14. Find the area of a square with 5 m sides. ____
15. Complete this pattern.

, , , ____, , ____

Tossing 3 coins

A 10c, a 20c and a $1 coin are tossed.

Complete this list to show the number of different outcomes.

10c	H	H	H					
20c	H	H	T					
$1	H	T	H					

Throw the 3 coins above, 16 times to find how often 3 heads occurs.

Fraction of tosses that gave 3 heads = ____ out of ____.

Fraction of outcomes that have 3 heads = ____ out of ____

 • *AUSTRALIAN SIGNPOST MATHS 5 MENTALS* • ISBN 978 1 4886 2189 5

16:3 ☐ out of 11

❶ 5971 + 1435

❷ 6984 + 1132

❸ 7823 + 1697

❹ $3\overline{)21}$

❺ $5\overline{)30}$

❻ $6\overline{)54}$

❼ 5 red and 4 green marbles are in a bowl.

What is the chance, as a fraction that a marble chosen would be:

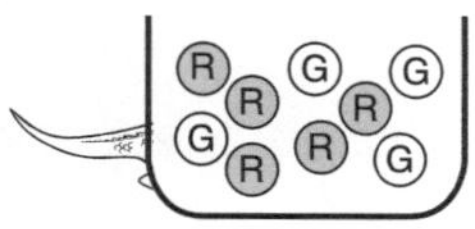

a red? ________

b green? ________

❽ Write the numerals shown.

a

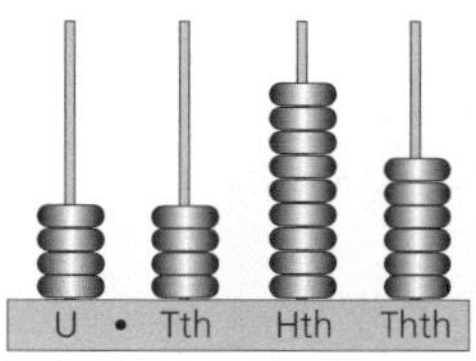

____

b

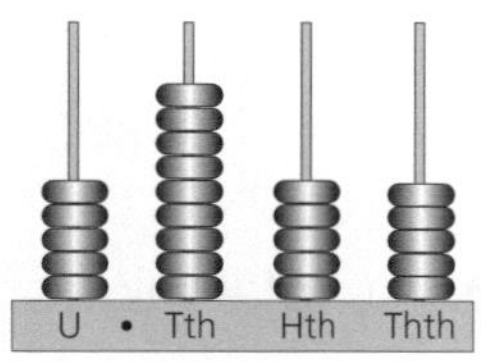

____

❾ **a** Draw an acute angle.

b Draw an obtuse angle.

❿ Write $2\frac{31}{100}$ as a decimal. ________

⓫ **a** 16, 24, 32, ________, ________, ________

b 80, 70, 60, ________, ________, ________

16:4 ☐ out of 5

Extension

❶ 3, 12, 21, 30, ________

a What is the rule in the pattern above? ________

b What would the 9th number be? ________

❷ Estimate how many times angle ***X*** would fit into:

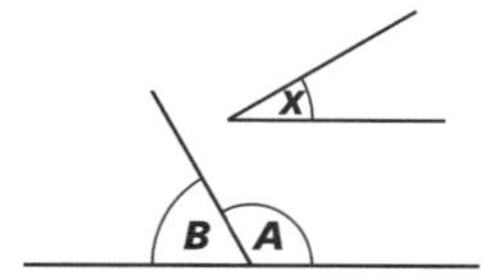

a angle ***A*** ________

b angle ***B*** ________

❸ What is the chance, as a fraction, that the spinner will land on:

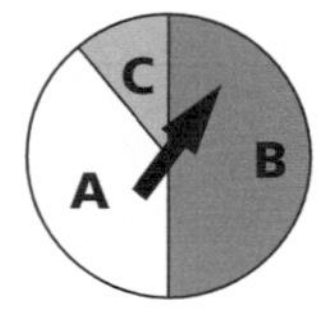

a **A** ________ **b** **B** ________

c **C** ________

❹ If # means 'add 15' and ^ means 'divide by 3', then the value of 9^^### is: ________

❺ ☐ × 7 = 42 ☐ = ________

Challenge

Write everything you know about the number 0·52.

____

____

____

____

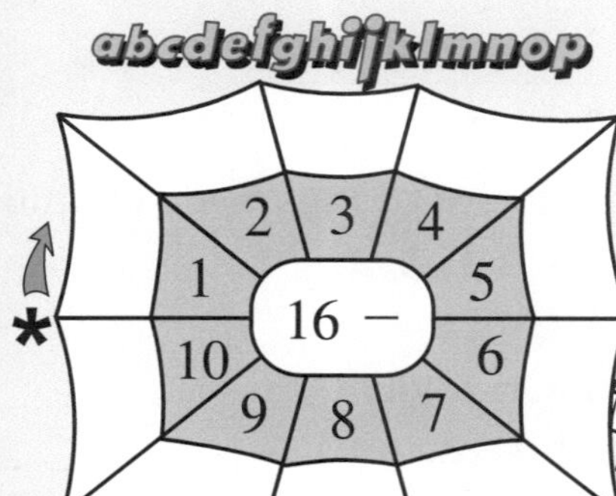

17:1 — out of 17

1. 13 + 5 ______
2. 7 × 7 ______
3. 14 – 6 ______
4. 18 ÷ 3 ______
5. $\begin{array}{r} 11 \\ \times\ 4 \\ \hline \end{array}$
6. 2 × 5 ______
7. 15 – 15 ______
8. 6 plus 73. ______
9. 2 groups of 12. ______
10. $\begin{array}{r} 38\text{m} \\ -21\text{m} \\ \hline \end{array}$
11. Show 8·07 on this abacus.

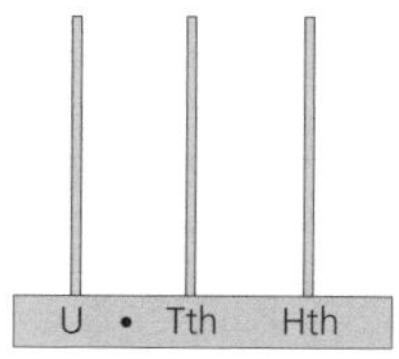

12. Does 1 hectare = 10 000 m^2? ______
13. Which ordinal number comes:
    a before 73rd? ______
    b two after 73rd? ______
14. Find the number of pencils in one share if 3 people share 18 pencils. ______
15. Which angle is:
    a an acute angle? ______
    b an obtuse angle? ______

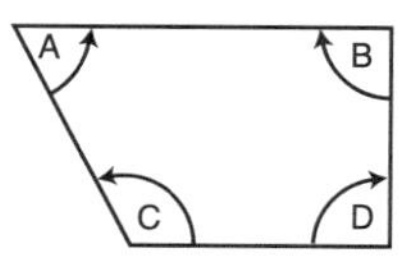

16. Is 30° acute, obtuse or reflex? ______
17. Write the numeral:
    a thirty-three point seven ______
    b eighty point five two ______

17:2 — out of 16

1. 45 + 25 ______
2. 6 × 4 ______
3. 28 – 9 ______
4. 4 × 3 ______
5. $\begin{array}{r} 1270 \\ +\ 650 \\ \hline \end{array}$
6. 90 – 82 ______
7. 80 take away 11. ______
8. 2 times 8. ______
9. 74 plus 6. ______
10. $\begin{array}{r} 1754 \\ +\ 689 \\ \hline \end{array}$
11. Complete the following:

    216·93 = ______ hundreds
    ______ tens
    ______ units
    ______ tenths
    ______ hundredths

12. Hectares in 20 000 m^2. ______
13. The total value of these notes. ______

14. a Write the digital time shown.
    ______
    b Write the analogue time shown.
    ______ to ______

15. How many 20 cent coins placed end to end, would reach 30 cm? ______
16. Square metres in 5 ha. ______

Using a graph

Crosses or dots can be used on a graph.

Draw a graph of these colour choices made by students.

B, R, R, G, P, B, O, R, B, R,G, P, O, R
G, B, P, O, Y, Y, R, B, O, G, G, B, B, P

a Which is the favourite colour? ______
b How many students chose green? ______
c How many more chose red than pink? ______

 • *AUSTRALIAN SIGNPOST MATHS 5 MENTALS* • ISBN 978 1 4886 2189 5

Answers

ID Card A

1 metres **2** millimetres **3** centimetres **4** kilometres **5** litres **6** millilitres **7** grams **8** kilograms **9** seconds **10** minutes **11** hours **12** square centimetres **13** square metres **14** hectares **15** cubic centimetres **16** cubic metres **17** degrees Celsius **18** 5 × 7 **19** 4 × 10 **20** 20 ÷ 5 **21** 42 ÷ 6 **22** counting numbers **23** even numbers **24** odd numbers **25** ordinal numbers **26** digits **27** 2 and 4 **28** 7 **29** 5 **30** remainder

ID Card B

1 line **2** straight line **3** curved line **4** wavy line **5** zigzag line **6** dotted line **7** parallel lines **8** perpendicular lines **9** horizontal line **10** vertical line **11** corner (or vertex) of an angle **12** arm of an angle **13** acute angle **14** right angle **15** obtuse angle **16** straight angle **17** reflex angle **18** revolution **19** tessellation **20** flip **21** slide **22** turn **23** axis of symmetry **24** axes of symmetry **25** number line **26** The coordinates of the dot are E2. **27** picture graph **28** tally **29** column graph **30** line graph

ID Card C

1 triangle **2** square **3** rectangle **4** parallelogram **5** rhombus **6** trapezium **7** quadrilaterals **8** pentagons **9** hexagons **10** octagon **11** circle **12** oval **13** regular shapes **14** irregular shapes **15** Shape B is rigid. **16** diagonals **17** 1 square metre **18** 1 hectare **19** 3 out of 8 **20** $\frac{3}{10}$ shaded **21** $\frac{24}{100}$ shaded **22** $\frac{3}{10}$ shaded **23** 0·3 shaded **24** 0·36 shaded **25** 3 tenths and 6 hundredths **26** 19 out of 100 **27** 62% shaded **28** 1·36 **29** 1·5 **30** $\frac{3}{10}$, $\frac{3}{10}$

ID Card D

1 face **2** vertex or corner **3** edge **4** cube **5** rectangular prism **6** triangular prism **7** hexagonal prism **8** triangular pyramid **9** square pyramid **10** rectangular pyramid **11** base **12** cylinder **13** cone **14** sphere **15** net of a cube **16** net of a square pyramid **17** net of a cylinder **18** net of a cone **19** net of a triangular prism **20** Side view is 3. **21** Front view is 1. **22** Top view is 2. **23** D will not roll. **24** 19:30 **25** 5:40 am **26** protractor **27** pair of compasses **28** thermometer **29** compass **30** tape measure

1:1

1 15 **2** 3 **3** 8 **4** 14 **5** 29 **6** 9 **7** 9 **8** 14 **9** 20 **10** 11 **11**

	Thousands	Hundreds	Tens	Units
a	4	2	8	0
b	2	8	9	3
c		7	2	4

12 a 9, 13 b 34, 6, 12 **13** 942 **14** $0.65 **15** 14 (cakes)

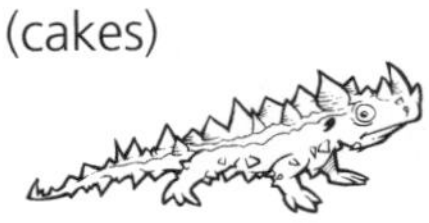

1:2

1 19 **2** 20 **3** 3 **4** 5 **5** 89 **6** 18 **7** 28 **8** 10 **9** 8 **10** 36 **11** a $0.85 b $1.15 **12** 10 (biscuits) **13** 20c, 10c **14** 10 out of 100 **15** 4 (pages) **16** 3622 **17** a 27 b 15

Activity

2, 4, 6, 8, 10, 12, 14, 16, 18, 20
4, 8, 12, 16, 20, 24, 28, 32, 36, 40

1:3

1 292 **2** 228 **3** 520 **4** 3 **5** 6 **6** 8 **7** 37 194 **8** 35 (sheep) **9** $\frac{37}{100}$ **10** 34, 54, 74, 94 **11** 33 **12** 4 (sides) **13** a 4 b 45 **14** 11 (grapes)

1:4

1 383 **2** a 1343 b 3612 **3** 16 (litres) **4** a 10 b 5 c 4 d 2 **5** 8 (coins) **6** 10 (outfits)

Challenge

A prism will be drawn.

Activity

Answers will vary.

2:1

1 15 **2** 21 **3** 1 **4** 20 **5** 12 **6** 16 **7** 18 **8** 7 **9** 10 **10** 59 **11** 8 **12** 80 cm **13** $1.30 **14** 28 **15** no **16** a 15 (minutes) b 25 (minutes) **17** a metres b centimetres

2:2

1 8 **2** 30 **3** 5 **4** 22 **5** 32 **6** 21 **7** 13 **8** 16 **9** 11 **10** 32 **11** 58 254 **12** 24 (flowers) **13** a 3 (weeks) b 10 (weeks) **14** a 2 m b 20 cm c 6 m d 1 m **15** a 3 (groups) b 2 (groups)

Activity

10, 50, 30, 100, 70, 40, 80, 20, 90, 60
5, 25, 15, 50, 35, 20, 40, 10, 45, 30

2:3

1 493 **2** 427 **3** 235 **4** 5 **5** 4 **6** 9 **7** 2 snakes will be shaded. **8** a 3 (hours) b 3 (hours) **9** summer **10** 12 (sweets) **11** a 57 (hundredths) b 43 out of 100 **12** $0.75 **13** 23 (biscuits) **14** 120 (minutes) **15** 42 (days)

2:4

1 a 100 b 75 c 125 **2** 28 (legs) **3** $22 **4** $4.75 **5** 17 (duck eggs) **6** a 88 (sides) b 112 **7** 540

 • *AUSTRALIAN SIGNPOST MATHS 5 MENTALS* • ISBN 978 1 4886 2189 5

Challenge

Horizontal lines will be drawn. Answers will vary.

Activity

1, 9, 5, 4, 0, 8, 2, 6, 3, 7
5, 1, 7, 6, 2, 10, 4, 8, 3, 9
odd, even

3:1

❶ 2 ❷ 12 ❸ 14 ❹ 18 ❺ 26 ❻ 24 ❼ 8 ❽ 12 ❾ 12 ❿ 21 ⓫ pyramid ⓬ $2.60 ⓭ **a** rectangle **b** oval **c** triangle **d** trapezium ⓮ 12 ⓯ 60 ⓰ 4 (digits)

3:2

❶ 19 ❷ 36 ❸ 21 ❹ 35 ❺ 42 ❻ 16 ❼ 1 ❽ 5 ❾ 10 ❿ 36 ⓫ 18 (coins) ⓬ yes ⓭ more ⓮ **a** 6 **b** 12 (edges) ⓯

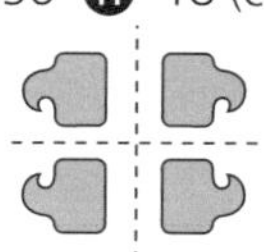

⓰ December and January (or July and August)

Activity

27, 21,18, 24, 3, 9, 12, 30, 15, 6
16, 36, 28, 8, 4, 40, 32, 24, 12, 20

3:3

❶ 127 ❷ 241 ❸ 386 ❹ 6 ❺ 8 ❻ 3 ❼ $13 ❽ no ❾ $2 ❿ no ⓫ June ⓬ 65c ⓭ 5 ⓮ **a** **B**, **C** **b** D ⓯ triangular pyramid

3:4

❶ 48 ❷ 64 (globes) ❸ 5 (cups) ❹ **a** $1.15 **b** 5c ❺ 13 (students) ❻ 320

Challenge

A pyramid will be drawn and described.
One answer could be:
This is a triangular pyramid. Its 4 faces are triangles. It has 6 edges and 4 corners. It can slide.

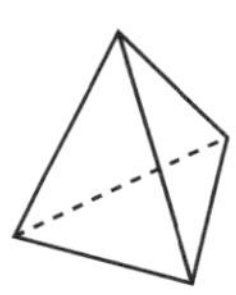

Activity

a 20 (names) **b** 306, 309, 360, 369, 390, 396

4:1

❶ 20 ❷ 21 ❸ 3 ❹ 10 ❺ 69 ❻ 2 ❼ 28 ❽ 12 ❾ 19 ❿ 22 ⓫ cube ⓬ 49 057 ⓭ **a** 7 000 **b** 60 ⓮ 4 (each) ⓯ 2 ⓰ **a** 5 000 **b** 50

4:2

❶ 10 ❷ 4 ❸ 24 ❹ 3 ❺ 80 ❻ 30 ❼ 4 ❽ 35 ❾ 6 ❿ 29 ⓫

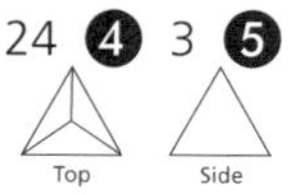

⓬ four thousand and ninety three ⓭ 600 000 ⓮ 4 (each) ⓯ 4 (each) ⓰ 90 745 ⓱ September, October, November ⓲ 231 508

Activity

30, 6, 18, 27, 3, 12, 21, 9, 15, 24
6, 54, 36, 18, 42, 48, 24, 30, 12, 60

4:3

❶ 709 ❷ 949 ❸ 1 234 ❹ B ❺ 721 523 ❻ Wednesday ❼ **a** 45 (minutes) **b** 90 (minutes) ❽ 4 698 557 should be circled. ❾ **a** 177 **b** 85 ❿ 1 400, 1 500,1 600 ⓫ **a** > **b** > ⓬ octagonal prism

4:4

❶ **a** 30 (faces) ❷ 11 packets (with 6 pens left) ❸ **a** $3\frac{1}{2}$ **b** $6\frac{1}{2}$ ❹ **a** 9:37 **b** 8:55 ❺ **a** 1 340 **b** 1 040 ❻ 9 weeks

Challenge

Answers will vary. Some answers include: 6 534 108 has 7 digits. It is an even number that is greater than 1 million. It rounds to 7 000 000 (nearest million).

Activity

1st picture	2nd picture	3rd picture	4th	10th
			10	22
			17	41

5:1

❶ 10 ❷ 5 ❸ 28 ❹ 2 ❺ 19 ❻ 10 ❼ 12 ❽ 13 ❾ 5 ❿ 82 ⓫ **a** 53 205 **b** 20 381 ⓬ 7:35 am ⓭ **a** 200 **b** $1 ⓮ 1 000 (metres) ⓯ 400 352 ⓰ **a** 6 (fish) **b** Matthew

5:2

❶ 16 ❷ 4 ❸ 6 ❹ 32 ❺ 58 ❻ 54 ❼ 24 ❽ 7 ❾ 40 ❿ 46 ⓫ 90 000 ⓬ 395 392 ⓭ 5 (each) ⓮ 7 (kilometres) ⓯ 1 900 247 ⓰ 2 951 633 should be circled. ⓱ 4 km 297 m ⓲ 3 300 ⓳ **a** 4 (hours) **b** 6 (hours) ⓴ triangular prism

Activity

14, 42, 7, 28, 70, 49, 21, 63, 35, 56
35, 21, 49, 63
odd

5:3

❶ 558 ❷ 389 ❸ 478 ❹ 3 395 637, 3 392 035, 3 359 574 ❺ 7 (books) ❻ 366 (days) ❼ **a** 400 **b** Answers will vary. Any number between 450 and 549 inclusive is correct. ❽ 1 000 (metres) ❾ 4:41 ❿ summer ⓫ 2 000 000 ⓬ **a** 5 (faces) **b** 8 (edges)

5:4

❶ 87 (months) ❷ ante meridiem (before midday) ❸ 90 or 91 ❹ **a** 84 **b** 112 ❺ ○ ❻ 20 (minutes)

Challenge

Answers will vary, eg $4\frac{1}{2}$

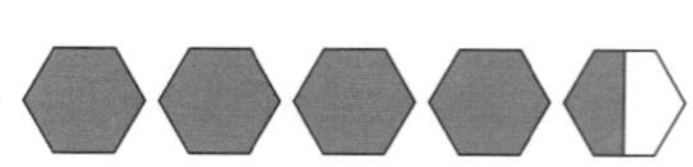

© PEARSON AUSTRALIA 2018 • *AUSTRALIAN SIGNPOST MATHS 5 MENTALS* • ISBN 978 1 4886 2189 5

Activity

4, 2, 8   6, 1, 2, 4   3, 2, 6   12, 4, 6, 3

6:1

1 15 **2** 12 **3** 14 **4** 5 **5** 59 **6** 4 **7** 8 **8** 8 **9** 4 **10** 39 **11** 2578 **12** 12 059 **13** 365 days (or 366 days in one leap year) **14** 2 cakes **15** 14 (days) **16** 1 m **17** 80 (balls) **18** **a** > **b** < **19** 6 023 403

6:2

1 8 **2** 24 **3** 15 **4** 6 **5** 8 **6** 10 **7** 51 **8** 15 **9** 13 **10** 83c **11** 8 781 344, 8 780 033, 8 768 367 **12** 5 books **13** June, July, August **14** 900 **15** half **16** **a** 12 hours **b** 61 (hours)

Activity

8, 16, 24, 32, 40, 48, 56, 64, 72, 80

a 56 (stickers) **b** 48 (ties)

6:3

1 702 **2** 410 **3** 7 toys **4** 9 km 72 m **5** 2 087 (m) **6** **a** 1:00 **b** 12:55 **7** 20 cm **8** Answers will vary. **9** 9:04 am **10** 6 000 000

6:4

1 **a** \$4 **b** \$8 **2** 250 m **3** 49 **4** 6 **5** **a** 410 **b** 120 **6** 40 (flowers) **7** **a** 20 (centuries) **b** 70 (decades)

Challenge

Answers will vary. One answer could be: A square has 4 equal sides and 4 right angles. It has 4 lines of symmetry.

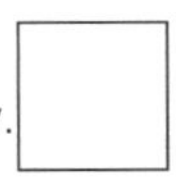

Activity

2, 1, 5   9, 27, 3

5, 6, 15   21, 7, 6

7:1

1 2 **2** 18 **3** 3 **4** 31 **5** 88 **6** 15 **7** 1 **8** 14 **9** 10 **10** 124 **11** 90 372 **12** 9000 (m) **13** **a** kilometres **b** centimetres **14** 12 cm **15** 6 { 3 (or 18) **16** 30 **17** 70 **18** 0·37 **19** 4007

7:2

1 9 **2** 13 **3** 5 **4** 18 **5** 70 **6** 9 **7** 9 **8** 36 **9** 21 **10** 89 **11** 9 (cards) **12** **a** 6 (hours) **b** 20 (hours) **13** **a** 8000 **b** 9 700 **14** 1 000 (m) **15** 3000 **16** 3656 **17**

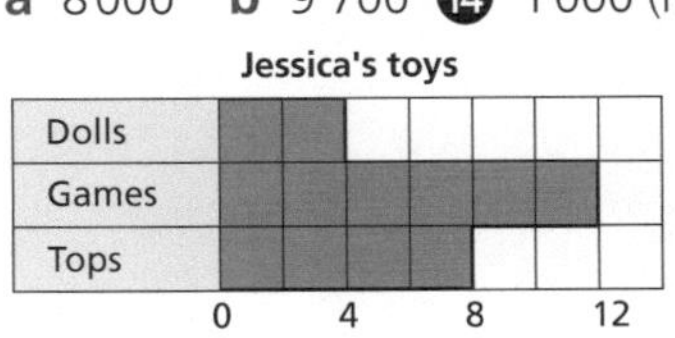

Activity

18, 54, 63, 27, 9, 45, 81, 36, 72, 90

9, 18, 27, 36, 45, 54, 63, 72, 81, 90

7:3

1 442 **2** 492 **3** 411 **4** 11 **5** 839 **6** 7 × 10^2 **7** 11 **8** **a** December **b** Christmas is in December. **c** 75 (sales) **9** 2 (km) **10** **a** min **b** h

7:4

1 **a** about 11 or 12 cm **b** about 4 or 5 cm **2** 90 or 91 **3** **a** 31 **b** 60 **4** **a** 64 × 3 = 192 **b** 387 ÷ 3 = 129 **5** 810

Challenge

Answers will vary.

One answer could be:

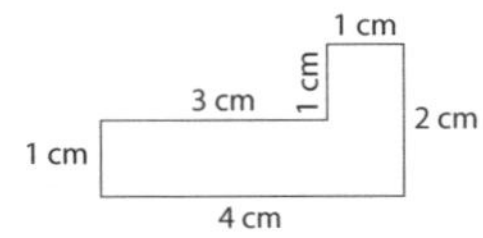

Activity

1 metres **2** millimetres **3** centimetres **4** kilometres **5** litres **6** millilitres **7** grams **8** kilograms **10** minutes **15** cubic centimetres

8:1

1 11 **2** 35 **3** 8 **4** 2 **5** 14 **6** 18 **7** 11 **8** 48 **9** 22 **10** 84 **11** $\frac{2}{6}$ **12**

Chickens	𝍸 III
Pigs	IIII
Cows	II

13 **a** < **b** > **14** 10, 12,14 **15** 600 **16**

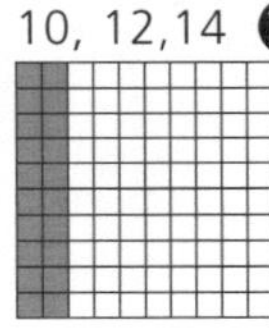

80 out of 100 (or 8 tenths or 4 fifths)

8:2

1 14 **2** 16 **3** 11 **4** 18 **5** 50 **6** 36 **7** 10 **8** 2 **9** 11 **10** 7 **11** 8 381 **12** 10 cm **13** 1 579 **14** 800 **15** six hundred and three thousand two hundred and eleven **16** **a** 8 tenths and 6 hundredths **b** 0·68 **17** 6

Activity

0, 3, 7, 8, 6, 4, 2, 5, 1, 9   6+ [9] = 15

7, 5, 9, 2, 8, 6, 0, 10, 3, 1   8+ [6] = 14

8:3

1 272 **2** 245 **3** 3 { 10^3 **4** 8cm **5** 3 (groups) **6** **a** 9 (pictures) **b** 12 (pictures) **7** 500, 505, 510 **8** **a** $\frac{2}{6}$ or $\frac{1}{3}$ **b** $\frac{4}{6}$ (or $\frac{2}{3}$) **c** $\frac{4}{6}$ **9** $\frac{9}{10}$

8:4

1 47 **2** **a** 24 **b** 24 **3** \$4.20 **4** 35 **5** 90 (bananas) **6** $\frac{1}{10}$ **7** 54

Challenge

Answers will vary.

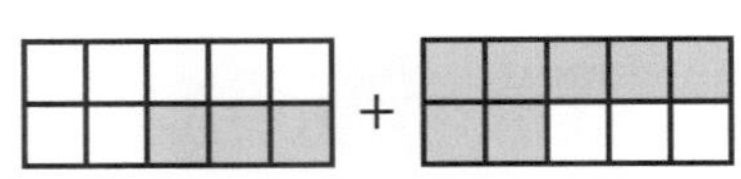

$\frac{3}{10} + \frac{7}{10} = 1$

Activity

27 friends had arrived by 7:30 pm.

9:1

1 10 **2** 6 **3** 6 **4** 1 **5** 12 **6** 27 **7** 17 **8** 5 **9** 18 **10** 97 **11** 3, 6, 9, 12, 15, 18 **12** 6879, 7684, 8147, 10000 **13** 1, 12, 2, 6, 3, 4 **14** flip **15** $2 **16** 60 (hundredths) **17** 100 (years)

9:2

1 12 **2** 45 **3** 2 **4** 8 **5** 38 **6** 9 **7** 11 **8** 42 **9** 27 **10** 9 **11** flip — reflection, slide — translation, turn — rotation **12** yes **13** $\frac{1}{8}, \frac{1}{4}, \frac{1}{2}$

14 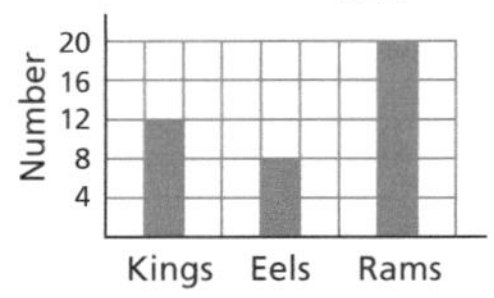

15 **a** $\frac{3}{9}$ (or $\frac{1}{3}$) **b** $\frac{6}{9}$ (or $\frac{2}{3}$) **c** $\frac{6}{9}$

Activity

a 2 **b** 6 (including the 2 squares) **c** 1

9:3

1 58 **2** 255 **3** 5, 10, 15, 20, 25, 30 **4** 1, 9, 3 **5** **a** $5 **b** $19 **c** $11 **6** **a**  **b** 51 (runs)

9:4

1 **a** left **b** right **2** **a** 6 **b** 27 **3** **a** 100 **b** 36 **4** 61 **5** 280

Challenge

Answers will vary. Some answers include:
a 2, 4, 6, 8, 10 **b** 3, 6, 9, 12 **c** 4, 8, 12,16 **d** 5,10,15, 20 **e** 6, 12, 18, 24

Activity

1 **a** 1200 **b** 1050 **c** 1053 **2** **a** 900 **b** 1050 **c** 1047 **3** **a** 6 **b** 300

10:1

1 12 **2** 63 **3** 7 **4** 3 **5** 10 **6** 24 **7** 30 **8** 8 **9** 6 **10** 20 **11** slide **12** translation **13** 17 **14** $1.15 **15** 1268 **16** cube **17** **a** 18 **b** 17

10:2

1 32 **2** 13 **3** 8 **4** 9 **5** 81 **6** 102 **7** 13 **8** 14 **9** 24 **10** 501 **11** 7, 14, 21, 28, 35, 42 **12** 17th **13** square 7, 14, 21, 28 pyramid **14** 1, 12, 2, 6, 3 ,4

15 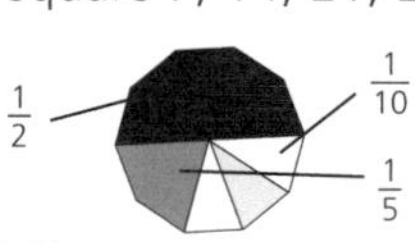

16 50 (hundredths)

Activity

Number	Possible factors						
16	(1)	(2)	3	(4)	6	(8)	(16)
25	(1)	2	3	(5)	10	(25)	50
18	(1)	(2)	(3)	4	(6)	(9)	(18)
9	(1)	2	(3)	4	5	6	(9)

Number	Possible factors						
12	(1)	(2)	(3)	(4)	(6)	(12)	24
28	(1)	(2)	(4)	6	(7)	(14)	(28)
81	(1)	(3)	(9)	18	(27)	40	(81)
121	(1)	3	7	9	(11)	22	(121)

10:3

1 267 **2** 179 **3** 33 **4** $\frac{1}{10}, \frac{1}{5}, \frac{1}{3}$

5 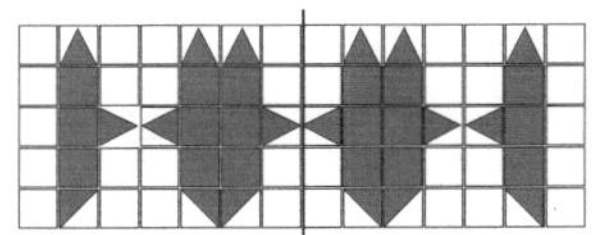

6 **a** 1, 8, 2, 4 **b** 70 **7** **a** 23 **b** March **c** Answers will vary. The team could have been on holidays.

10:4

1 **a** 5 **b** 2 **2** **a** 32 **b** 24 **3** 31, 63 **4** **a** $10 **b** $30 **5** **a** 61 **b** 30

Challenge

Answers will vary. A symmetrical design will be drawn.

Activity

a 4, 8, 12,16, 20 **b** 10, 20, 30, 40, 50 **c** 4, 8, 12, 16, 20 **d** 10, 20, 30, 40, 50 **e** 0, 0, 0, 0, 0 **f** 4, 7, 3, 9, 6

11:1

1 42 **2** 11 **3** 4 **4** 3 **5** 22 **6** 11 **7** 20 **8** 35 **9** 4 **10** 483 **11** **a** butterfly **b** cube **c** umbrella **12** **a** $1.65 **b** 12 **13** 1304, 1473, 1692, 1724 **14** odd **15** 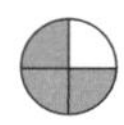 **16** **a** 3650 **b** 2401

11:2

1 4 **2** 10 **3** 2 **4** 20 **5** 16 **6** 4 **7** 42 **8** 2 **9** 49 **10** $26 **11** **a** C **b** A **c** B **12** 8 **13** 2000 + 50 + 3 **14** C **15** yes

Activity

1 B **2** F

11:3

1 880 **2** $5.75 **3** $12.34 **4** **a** rectangle **b** 3A **c** 2B **5** 75° **6** 1240, 1250, 1260, 1270, 1280 **7** 2 (right angles) **8** square pyramid **9** turn **10** reflection

11:4

1 23 **2** 36 **3** **a** 93 **b** 81 **4** 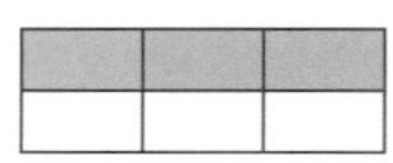 **5** **a** 14 toys **b** 7 toys

Challenge

Answers will vary.

Activity

10, 20, 30, 40, 50, 60, 70, 80, 90, 100
5, 10, 15, 20, 25, 30, 35, 40, 45, 50

12:1

1 40 **2** 0 **3** 5 **4** 9 **5** $137 **6** 7 **7** 64 **8** 20 **9** 1 **10** 40 **11** your estimate, 5 cm **12** 9 (plants) **13** **a** 650 (cents) **b** $3.75 **14** 4 (faces) **15** 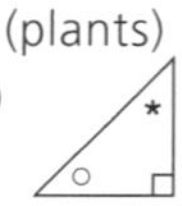

12:2

❶ 3 ❷ 13 ❸ 12 ❹ 3 ❺ 55c ❻ 20 ❼ 16 ❽ 28 ❾ 4 ❿ 22 ⓫ $17 ⓬ 70° ⓭ one hundred and nine thousand seven hundred and three ⓮ **a** 5 000 **b** 5 times ⓯ **a** ✪ **b** ♥ **c** ✔ **d** ✎

Activity

a Monday **b** Tuesday **c** 8 (days) **d** 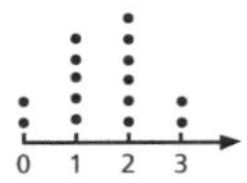

12:3

❶ $5.28 ❷ $1.48 ❸ 8 (weeks) ❹ 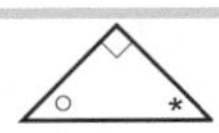 ❺ 40 (5c coins) ❻ 4 360, 4 365 ❼ obtuse ❽ $4.00 ❾ **a** about 8 150 **b** 1993 ❿ A

12:4

❶ $97 ❷ **a** 3 **b** 4 ❸ **a** 128 **b** 160 ❹ 184 ❺ **a** 48 **b** 53

Challenge

Answers will vary. One answer is: 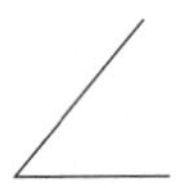
acute angle

Activity

(4) cube **(5)** rectangular prism **(6)** triangular prism **(7)** hexagonal prism **(8)** triangular pyramid **(9)** square pyramid **(12)** cylinder **(13)** cone

13:1

❶ 30 ❷ 11 ❸ 42 ❹ 28 ❺ 896 ❻ 20 ❼ 11 ❽ 34 ❾ 4 ❿ 384 ⓫ 4 (groups), 2 (left over) ⓬ square pyramid ⓭ 28 (cows) ⓮ **a** < **b** > ⓯ $\frac{34}{100}$

13:2

❶ 32 ❷ 100 ❸ 450 ❹ 2 ❺ 39 ❻ 160 ❼ 6 ❽ 33 ❾ 8 ❿ 6 ⓫ 7 069 ⓬ $12 ⓭ $25 ⓮ 130° ⓯ square pyramid ⓰ 5, $5\frac{1}{2}$, 6 ⓱ 1·4 ⓲ **a** 4"6 (hundredths) **b** 46 out of 100 **c** 0"46

Activity

a 2 **b** 2 (times) **c** 7 (goals) **d** 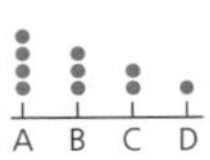

13:3

❶ $4.65 ❷ $2.15 ❸ **a** 6r4 **b** 9r5 ❹ **a** 14 cm **b** 6 cm^2 ❺ 3 (flowers) ❻ 21 (days) ❼ 10 ❽ $\frac{2}{3}$ ❾ acute ❿ 43 ⓫ $\frac{7}{10}$ (or $\frac{70}{100}$)

13:4

❶ $3.15 ❷ 0·22, 0·24, 0·26 ❸ **a** 51 **b** 12 ❹ 2 (oranges) ❺ **a** $\frac{1}{3}$ **b** $\frac{3}{8}$ ❻ 60

Challenge

Answers will vary. One answer is: 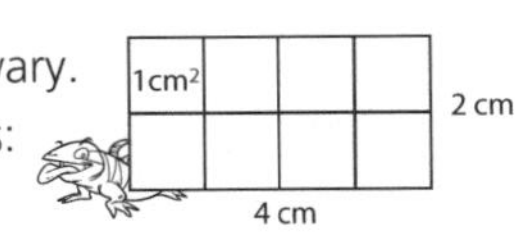

Activity

a 7 cm^2 **b** 6 cm^2 **c** 11 cm^2

14:1

❶ 30 ❷ 11 ❸ 14 ❹ 42 ❺ 458 ❻ 14 ❼ 36 ❽ 93 ❾ 17 ❿ 18 ⓫ $\frac{1}{10}$ ⓬ **a** $\frac{6}{8}$ (or $\frac{3}{4}$) **b** $\frac{2}{8}$ ($\frac{1}{4}$) ⓭ 11 (stickers) ⓮ 12, 14, 16, 18 ⓯ 0·33 ⓰ four thousand and seventy ⓱ **a** 15 (stars) **b** 28 (beads)

14:2

❶ 9 ❷ 13 ❸ 15 ❹ 5 ❺ 72 ❻ 280 ❼ 8 ❽ 18 ❾ 5 ❿ 80 ⓫ **a** 0·3 **b** 0·7 **c** 0·5 **d** 1·1 ⓬ **a** 12 (pairs) **b** 9 (pairs) ⓭ 16, 19, 22 ⓮ 30 m^2 ⓯ One share = 3, Left over = 3 ⓰ $\frac{63}{100}$ ⓱ $\frac{67}{100}$

Activity

a 6 coins each with 2 left over **b** 6 cards each with 3 left over

14:3

❶ 289 ❷ 430 ❸ 266 ❹ 5 r 4 ❺ 9 r 4 ❻ 0·11, 0·12, 0·13 ❼ One share = 4, Left over = 3 ❽ **a** 10 cm **b** 6 cm^2 ❾ $1.50 ❿ 4 (digits) ⓫ 5 (faces) ⓬ 42, 48, 54 ⓭  ⓮ **a** $\frac{52}{100}$ **b** $\frac{48}{100}$

14:4

❶ $\frac{1}{4}$ is 1 out of 4 but $\frac{1}{8}$ is only 1 out of 8. 2 out of 8 is equal to $\frac{1}{4}$. ❷ **a** 17 **b** 67 ❸ **a** 30 **b** 30 ❹ 8 (lights)

Challenge

Answers will vary. Examples include: classroom floor, windows, blinds and display boards.

Activity

3, 6, 9, 12, 15, 18, 21, 24, 27, 30
6, 12, 18, 24, 30, 36, 42, 48, 54, 60

15:1

❶ 21 ❷ 0 ❸ 40 ❹ 6 ❺ 126 ❻ 17 ❼ 25 ❽ 4 ❾ 28 ❿ 48 ⓫ 4 (right angles) ⓬ **a** $\frac{4}{6}$ (or $\frac{2}{3}$) **b** $\frac{2}{6}$ (or $\frac{1}{3}$) ⓭ **a** $5 **b** $15 ⓮ One share = 6, left over = 3) ⓯ **a** cylinder **b** sphere

15:2

❶ 16 ❷ 10 ❸ 8 ❹ 21 ❺ 81 ❻ 1 ❼ 93 ❽ 11 ❾ 12 ❿ 575 ⓫ 20° ⓬ irregular ⓭ Sunday ⓮ 35 minutes ⓯ 2·63 ⓰  ⓱ 24 (shoes) ⓲ 4 groups and 3 left over

Activity

a 9 groups, with 1 left over **b** 12 lots, with 3 left over

15:3

❶ 184 ❷ 203 ❸ 107 ❹ 3 r 5 ❺ 8 r 4 ❻ **a**  **b**  ❼ 3 (groups), 1 (left over) ❽ gold ❾ false ❿ 15 ⓫ yes ⓬ 36 cm^2 ⓭ **a** 16, 20 **b** 17, 27

15:4

1  **2** **3** a 4 b 2 **4** a 40 b 33 **5** 9 and 8

Challenge

Answers will vary. One answer could be: 6, 12, 18, 24, 30, 36
The rule is add 6.

Activity

4, 7, 0, 10, 5, 2, 9, 6, 3, 8
0, 8, 2, 7, 10, 3, 6, 9, 4, 5

16:1

1 14 **2** 1 **3** 45 **4** 24 **5** 590 **6** 28 **7** 42 **8** 15 **9** 93 **10** 172 **11** 16, 20, 24, 28, 32 **12** 4 (digits) **13** 83·69 **14** a $20 b $60 **15** $9 **16** 8 **17** a A, E (and perhaps D) b C, F

16:2

1 30 **2** 50 **3** 12 **4** 96 **5** 40 **6** 70 **7** 7 **8** 6 **9** 35 **10** 52 mL **11** a acute b obtuse **12** cone **13** a C, B, D, A b reflex c right **14** 25 m^2
15 

Activity

10c	H	H	H	H	T	T	T	T
20c	H	H	T	T	T	T	H	H
$1	H	T	H	T	T	H	T	H

Fraction of outcomes that have 3 heads = 1 out of 8
Results will vary for the experiment.

16:3

1 7406 **2** 8116 **3** 9520 **4** 7 **5** 6 **6** 9
7 a $\frac{5}{9}$ b $\frac{4}{9}$
8 a 4·496 b 5·955 **9** a 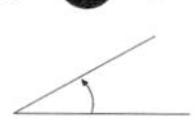 b 
10 231 **11** a 40, 48, 56 b 50, 40, 30

16:4

1 a add 9 b 75 **2** a 4 times b 2 times **3** a $\frac{3}{8}$ b $\frac{1}{2}$ c $\frac{1}{8}$ **4** 46 **5** 6

Challenge

Answers will vary. One answer could be: 0·52 is a decimal, less than one. It is greater than, but almost equal to a half. It is equal to $\frac{52}{100}$, $\frac{26}{50}$ and $\frac{13}{25}$.

Activity

14, 13, 12, 11, 10, 9, 8, 7, 6, 5
15, 14, 13, 12, 11,10, 9, 8, 7

17:1

1 18 **2** 49 **3** 8 **4** 6 **5** 44 **6** 10 **7** 0 **8** 79
9 24 **10** 17 m **11**  **12** yes **13** a 72nd b 75th
14 6 (each) **15** a A b C **16** acute **17** a 33″7 b 80″52

17:2

1 70 **2** 24 **3** 19 **4** 12 **5** 1920 **6** 8 **7** 69 **8** 16 **9** 80 **10** 2443 **11** 2 hundreds, 1 ten, 6 units, 9 tenths and 3 hundredths **12** 2 (hectares) **13** $175 **14** a 12:38 b 22 to 1 **15** 11 **16** 50 000 m^2

Activity

(Answers will vary.) a blue b 5 (students) c 2

17:3

1 2543 **2** 2815 **3** 1316 **4** 9 r 1 **5** 5 r 2 **6** a $\frac{1}{2}$ b $\frac{1}{4}$ **7** 60 000 m^2 **8** a A, B b A, B c A, C **9** 3 410 **10** ha **11** a 5″778 b 9″378

17:4

1 a 14 b 20 **2** a < b < **3** 0 **4** a 376 b 354 c 476
5 Monday

Challenge

Answers will vary. Some answers include:
cm^2: a coin, a DVD ha: a park, a farm

Activity

(3) curved line **(4)** wavy line **(5)** zigzag line **(6)** dotted line **(7)** parallel lines **(8)** perpendicular lines **(19)** tessellation **(20)** flip **(21)** slide **(22)** turn

18:1

1 120 **2** 42 **3** 11 **4** 100 **5** 315 **6** 9 **7** 4
8 102 **9** 25 **10** 556 **11** ha **12** 7 cm^3
13 1710 **14** six thousand eight hundred and forty-nine
15 89 and 94 will be circled. **16** $8 **17** true
18 a 90 (degrees) b 180 (degrees)

18:2

1 4 **2** 17 **3** 18 **4** 36 **5** 5327 **6** 40 **7** 13 **8** 13
9 9 **10** 2635 **11** 9 (hectares) **12** 108 **13** 6993
14 2203, 2213, 2223, 2233 **15** 9730 **16** 4 **17** 4000
18 27cm^3 **19** a 49″21 b 60″89

Activity

a 352 b 681

18:3

1 1564 **2** 3503 **3** $\frac{2}{7}$ **4** $\frac{3}{6}$ (or $\frac{1}{2}$) **5** 32 cm^3
6 70 (days) **7** a 71 m^2 b 24 m^2 **8** 30 000 m^2
9 1 hundred, 3 tens, 4 units, 5 tenths, 8 hundredths

18:4

1 36 **2** 12 (weeks) **3** a 17 r 2 b 23 r 1 **4** 77
5 180° or 360° **6** a 160 b 460 c 1460

Challenge

a
4999 + 1
~~5000~~
− 2537
2462 + 1
= 2463

b
7999 + 1
~~8000~~
− 4291
3708 + 1
= 3709

Activity

14, 42, 7, 28, 70, 49, 21, 63, 35, 56
16, 48, 8, 32, 80, 56, 24, 72, 40, 64

19:1

1 3 **2** 13 **3** 48 **4** 12 **5** 1027 **6** 24 **7** 180 **8** 35 **9** 4 **10** 517 **11** 52 cm^3 **12** yes **13** right angle **14** $1.83 **15** 0·54 **16** **a** 6:20 **b** 20 past 6 **17** 3, 6, 9, 12,15 **18**

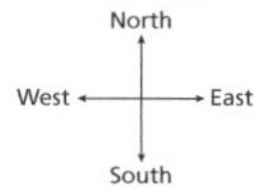

19 31 (days) **20** 1, 20, 2, 10, 4, 5

19:2

1 5 **2** 17 **3** 56 **4** 5 **5** 348 **6** 1 **7** 35 **8** 24 **9** 42 **10** 914 **11** **a** 36 cm^3 **b** 100 cm^3 **12** 320 **13** **a** 6·09 **b** 19·3 **14** **a** divided bar graph **b** 30 minutes **c** 1 hour **d** 45 minutes **e** $1\frac{1}{4}$ hours (or 75 minutes)

Activity

a south-east **b** south-west **c** north-west

19:3

1 5369 **2** 3778 **3** 6576 **4** 2 r 4 **5** 6 r 1 **6** 736 **7** $\frac{35}{100}$ or 0·35 **8** **a** 0·17 **b** 0·09 **9** 1, 32, 2, 16, 4, 8 **10** 100 (cm) **11** 1300 m^2 **12** 2 hundreds, 0 tens, 1 unit, 7 tenths, 9 hundredths

19:4

1 27 (cubes) **2** 4079 **3** 9 **4** 7·8 cm and 8·8 cm **5** 1382

Challenge

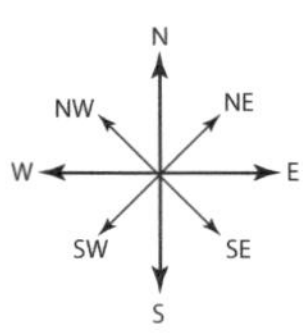

Activity

8, 32, 48, 24, 40, 64, 16, 72, 56, 80
6, 24, 36, 18, 30, 48, 12, 54, 42, 60

20:1

1 21 **2** 13 **3** 27 **4** 10 **5** 282 **6** 100 **7** 106 **8** 9 **9** 20 **10** 41 **11** 7 **12** 8 **13** 4 **14** **a** straight **b** acute **c** obtuse **d** acute **15**

E	S	U	F	M
||||	|||	|	||	|

16 1, 9, 3 **17** 36

20:2

1 0 **2** 14 **3** 55 **4** 2 **5** 309 **6** 48 **7** 50 **8** 6 m **9** 24 **10** 818 **11** 374 **12** 0·37 **13** **a** car **b** boy **c** bus **d** house **14** 30, 36 **15** **a** > **b** > **16** 24 cm^3

Activity

1, 8, 5, 2, 7, 9, 3, 10, 6, 4
5, 1, 10, 6, 2, 8, 4, 7, 3, 9
[8] × 3 = 24, [8] × 6 = 48

20:3

1 3250 **2** 5750 **3** 6957 **4** 41 **5** 23 **6** 12 **7** 662 **8** **a** 3 hundredths **b** 1 tenth **9** trapezium **10** 1, 18, 2, 9, 3, 6 **11** **a** 0·8 **b** 1·2 **12** 272

20:4

1 E **2** **a** $\frac{1}{2}$ **b** $\frac{1}{4}$ **3** 24th March 2012 **4** 2 (birds) **5** 16

Challenge

83·561 is greater than $83\frac{1}{2}$. It has 8 tens, 3 units, 5 tenths, 6 hundredths and 1 thousandth. It rounds to 84 (nearest whole number) and 80 (nearest ten).

Activity

1 **a** dog **b** fish **c** cake **d** bird **2** **a** M **b** P **c** P **d** C

21:1

1 35 **2** 6 **3** 21 **4** 2 **5** 83 **6** 82 **7** 40 **8** 66 **9** 15 **10** 54 **11** 3 **12** 6 **13** 6 **14** 12 cm^3 **15** yes **16** **a** B2 **b** D3 **c** dam **d** stable

21:2

1 31 **2** 60 **3** 7 **4** 97 **5** 12 **6** 54 **7** 7 **8** 54 **9** 106 **10** 912 **11** 512 **12** $\frac{52}{100}$ (or $\frac{26}{50}$) **13** **a** yes **b** yes **14** 20 (boys) **15** 130° **16** 45 cm^3 **17** **a** 0·4 **b** 0·71

Activity

1 **a** C **b** A **2** B **3** 14

21:3

1 4679 **2** 4630 **3** 179 **4** 21 **5** 22 **6** 13 **7** 0·14 **8** 24 cm^3 **9** 6024 **10** 7 **11** **a** C **b** 4 (times) **12** 1, 24, 2, 12, 3, 8, 4, 6

21:4

1 **a** 36 **b** 144 cm^3 **2** 22·5 **3** $3.30 **4** **a** 3 **b** 9 **5** **a** 30 **b** 60 **6** 85

Challenge

Answers will vary. One answer could include: Half of the group (or 50%) chose blue as their favourite colour. One quarter of the group (or 25%) chose red. Pink was the least favourite colour. Green was not as popular as blue or red, but more popular than pink.

Activity

a 2 **b** 8 **c** 10 **d** 12

22:1

1 60 **2** 50 **3** 6 **4** 36 **5** 1099 **6** 13 **7** 150 **8** 72 **9** 180 **10** 8544 **11** 10 cm^3 **12** $\frac{2}{4}$ (or $\frac{1}{2}$) **13** **a** 3:15 **b** 3:45 **14** 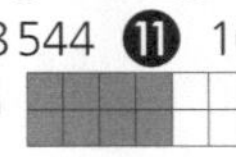 **15** 9 (each) **16** 1000 (mL) **17** 300 **18** eight thousand seven hundred and forty

22:2

1 14 **2** 10 **3** 180 **4** 108 **5** 430 **6** 56 **7** 1 **8** 230 **9** 30 **10** 5529 **11** 363

 • *AUSTRALIAN SIGNPOST MATHS 5 MENTALS* • ISBN 978 1 4886 2189 5

12 a yes b C **13** post meridiem (after midday)
14 a 12 (students) b no c 25 (students)

Activity

54 m

22:3

1 600 **2** 150 **3** 400 **4** 331 **5** 431 **6** 131
7 80 cm^3 **8** 3 (students) **9** a 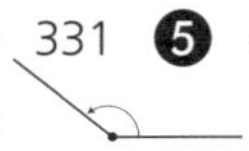 b Answers will vary. An obtuse angle will be between 90 and 180 degrees.
10 $\frac{5}{8}$ **11** a 12 pm b 9 pm c 1 am d 3 am
12 a 7213 b 2922

22:4

1 30 ° **2** 12 (cards) **3** a $\frac{5}{10}$ (or $\frac{1}{2}$ or 0·5) b $1\frac{5}{10}$ (or $1\frac{1}{2}$ or 1·5) **4** 14 (squares) **5** 3

Challenge

Answers will vary.

Activity

(1) triangle (2) square (3) rectangle (5) rhombus
(6) trapezium (8) pentagons (9) hexagons (10) octagon
(11) circle (12) oval

23:1

1 18 **2** 38 **3** 270 **4** 3 **5** 1098 **6** 8 **7** 21
8 16 **9** 36 **10** 1052 **11** 18:00 **12** a T b F
13 a 400 b 6 **14** 31 (days) **15** a 120 (months) b 1200 (months) **16** a \$50 b \$150 **17** 19, 22, 25, 28 **18** 9630

23:2

1 7 **2** 88 **3** 35 **4** 130 **5** 973 **6** 15
7 54 **8** 240 **9** 19 **10** 340 **11** a 6:00 pm b 9:00 pm **12** 6429 **13** $4\frac{1}{2}$ hours **14** a $\frac{7}{12}$ b $\frac{5}{12}$
15 a B b A **16** seven thousand and thirty-one **17** $\frac{9}{10}$

Activity

2, 6, 3, 9, 7, 4, 10, 8, 5, 1
2, 5, 8, 1, 7, 9, 3, 6, 4, 10

23:3

1 120 **2** 700 **3** 210 **4** 20 **5** 34 **6** 70 r 3
7 a 8:00 pm b 7:00 am **8** a 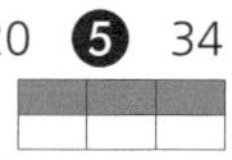 b $\frac{1}{6}$
9 240 (melons) **10** a A b A **11** a 9:56 am b 2:33 pm
12 1 (or $\frac{3}{3}$)

23:4

1 a 6:18 b 11:50 **2** 108 **3** a 110 b 44 **4** 10 and 11 **5** \$10 **6** a 4323 b 5524

Challenge

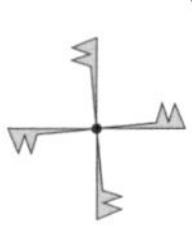

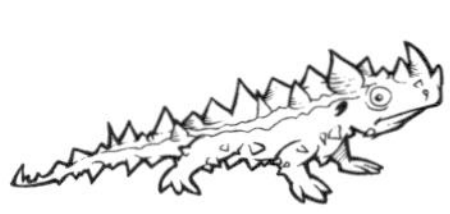

Activity

a 8 b 15 c 60 d 120 e 65 f 160 g XXII h CV
i CCXII j LXIII k LXXV l CCCLI

24:1

1 29 **2** 61 **3** 28 **4** 7 **5** 2698 **6** 800 **7** 6 **8** 22
9 440 **10** 25 **11** 200 **12** six dollars fifty **13** 8
14 April, June, September, November **15** 14 (vehicles)
16 1, 6, 2, 3 **17** a F b F

24:2

1 8 **2** 13 **3** 530 **4** 24 **5** \$6.00 **6** 39 **7** \$180
8 48 **9** 15 **10** \$1.80 **11** 65c **12** a 3 b 3
13 86, 96, 106 **14** 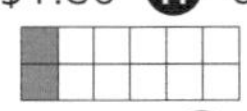 **15** 12, 15, 18, 21
16 4 (groups) **17** 7 (coins) **18** February **19** 18
20 4 **21** 1 (or $\frac{4}{4}$)

Activity

5, 7, 1, 12, 9, 17, 15, 21, 25, 27
1, 20, 32, 11, 3, 6, 4, 39, 28, 24
10, 14, 7, 32, 41, 24, 0, 19, 8, 30

24:3

1 52 **2** 41 r 7 **3** 34 r 1 **4** 61771 **5** 41768
6 a $\frac{6}{12}$ (or $\frac{1}{2}$) b $\frac{3}{12}$ (or $\frac{1}{4}$) **7** 16, 8 and 4 will be circled.
8 8 (runs) **9** a true b true **10** 32 **11** 7 **12** 13 **13** VIII
14 1 (or $\frac{4}{4}$)

24:4

1 a XXVI b LII **2** 80c (or \$0.80) **3** a 10 cm b 30 cm
4 a 67 b 14

Challenge

Answers will vary. See 22:2 (Q12).

Activity

5, 1, 7	20, 10, 4
8, 2, 6	6, 16, 36

25:1

1 8 **2** 18 **3** 13 **4** 6 **5** 1989 **6** 15 **7** 3 **8** 740
9 5 **10** 1144 **11** 3, 6, 9, 12, 15, 18 **12** 24 (books) **13** 20
14 90, 95, 100 **15** 50 (cubes) **16** 8 **17** 1, 14, 2, 7
18 a T b F

25:2

1 12 **2** 33 **3** 41 **4** 180 **5** 838 **6** 5 **7** 66
8 111 **9** \$140 **10** 1000 **11** 5 m^3 **12** 20 **13** a 1 Oct b 2·5 cm **14** \$8 **15** 12, 3, 6 and 15 will be circled.
16 a $\frac{1}{4}$ b $\frac{1}{4}$

Activity

0, 15, 24, 9, 30, 18, 27, 6, 21, 12
0, 30, 48, 18, 60, 36, 54, 12, 42, 24

25:3

1 101 **2** 309 **3** 106 **4** 811 **5** 831 **6** 742

 ISBN 978 1 4886 2189 5

7 XIX **8** a $\frac{7}{10}$ b $\frac{8}{10}$ (or $\frac{4}{5}$) c $\frac{10}{10}$ (or 1) d $\frac{8}{10}$ (or $\frac{4}{5}$)
9 30, 50 and 75 will be circled. **10** 14 cm^3 **11** cm^3
12 12 s **13** $\frac{8}{10}$ (or $\frac{4}{5}$)

25:4

1 a 116 b 260 **2** a 198 b 315 **3** 200
4 The drawing will be copied. **5** 84 **6** 497

Challenge

Answers will vary. Some answers include lunch box (cm^3), room (m^3).

Activity

1 a 25 b 13 c 3 **2** a 15 b 6

26:1

1 11 **2** 170 **3** 48 **4** 10 **5** 114 **6** 6 **7** 6
8 63 **9** 220 **10** 996 **11** a $\frac{2}{8}$ b $\frac{5}{8}$ c $\frac{7}{8}$ d $\frac{1}{8}$
12 26 **13** 10, 5, 0 **14** cylinder **15** 13 cm^3 **16** 1, 32, 2, 16, 4, 8 **17** a $\frac{3}{4}$ b $\frac{5}{6}$

26:2

1 9 **2** 50 **3** 560 **4** 5 **5** 1 020 **6** 720 **7** 9
8 13 **9** 5 **10** 75 **11** 7, 14, 21, 28, 35, 42 **12** square pyramid **13** 48 **14** a 8 m^3 b 72 m^3 **15** a $\frac{5}{8}$
b $\frac{6}{8}$ (or $\frac{3}{4}$) c $\frac{7}{8}$ d $\frac{7}{8}$

Activity

9, 18, 27, 36, 45, 54, 63, 72, 81, 90
7, 14, 21, 28, 35, 42, 49, 56, 63, 70

26:3

1 9; 72 **2** 8; 800 **3** 9 **4** 8 **5** 10 r 2 **6** VII
7 a $\frac{3}{10}$ b $\frac{2}{5}$ **8** 25 m^3 **9** a 6°C b 10 am **10** m^3

26:4

1 a XCV b CL **2** a 260 b 98 **3** a 276 b 135
4 a yes b 0·35 c 0·35 d 0·05 **5** a 18 b 12 c 21
6 13, 26, 39, 52

Challenge

Answers will vary.

Activity

Answers may vary.

a

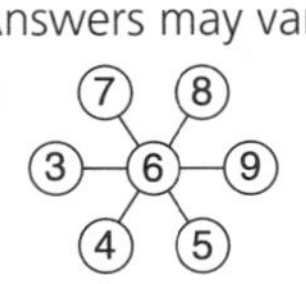

b

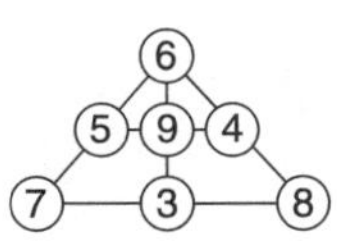

27:1

1 23 **2** 120 **3** 8 **4** 48 **5** 5 **6** 2 **7** 16
8 9 **9** 22 **10** 993 **11** a $\frac{4}{10}$ (or $\frac{2}{5}$) b $\frac{2}{10}$ (or $\frac{1}{5}$) **12** 10 (mm)
13 94, 172, 186, 261 **14** perimeter **15**

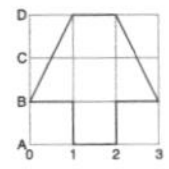

16 20, 24, 28 **17** a 1 (or $\frac{4}{4}$) b $\frac{3}{4}$

27:2

1 140 **2** 5 **3** 12 **4** 19 **5** 594 **6** 8 **7** 38
8 13 **9** 24 **10** 834 **11** a $\frac{1}{3}$ b $\frac{4}{10}$ (or $\frac{2}{5}$)
12

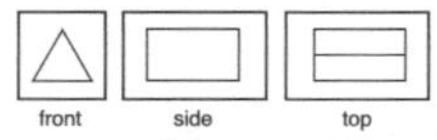

13 1·62 **14** a 32 m b 18 m
15 36 mm **16** 24 **17** multiply top by 3 **18** a m^3 b cm^3

Activity

a 12 cm b 11 cm c 12 cm d 10 cm

27:3

1 8; 80 **2** 4; 400 **3** 407 **4** 403 **5** 104
6 68 **7** Your estimate; 6·5 cm (or 65 mm) **8** 2·37
9 rectangular prism **10** 31 m^3 **11** a $7\frac{1}{2}$ b $2\frac{1}{2}$
12 a $\frac{13}{5}$ b $\frac{10}{3}$ **13** a X b XIX

27:4

1 a 23 b 79 **2** 8 cm **3** 137 runs **4** a 585 cm
b 1 460 cm **5** a 15 cm b 45 cm **6** 160

Challenge

Answers will vary.

Activity

(20) 20 ÷ 5 **(21)** 42 ÷ 6 **(22)** counting numbers
(23) even numbers **(24)** odd numbers **(25)** ordinal numbers
(26) digits **(28)** 7

28:1

1 45 **2** 3 **3** 11 **4** 21 **5** 601 **6** 12 **7** 5
8 40 **9** 24 **10** 287 **11** B (3 cm) will be circled.
12 12 cm **13** 10 past 8 (or 8:10) **14** 3 **15** 29 (birds)
16 a 18 cm b 20 cm^2

28:2

1 3 **2** 88 **3** 28 **4** 6 **5** 184 **6** 12 **7** 44
8 9 **9** 24 **10** 1374 **11** 189 **12** 222
13 Your estimate; 42 mm **14** a D3 b D2 c C2 d D1
15 79 mm **16** a $\frac{1}{5}$ b $\frac{2}{5}$

Activity

a 16 cm b 20 cm

28:3

1 866 **2** 203 **3** 598 **4** 4 r 2 **5** 5 r 3 **6** 29·34
7 13 (millimetres) **8** a 8 cm b 3 cm^2 **9** $\frac{5}{8}$ **10** 24 cm
11 a 3 cm 2 mm b 26 (mm) **12** 10, 15, 20, 25 **13** 30, 36, 42 **14** LV

28:4

1 a LIV b XCIX c CCCLXXVI **2** a 250 (cm) b 25 (mm)
3 24 (metres) **4** 2:12 **5** 52 (runs) **6** 80

 • • ISBN 978 1 4886 2189 5

Challenge

Answers will vary. Lines could include:

straight line, curved line, zigzag line, dotted line, parallel lines and perpendicular lines.

Activity

a

23	27	31	35	39	43

b

2	4	8	16	32	64

c

82	73	64	55	46	37

d

88	99	110	121	132	143

e

3	7	15	31	63	127

f

16	18	24	42	96	258

29:1

1 22 **2** 240 **3** 10 **4** 12 **5** 89 **6** 240 **7** 20 **8** 9 **9** 22 **10** 1 191 **11** 1 (or 1·0), 1·1, 1·2 **12** a 8 b 10 **13** 172 (cm) **14** September, October, November **15** 24 **16** 4 (groups) **17** 3 (h) **18** a 5 cm² b 12 cm

29:2

1 30 **2** 33 **3** 43 **4** 14 **5** 718 **6** 5 **7** 89 **8** 162 **9** 72 **10** 62 **11** a 10 past 7 b 20 past 10 **12** a 30 (months) b December, January, February **13** 17 ÷ 3 **14** 12 (quarters) **15** 90 **16** 6 (apples) **17** a $\frac{19}{100}$, $\frac{18}{100}$, $\frac{17}{100}$ b subtract $\frac{1}{100}$ **18** a 5·2 b 3·3

Activity

a 26 cm b 27 cm c 16 cm

29:3

1 140 **2** 168 **3** 228 **4** 204 **5** a Asia b Africa c South America d F2 **6** 6·5, 8·5 **7** 14 cm **8** 27 mm

29:4

1 a CLX b 194 **2** 16 cm **3** 9 o'clock and 3 o'clock **4** a 48 (petals) b 25 (flowers) **5** a 52 r 1 b 31 r 2

Challenge

Answers will vary.

Activity

18, 42, 12, 36, 54, 6, 30, 0, 24, 48

49, 7, 56, 42, 21, 63, 28, 70, 35, 77

88, 40, 24, 48, 72, 64, 16, 56, 0, 32

30:1

1 19 **2** 27 **3** 20 **4** 12 **5** 1 156 **6** 9 **7** 66 **8** 340 **9** 32 **10** 938 **11** 4:11 am **12** red **13** 0·74, 0·75, 0·76 **14** a 19 cm² b 32 cm

30:2

1 13 **2** 6 **3** 48 **4** 6 **5** 658 **6** 49 **7** 17 **8** 6 **9** 33 **10** 418 **11** 0·39, 0·38, 0·37 **12** 30 (days) **13** 66 **14** 4 to 12 **15** 7:30 am **16** a 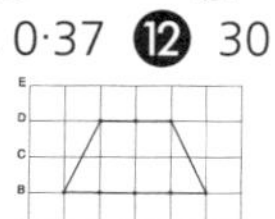 b trapezium

Activity

The game is not fair. The girl on the right has more chance of winning. Results will differ.

30:3

1 538 **2** 644 **3** 131 **4** 157 **5** 121 r 2 **6** $\frac{11}{100}$, $\frac{15}{100}$, $\frac{21}{100}$ **7** no **8** 20 **9** 37 **10** $\frac{4}{8}$ (or $\frac{1}{2}$) **11** a 3:32 pm b 6:09 pm c 8:23 am d 4:58 am **12** 9·6 **13** 9·7

30:4

1 a 127 b 309 **2** a 3B b 6B **3** a 12:49 (or 11 to 1) b 13 past 7 (or 7:13) **4** 21 **5** a 10 minutes b 20 minutes **6** $91

Challenge

Answers will vary. Some answers include:

603 730 has 6 digits. It is an even number that is divisible by 10.

Activity

(1) *face* **(2)** *vertex* or *corner* **(3)** *edge* **(11)** *base* **(15)** net of a *cube* **(20)** Side view is *3*. **(21)** Front view is *1*. **(22)** Top view is *2*. **(23)** *D* will not roll. **(26)** *protractor*

31:1

1 16 **2** 42 **3** 4 **4** 40 **5** 1 039 **6** 8 **7** 4 **8** 25 **9** 3 **10** 4 090 **11** 1 308 **12** 24 **13** a 149 cm b 205 cm **14** 44 + 32 = 76 **15** 38 **16** 256 **17** a 3:04 am b 7:22 pm

31:2

1 4 **2** 27 **3** 34 **4** 550 **5** 1 021 **6** 12 **7** 680 **8** 15 **9** 12 **10** 437 **11** pm **12** 5:30 pm **13** a C b A **14** 36 **15** 250 mL **16** a 5 b 4 c 4 d 5

Activity

18, 3, 12, 0, 24, 15, 27, 6, 21, 30

30, 45, 15, 35, 10, 50, 25, 40, 20, 0

9, 81, 72, 36, 54, 18, 45, 0, 63, 27

31:3

1 186 **2** 194 **3** 423 **4** Estimate may vary. a E = 150 + 70 = 220 b E = 600 – 300 = 300 **5** $\frac{2}{8}$ (or $\frac{1}{4}$) **6** a LV b CIX **7** 60 (wheels) **8** 36 (months) **9** a $\frac{1}{4}$ b $\frac{1}{4}$ c $\frac{3}{8}$ d $\frac{16}{16}$ **10** a 17:00 b 04:00 **11** yes

31:4

1 a 0·4 (or 0·40), 0·42, 0·44 b 0·74, 0·78, 0·82 **2** 264 **3** a 11:57 am b 12:15 pm **4** 15 **5** a 7 b 10 c A **6** 24

Challenge

Answers will vary. Answers may include:

a $\frac{1}{2} = \frac{2}{4}, \frac{3}{6}, \frac{4}{8}, \frac{5}{10}$ **b** $\frac{1}{3} = \frac{2}{6}, \frac{3}{9}, \frac{4}{12}, \frac{5}{15}$
c $\frac{1}{4} = \frac{2}{8}, \frac{3}{12}, \frac{4}{16}, \frac{5}{20}$

Activity

a false (or 2403/) **b** true (or *8(/) **c** true (or *8(/)

32:1

1 0 **2** 44 **3** 12 **4** 5 **5** 224 **6** 500 **7** 114 **8** 34 **9** 36 **10** 281 **11** litres **12** 4 **13** 500 **14** 320 (cents) **15** 15 m **16** 300 (cm) **17** 2 022 **18** **a** $\frac{1}{3}$ **b** $\frac{4}{5}$

32:2

1 74 **2** 21 **3** 10 **4** 29 **5** 709 **6** 740 **7** 54 **8** 820 **9** \$37 **10** \$39 **11** L **12** 27 past 3 **13** 8 m **14** 80 (books) **15** \$20 will be circled. **16** reflex (angle) **17** **a** $\frac{1}{8}$ **b** $\frac{7}{8}$ **18** 1:43 pm

Activity

4, 10, 6, 2, 8, 7, 1, 3, 9, 5
2, 5, 3, 1, 4, 9, 7, 10, 8, 6

32:3

1 972 **2** 10 440 **3** 6 810 **4** Estimates may vary. E = 440 + 40 = 480 **5** Estimates may vary. E = 500 – 200 = 300 **6** 4 (caps) **7** between 180° and 360° **8** 96 (nails) **9** **a** acute **b** obtuse **10** 9 (pens) **11** **a** 160 **b** 460 **c** 5 460 **12** **a** $\frac{15}{20}$ **b** $\frac{10}{20}$ **c** $\frac{1}{10}$ **d** $\frac{5}{10}$

32:4

1 CCCXXIX **2** **a** 5·5, 6·5, 7·5 **b** 1·4, 1·6, 1·8 **3** 99 (minutes) **4** $\frac{11}{24}$ **5** **a** 2 500 mL **b** 0·8 L **6** **a** 7 **b** 9 **7** **a** 5 **b** 9

Challenge

Answers will vary. Answers may include straight angle, right angle, acute angle, obtuse angle and reflex angle

Activity

a

10c	H	H	H	H	T	T	T	T
20c	H	H	T	T	T	T	H	H
\$1	H	T	H	T	T	H	T	H

b

9	4	5
2	6	10
7	8	3

c

8	3	10
9	7	5
4	11	6

33:1

1 77 **2** 34 **3** 7 **4** 109 **5** 6 518 **6** 6 **7** 92 **8** 64 **9** 36 **10** 5 910 **11** **a** 800 **b** 600 **12** \$5 **13** **a** G = 8; S = 12; B = 16 **b** Bronze **c** 8 **14** **a** 3 **b** 4 **15** 1 000 (m)

33:2

1 32 **2** 18 **3** 9 **4** 50 **5** 5 993 **6** 72 **7** 590 **8** 89 **9** 110 **10** 118 **11** **a** $\frac{2}{6}$ **b** $\frac{12}{15}$ **12** 500 mL (or 0·5 L) **13** 5 500 mL **14** **a** $\frac{6}{12}$ **b** $\frac{3}{4}$ **15** 17 (marks) **16** **a** 28 **b** 39

Activity

(9) horizontal line **(10)** vertical line **(12)** arm of an angle **(14)** right angle **(15)** obtuse angle **(16)** straight angle **(17)** reflex angle **(18)** revolution **(24)** axes of symmetry **(26)** The coordinates of the dot are E2.

33:3

1 848 **2** 812 **3** 3 042
4 Answers may vary. E = 30 × 10 = 300
5 Answers may vary. E = 40 × 300 = 12 000
6 **a** $\frac{3}{8}$ **b** $\frac{5}{8}$ **7** 1 L 700 mL (or 1·7 L or 1 700 mL)
8 12 (glasses) **9** 4 (right angles) **10** 4 500 (g)
11 **a** 150 **b** 450 **c** 4 450 **12** **a** $\frac{6}{12}$ **b** $\frac{3}{12}$

33:4

1 no **2** 6 500 **3** 390 (tigers) **4** **a** heptagon **b** nonagon **5** **a** 10 **b** 12

Challenge

Answers will vary.

Activity

1 **a** 39 **b** 40 **c** 304 **d** 400 **e** 621 **f** 1 551
2 **a** LXV **b** CCXL **c** CMLXVI **d** MMD **e** CCCXCII **f** MCMXCIX

34:1

1 3 **2** 20 **3** 14 **4** 25 **5** 1 392 **6** 10 **7** 13 **8** 13 **9** 240 **10** 615 **11** **a** 117 cm **b** 3 m 51 cm **12** 9 (weeks) **13** 50 g **14** **a** 4 (white cars) **b** green **c** red **d** 16 (cars) **e** 30 (cars) **15** **a** 500 (g) **b** 1 500 (g)

34:2

1 24 **2** 69 **3** 31 **4** 90 **5** 920 **6** 9 **7** 47 **8** 15 **9** 74 **10** 852 **11** 4 000 g **12** 1 m 17 cm **13** 1 000 **14** 17 (tonnes) **15** **a** $\frac{2}{6}$ **b** $\frac{8}{10}$ **16** 64 000 kg **17** **a** 18 **b** 22

Activity

Answers will vary. 7 is the easiest total to throw using two dice.

34:3

1 \$96.76 **2** 3 200 **3** 13 860 **4** Answers may vary. E = 40 × 10 = 400 **5** Answers may vary. E = 500 × 30 = 15 000 **6** 680 (cm) **7** 4 000 (g) **8** 57 000 **9** \$44.60 **10** **a** $\frac{6}{8}$ **b** $\frac{8}{12}$ **11** 870 mL **12** **a** 279 **b** 579 **c** 4 579

34:4

1 73 g, 73 g, 73 g, 99 g **2** 3 (oranges) **3** 13 (trips) **4** 384 (times)

Challenge

Answers will vary.

Activity

90, 27, 18, 45, 81, 63, 99, 36, 54, 72
2, 4, 6, 3, 8, 5, 7, 9, 1, 10

35:1

1 1 **2** 23 **3** 32 **4** 35 **5** 825 **6** 160
7 12 **8** 8 **9** 11 **10** 186 **11** yes **12** 300 (cm)
13 7 **14** $3.50 **15** **a** 200 g **b** 37 kg **16** 5
17 The drawing will be enlarged. **18** 70 cm **19** 100 (cm)
20 2 000 (g)

35:2

1 17 **2** 54 **3** 28 **4** 19 **5** 710 **6** 600
7 33 **8** 11 **9** $18 **10** 2 548 **11** 4 m 87 cm
12 $36.90 **13** 3 270 g **14** 38° **15** 3 (tonnes)
16 $20.60; $5.40

Activity

1 **a** $20 **b** $17.70 **c** $21.00 **d** $33.35 **e** $18.95
f $46.95 **g** $52.50

35:3

1 $84 **2** $75.66 **3** $55.41 **4** 169 **5** 145 r 2
6 244 cm **7** 2 m **8** $23.75; $16.25 **9** 5 000 (kg)
10 The drawing will be enlarged. The enlargement factor is 2.

35:4

1 5 **2** **a** 11 (matchsticks) **b** 30 **3** **a** $\frac{16}{35}$ **b** yes **4** 36

Challenge

Answers will vary.

Activity

10 kg	2	2	2	1	1	1	0	0
5 kg	1	0	0	3	2	2	4	4
2 kg	0	2	1	0	2	1	2	1
1 kg	0	1	3	0	1	3	1	3

36:1

1 28 **2** 2 **3** 6 **4** 26 **5** 4 269 **6** 21
7 8 **8** 5 **9** 16 **10** 2 627 **11** m **12** 100 (cm)
13 14 (kg) **14** 239 (cm) **15** 5 out of 8 **16** 5 (L)
17 4 600 (g) **18** $33 **19** no **20** litres or millilitres
21 200 (cm)

36:2

1 11 **2** 7 **3** 90 **4** 10 **5** 10 636 **6** 11
7 64 **8** 88 **9** 80 **10** 3 228 **11** 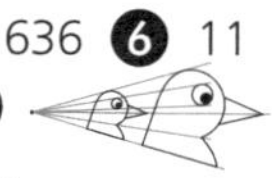
12 **a** 10 (matches) **b** Rachel **c** Heather

Activity

20, 32, 24, 0, 16, 36, 8, 28, 12, 40
45, 72, 54, 0, 36, 81, 18, 63, 27, 90

36:3

1 $41.65 **2** $120.90 **3** $62.15 **4** 250 **5** 46
6 27 r 3 **7** $\frac{1}{6}$ **8** **a** $100 **b** $300 **9** **a** $16.70
b $1.25 **10** 9·3 cm **11** 1 000 (g) **12** 3 m (or 300 cm)

36:4

1 6 kg 936 g **2** 5 **3** **a** 5 **b** 11 **4** 8
5 225 (diagonals)

Challenge

Answers will vary.

Activity

a 7 **b** 3 and 8 **c** 14

37:1

1 94 **2** 78 **3** 81 **4** 6 **5** 8 250 **6** 32 **7** 100
8 48 **9** 56 **10** 2 916 **11** cm **12** 68 out of 100
13 October **14** 15 (halves) **15** 2 021 **16** 21 (days)
17 40 **18** $1.25 **19** **a** $11.80 **b** 4 **20** 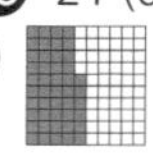

37:2

1 63 **2** 9 **3** 4 **4** 64 **5** 7·61 **6** 5 **7** 72
8 65 **9** 86 **10** $4.26 **11** $\frac{34}{100}$; 0·34 **12** acute (angle)
13 6 307, 6 370, 6 730 **14** 2 m 73 cm **15** **a** 14 (trophies)
b 2 (trophies) **c** 24 (trophies)

Activity

(19) 3 out of 8 **(20)** $\frac{3}{10}$ shaded **(21)** $\frac{24}{100}$ shaded
(22) $\frac{3}{10}$ shaded **(23)** 0·3 shaded **(24)** 0·36 shaded
(26) 19 out of 100 **(27)** 62% shaded **(28)** 1·36
(30) $\frac{3}{10}$, $\frac{3}{100}$

37:3

1 7 274 **2** $37.67 **3** $81.00 **4** 67 **5** 415
6 76 **7** 400 **8** **a** 0·37, 37% **b** 0·96, 96%
9 5:1 or '5 to 1' **10** $21.70 **11** 126 (pages) **12** 713
13 *43* out of *100* = *43*% **14** **a** *9* m *37* cm **b** 5·23 m

37:4

1 2 dolls, 2 yo-yos **2** **a** 0·1 **b** 0·07 **c** 0·35 **d** 0·14
3 **a** $870 **b** $1 044 **4** 16 **5** 225 (minutes)
6 7 **7** $16.71

Challenge

Answers will vary for the last two rows.

Fraction	Decimal	Percentage
$\frac{20}{100}$	0·20	20%
$\frac{41}{100}$	0·41	41%
$\frac{86}{100}$	0·86	86%

Activity

Answers will vary.

 • *AUSTRALIAN SIGNPOST MATHS 5 MENTALS* • ISBN 978 1 4886 2189 5

17:3 ☐ out of 11

1 $\begin{array}{r} 4325 \\ -\,1782 \\ \hline \end{array}$

2 $\begin{array}{r} 5000 \\ -\,2185 \\ \hline \end{array}$

3 $\begin{array}{r} 6308 \\ -\,4992 \\ \hline \end{array}$

4 $3\overline{)28}$ r

5 $9\overline{)47}$ r

6 What is the chance, as a fraction, that the spinner will land on:

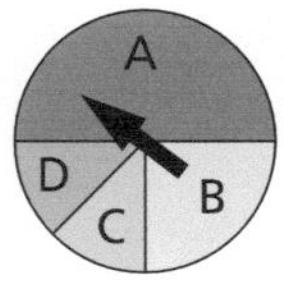

a **A**? ________ **b** **B**? ________

7 Square metres in 6 ha. ________

8

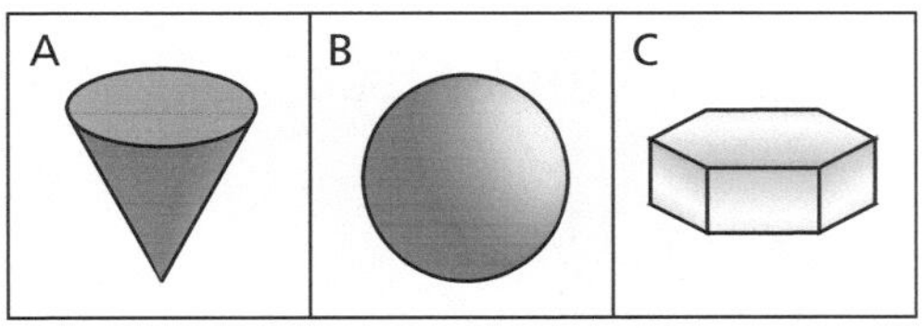

a Which of these solids have a curved surface? ________

b Which solids will roll? ________

c Which have a flat surface? ________

9 What number follows 3409? ________

10 The symbol for 'hectare'. ________

11 Write the numerals shown.

a

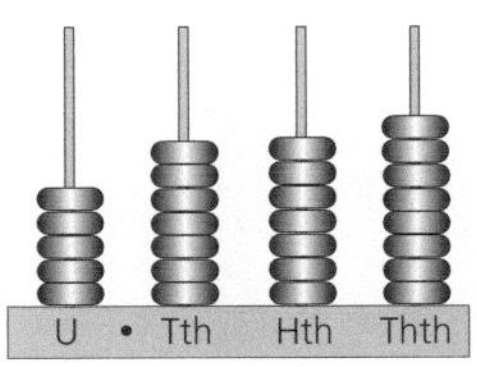

____

b

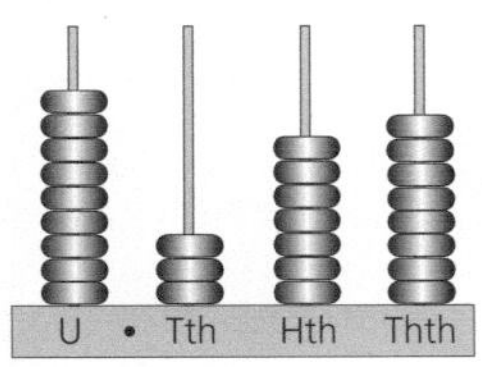

____

17:4 Extension ☐ out of 5

1 If the shaded part has the value given, find the value of the whole.

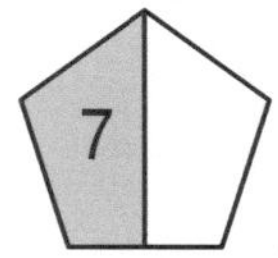

____

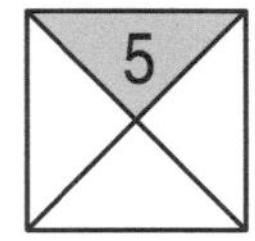

____

2 If '<' means 'is less than' and '>' means 'is greater than', choose the sign that makes the number sentence true.

a $6\frac{1}{2} \triangle 7$? $\triangle =$ ________

b 0·20 △ 0·9? $\triangle =$ ________

3 $0 \times 3 \times 40$ ________

4 **a** 255 more than 121. ________

b 243 more than 111. ________

c 372 more than 104. ________

5 If May 10th was a Monday, what day was May 31st? ________

Challenge

List areas that would be measured in:

cm^2	ha

Turn to ID Card B on page 7.

Give the answers for these numbers.

(3) ________	line	(4) ________	line
(5) ________	line	(6) ________	line
(7) ________	lines	(8) ________	lines
(19) ________		(20) ________	
(21) ________		(22) ________	

18:1 ☐ out of 18

1. 70 + 50 ______
2. 6 × 7 ______
3. 16 – 5 ______
4. 12 + 88 ______
5.
```
  915
– 600
```
6. 19 – 10 ______
7. 3 × ______ = 12
8. Double 51. ______
9. 5 × 5 ______
10.
```
  864
– 308
```
11. The short way of writing hectares. ______
12. If each cube has a volume of one cubic centimetre, what is the volume of this shape? ______

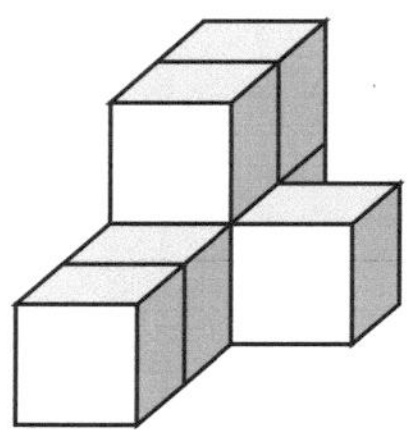

13. Which number is larger, 1 609 or 1 710? ______
14. Write the number 6 849 in words.

______

______

15. Circle the numbers that round off to 90, if we round to the nearest 10.

    62 89 40 19 94 99

16. \$2 + \$2 + \$2 + \$2 ______
17. True or false? An obtuse angle is larger than an acute angle. ______
18. **a** Degrees in a right angle. ______

    b Degrees in a straight angle. ______

18:2 ☐ out of 19

1. 10 – 6 ______
2. 8 + 9 ______
3. 6 × 3 ______
4. 9 × 4 ______
5.
```
  8000
– 2673
```
6. 5 × 8 ______
7. 22 subtract 9. ______
8. Half of 26. ______
9. 5 + 7 – 3 ______
10.
```
  2197
+  438
```

11. Hectares in 90 000 m^2. ______
12. 300 – 192 = 299 + 1 – 192 = ______
13. The number 7 before 7 000. ______
14. 2 173, 2 183, 2 193, ______, ______, ______, ______
15. Make the largest possible number using 3, 0, 7, 9. ______
16. Using notes only, in how many different ways can you make \$20? ______
17. What is the value of the 4 in 4 891? ______
18. Write 27 cubic centimetres in short form. ______
19. Write the numeral:

    a forty-nine point two one ______

    b sixty point eight nine ______

The jump strategy

We can do this on a number line or as a mental strategy.

Example:

347 + 34

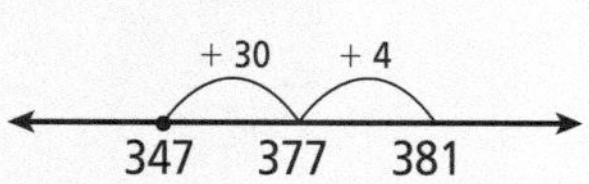

Use the jump strategy for these:

a 778 – 426 = ______

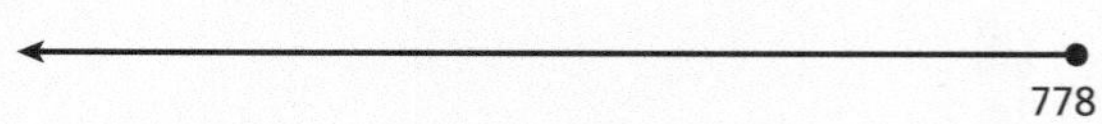

b 649 + 32 = ______

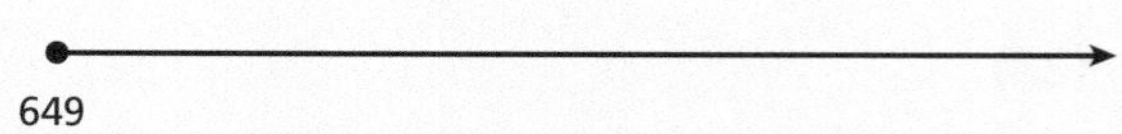

18:3 ☐ out of 9

❶
$$\begin{array}{r} \overset{\curvearrowright}{2999+1} \\ \not{3000} \\ -1436 \\ \hline +1 \\ \hline = \quad\quad \end{array}$$

❷
$$\begin{array}{r} \overset{\curvearrowright}{5999+1} \\ \not{6000} \\ -2497 \\ \hline +1 \\ \hline = \quad\quad \end{array}$$

❸ **Colour of balloons used**

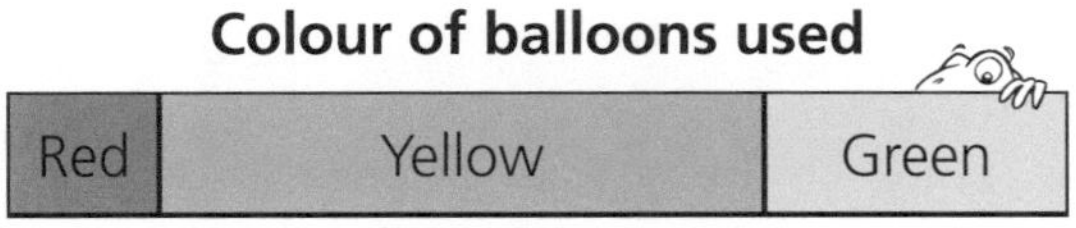

What fraction of the balloons shown in the bar graph was green? ______

❹ Write the fraction shaded.

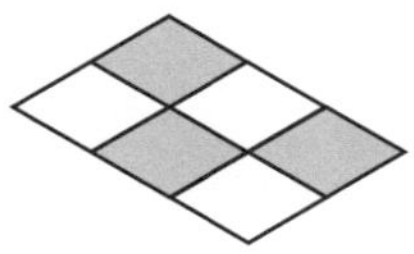

______

❺ Find the volume of a rectangular prism with sides 4 cm, 4 cm and 2 cm. ______

❻ Days in 5 fortnights. ______

❼ a

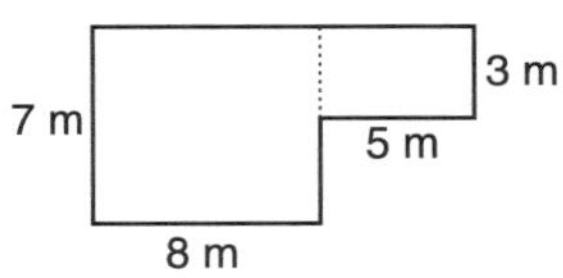

b

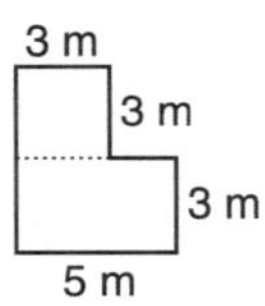

Area = ______ Area = ______

❽ Square metres in 3 ha. ______

❾ Complete the following:

134·58 = ______ hundreds
______ tens
______ units
______ tenths
______ hundredths

18:4 Extension ☐ out of 6

❶ Which of 9, 21, 32 and 36 is both 'even' and 'a multiple of 3'? ______

❷ How many weeks would it take Taya to save \$18 for a pet budgie if she saves \$1.50 each week?

______

❸ **a** 70 ÷ 4 ______ r ______
b 70 ÷ 3 ______ r ______

❹ 17 + 4 + 8 + 13 + 9 + 6 + 20 ______

❺ What is the size of the largest angle that can be made by the hour and minute hands of a clock? ______

❻ **a** 108 more than 52. ______
b 108 more than 352. ______
c 108 more than 1 352. ______

Challenge

Use the subtraction from thousand strategy in 18:3 question 1 to find:

a 5 000 – 2 537 *b* 8 000 – 4 291

19:1 ☐ out of 20

1. 6 ÷ 2 ______
2. 17 – 4 ______
3. 6 × 8 ______
4. 2 × 6 ______
5. 4000 − 2973
6. 10 + 14 ______
7. 2 groups of 90. ______
8. Add 18 and 17. ______
9. 16 ÷ 4 ______
10. 173 + 344
11. Use the short form to write 52 cubic centimetres. ______
12. Is 0·6 the same size as 0·60? ______
13. What is the name of the angle at the corner of a page? ______
14. Write 183 cents as dollars. ______
15. 54 hundredths as a decimal. 0· ______
16. Write the time shown as:

   a digital time: ______

   b analogue time:

   ______ past ______
17. Write down the first 5 multiples of 3.

   ______
18. Fill in the missing words.

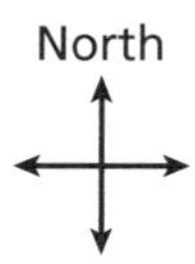

19. Days in August. ______
20. Write all the factors of 20.

   ______

19:2 ☐ out of 14

1. 10 – 5 ______
2. 11 + 6 ______
3. 8 × 7 ______
4. 13 – 8 ______
5. 1787 − 1439
6. 2 + 4 – 5 ______
7. 7 × 5 ______
8. 3 lots of 8. ______
9. 66 take away 24. ______
10. 564 + 350
11. a

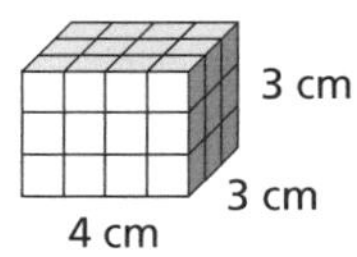

   b

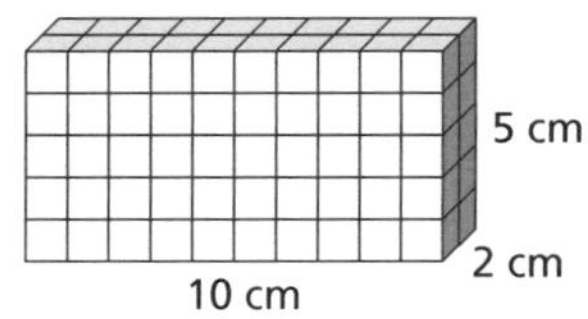

   Volume = ______ Volume = ______
12. 197 + 123 ______

13. Which number is larger:

   a 6·09 or 4·87? ______

   b 17·25 or 19·3? ______
14.

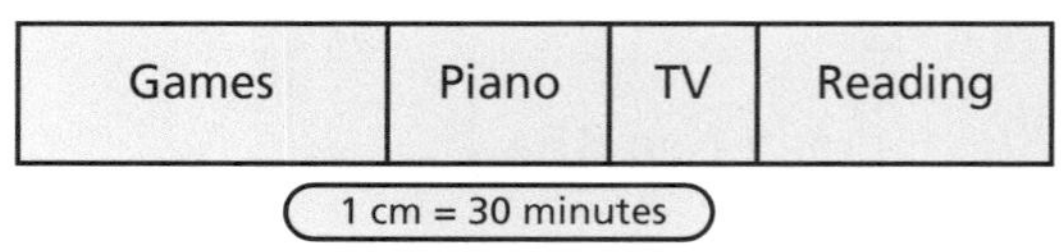

   a What kind of graph is this? ______

   What fraction of the time was spent:

   b watching TV? ______ c reading? ______

   How much time was spent on:

   d the piano? ______ e games? ______

Compass points

The direction halfway between north and east is called north-east.

What is the direction halfway between:

a south and east? ______

b south and west? ______

c north and west? ______

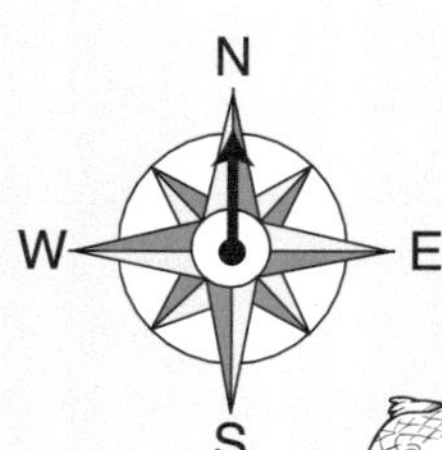

 • *AUSTRALIAN SIGNPOST MATHS 5 MENTALS* • ISBN 978 1 4886 2189 5

19:3 ☐ out of 12

1 6312 − 943 = ____

2 4431 − 653 = ____

3 9013 − 2437 = ____

4 $5\overline{)14}$ ____ r ____

5 $3\overline{)19}$ ____ r ____

6 Use the jump strategy for 763 – 27. ________

7 The part shaded is:

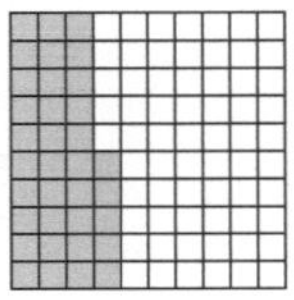

$\frac{\quad}{100}$ or 0·________

8 Circle the smaller decimal:

a 0·8 0·17 **b** 0·7 0·09

9 The factors of 32. ________

10 Centimetres in one metre. ________

11 What is the area of this battleaxe block?

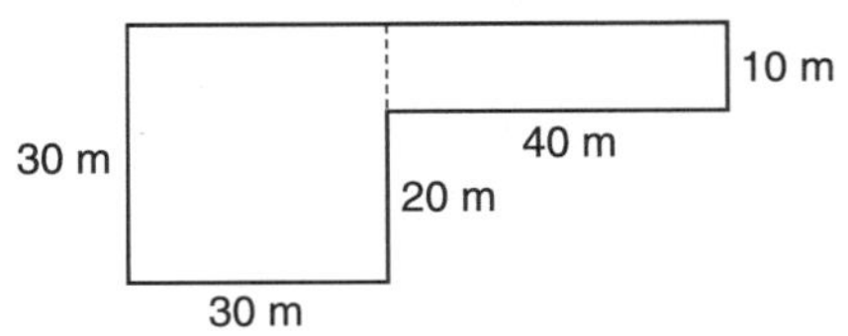

____

12 Complete the following:

201·79 = ________ hundreds

________ tens

________ units

________ tenths

________ hundredths

19:4 Extension ☐ out of 5

1 I need 8 cubes to make a 2 × 2 × 2 stack like this. How many cubes do I need to make a 3 × 3 × 3 stack? ________

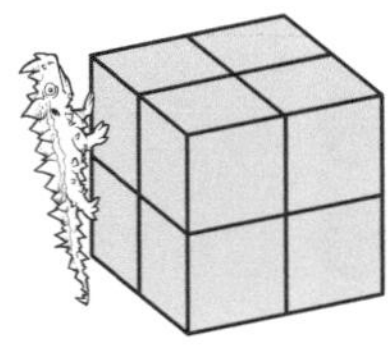

2 8000 – 3921 = 7999 + 1 – 3921 = ________

3 A zoo wants to buy 10 lions and tigers. There must be at least one of each. How many different possible choices could they make? ________

4 The length of a straw can be 7·8 cm, 8·8 cm or 9·8 cm. What two straws have a total length of 16·6 cm? ________

5 1339 + 43 ________

Challenge

Draw and label a compass rose with N, NE, E, SE, S, SW, W and NW.

20:1 ☐ out of 17

1. 3 × 7 ____
2. 16 − 3 ____
3. 10 + 17 ____
4. 80 ÷ 8 ____
5. $\begin{array}{r} 154 \\ +128 \\ \hline \end{array}$
6. 32 + 37 + 31 ____
7. 112 minus 6. ____
8. 3 × 3 ____
9. Halve 40. ____
10. $\begin{array}{r} 43 \\ -\ 2 \\ \hline \end{array}$
11. $6\overline{)42}$
12. $7\overline{)56}$
13. $9\overline{)36}$
14. What kind of angle is shown in each?

a ________

b ________

c ________

d ________

15. Make a tally for the letters E, S, U, F and M from these children's names.
Jessica, Shaun, Mary, Geoffrey, Kyle

E	S	U	F	M

16. The factors of 9. ____
17. 6 + 6 + 6 + 6 + 6 + 6 ____

20:2 ☐ out of 16

1. 5 − 5 ____
2. 10 + 4 ____
3. 5 × 11 ____
4. 12 ÷ 6 ____
5. $\begin{array}{r} 212 \\ +\ 97 \\ \hline \end{array}$
6. 8 × 6 ____
7. 14 + 36 ____
8. 17 m − 11 m ____
9. Sum of 7, 8 and 9. ____
10. $\begin{array}{r} 1293 \\ -475 \\ \hline \end{array}$
11. Use the jump strategy for 327 + 47. ____

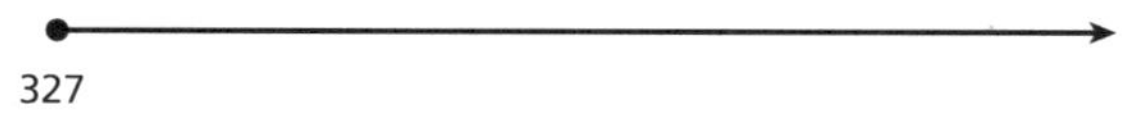

12. Write $\frac{37}{100}$ as a decimal. ____
13. On the map, Kristen is standing at **X**. What does she see if she looks:

a west? ____
b east? ____
c south-east? ____
d north-west? ____

14. Fill in the missing multiples of 6.

12, 18, 24, ______ , ______ , 42

15. Use < or > in:
a 2·986 ______ 2·298
b 1·342 ______ 0·987
16. Find the volume of a rectangular prism with sides 2 cm, 6 cm and 2 cm. ____

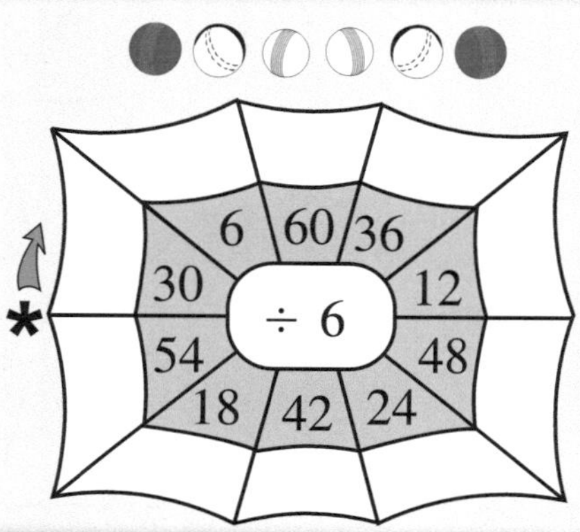

☐ × **3** = **24**
☐ × **6** = **48**

 ISBN 978 1 4886 2189 5

20:3 ☐ out of 12

❶
$$\begin{array}{r} 4000 \\ -\ 750 \\ \hline \end{array}$$

❷
$$\begin{array}{r} 6000 \\ -\ 250 \\ \hline \end{array}$$

❸
$$\begin{array}{r} 9000 \\ -\ 2043 \\ \hline \end{array}$$

❹ $2\overline{)82}$ ❺ $3\overline{)69}$ ❻ $6\overline{)72}$

❼ Use the jump strategy for 933 – 271. ______

❽ The value of the bold digit:

a 6·5**3** ______ **b** 8·**1**9 ______

❾ 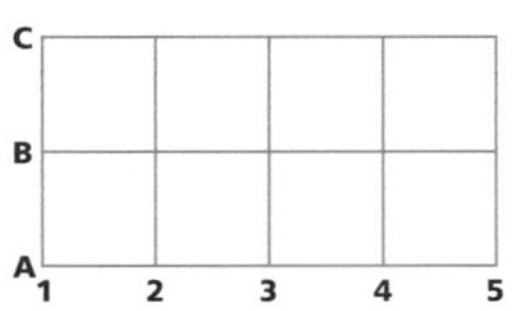

1A, 3C, 4C, 5A, 1A

Plot this set of points. Join each one to the next. Then name the shape you have drawn.

______

❿ Write down all the factors of 18.

______

⓫ Circle the larger decimal in each pair.

a 0·8 0·67

b 0·99 1·2

⓬ 700 – 428 = 699 + 1 – 428 ______

20:4 ☐ out of 5

Extension

❶ I started at **X**, went 3 km east, then 3 km north, then travelled 3 km south east. Through which letter did I pass?

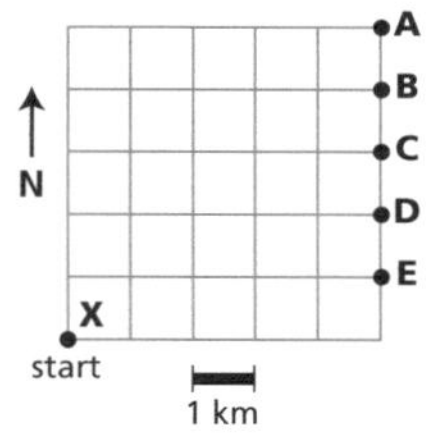

______

❷ I tossed 2 coins 40 times. This tally shows the results.

2 heads	𝍸 𝍸
2 tails	𝍸 𝍸
head and tail	𝍸 𝍸 𝍸 𝍸

What fraction of the time did I get:

a head and tail? ______

b 2 heads? ______

❸ If it is 25 February 2012 today, what will the date be in four weeks time? ______

❹ I keep rabbits and birds. There are 5 heads and and 16 feet. How many birds do I have? ______

❺ If # means 'add 7' and ^ means 'divide by 7', then 14^## = ______

Challenge

Write everything you know about the number 83·561.

______

______

______

______

Concept

1 What object is:

a north of **A**? ______ **b** east of **A**? ______

c west of **A**? ______ **d** south of **A**? ______

2 Where do you end up if you start at S and move:

a 3 spaces east, 2 north, then 1 west? ______

b 5 spaces north, 5 east, then 4 south? ______

c 4 north, 3 south, then 5 east? ______

d 1 north, 5 east, then 3 west? ______

21:1 ☐ out of 16

1. 7×5 ______
2. $10 - 4$ ______
3. $12 + 9$ ______
4. $14 \div 7$ ______
5. $57 + 26$ ______
6. $90 - 8$ ______
7. 20×2 ______
8. 17 plus 49. ______
9. Triple 5. ______
10. $99 - 45$ ______
11. $8\overline{)24}$
12. $8\overline{)48}$
13. $9\overline{)54}$
14. How many cubic centimetres would be in this prism?

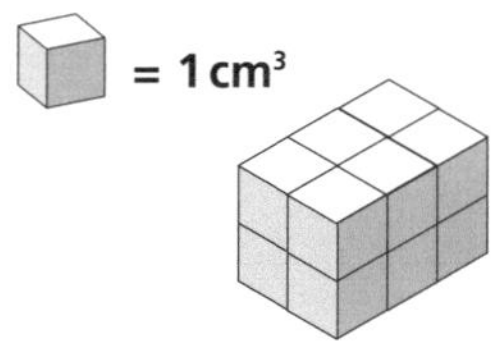

Volume = ________ cm³

15. 
Does this shape have rotational symmetry? ________

16. 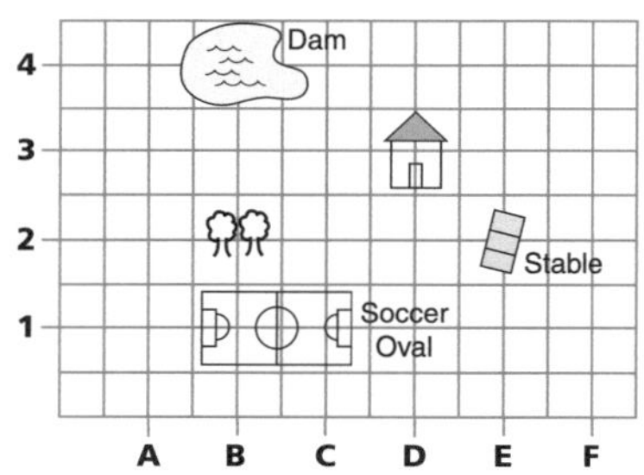

Write the coordinates of:

a  ________ b  ________

What is located at:

c **B4**? ________ d **E2**? ________

21:2 ☐ out of 17

1. $27 + 4$ ______
2. 6×10 ______
3. $21 \div 3$ ______
4. $100 - 3$ ______
5. $80 - 68$ ______
6. 9×6 ______
7. $28 \div 4$ ______
8. 6 rows of 9. ______
9. 113 take away 7. ______
10. $852 + 60$ ______

11. $387 + 125$ ______

12. Write 0·52 as a fraction. ______
13. **a** Is 5 a factor of 20? ______
    b Is 20 a multiple of 5? ______
14. There were 50 people at a concert. Was the number of boys about 10, 20, 30 or 40? ______

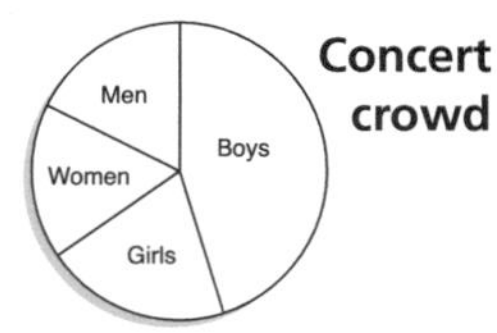

15. The size of this angle is: ______

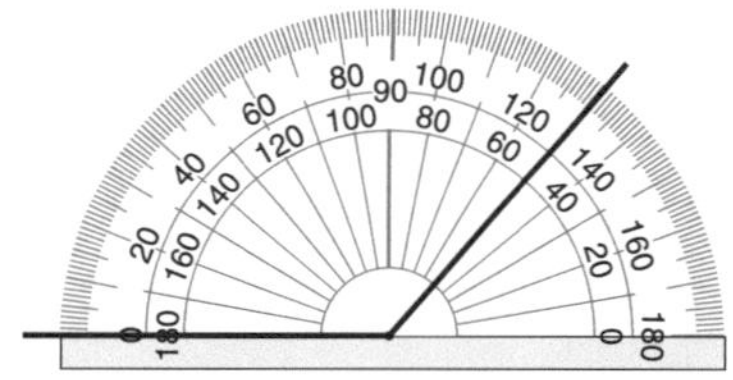

16. Find the volume of a rectangular prism with sides 5 cm, 9 cm and 1 cm. ______
17. Circle the larger decimal in each part.
    a 0·27 or 0·4 **b** 0·71 or 0·7

1 Which shape could be the result, if:
   a I rotate the top heptagon? ______
   b I reflect the top heptagon? ______
2 Which of the diagrams has an axis of symmetry? ______
3 How many diagonals has a heptagon? ______

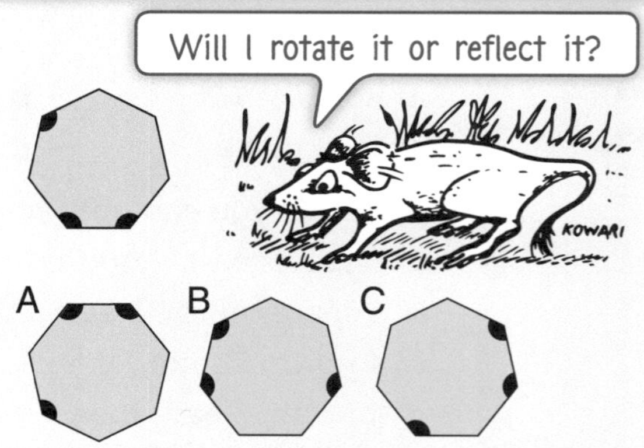

21:3 ☐ out of 12

❶
```
  7351
– 2672
```

❷
```
  5000
–  370
```

❸
```
  2000
– 1821
```

❹ $2\overline{)42}$

❺ $4\overline{)88}$

❻ $7\overline{)91}$

❼ Circle the smallest decimal.

0·14   0·43   2·1   1·09

❽ What is the volume of a prism with measurements 3 cm × 2 cm × 4 cm? ______

❾ 6000 + 20 + 4 ______

❿ 

What is the order of rotational symmetry on this shape? ______

⓫ **A**  **B** 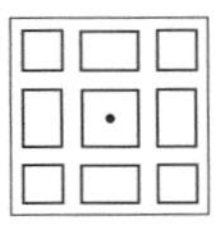 **C** 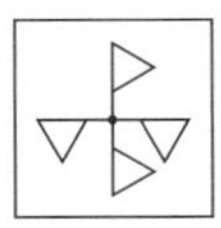

a Which of these patterns does not have turning symmetry? ______

b How many times does a tracing of pattern **A** exactly match the original as it turns through a full turn? ______

⓬ Write down all the factors of 24.

______

21:4 Extension ☐ out of 6

❶ If the length, breadth and height of this model are all multiplied by 2, how many cubes will be used in the new model's:

a top view? ______

b total volume? ______

❷ Four equal angles make up a right angle. How big is each angle? ______

❸ One ice-cream sundae costs 55c. Find the cost of six.

______

❹ **a** $\frac{1}{4}$ of 12 ______

b $\frac{3}{4}$ of 12 ______

❺ **a** (3 × 6) + (2 × 6) ______

b (3 × 6) + (7 × 6) ______

❻ 18 + 23 + 32 + 7 + 5 ______

Challenge

List information displayed in this graph.

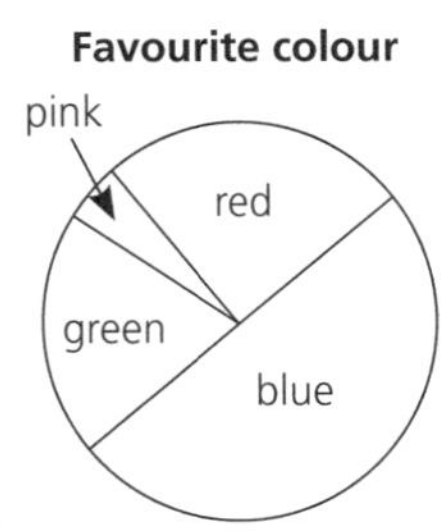

______

______

______

______

For each grid, find how many ways there are of getting three crosses in a line, either across, down or diagonally.

a 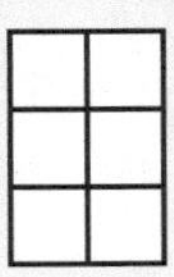 ______

b 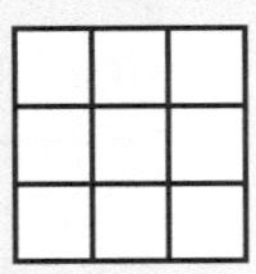 ______

c 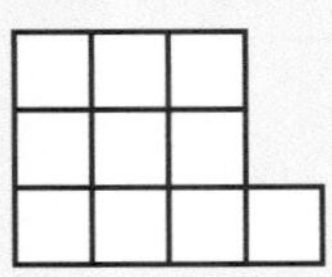 ______

d 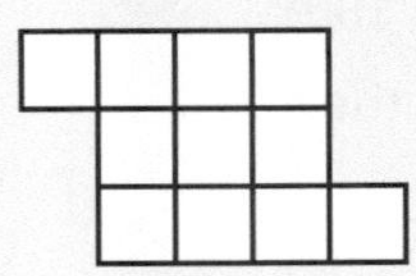 ______

22:1 — out of 18

1. 90 – 30 ______
2. 42 + 8 ______
3. 48 ÷ 8 ______
4. 12 × 3 ______
5. 983 + 116 ______
6. 3 + 8 + 2 ______
7. 15 ×10 ______
8. 80 take away 8. ______
9. 18 tens. ______
10. 8925 – 381 ______
11. Write the volume of this model in cm^3. ______

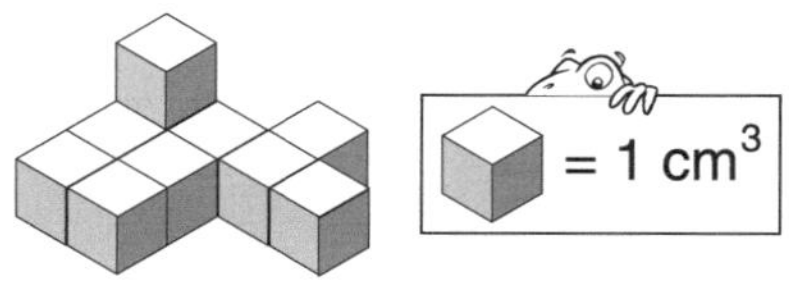

12. $\frac{1}{4} + \frac{1}{4}$ 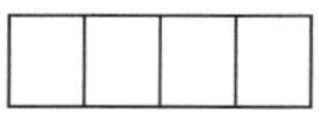 ______
13. Write the digital time for:
    - **a** quarter past 3.
    - **b** quarter to 4.

14. Shade $\frac{8}{12}$ of this shape.

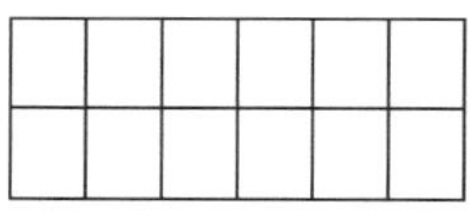

15. Share 36 cakes among 4 children ______ each
16. Millilitres in 1 litre. ______
17. The value of the 3 in 4321. ______
18. Write 8740 in words.

______

______

22:2 — out of 14

1. 5 + 9 ______
2. 20 ÷ 2 ______
3. 18 × 10 ______
4. 112 – 4 ______
5. 630 – 200 ______
6. 7 × 8 ______
7. 6 – 2 – 3 ______
8. 23 tens. ______
9. Add 13 and 17. ______
10. 2073 + 3456 ______
11. 239 + 124 ______

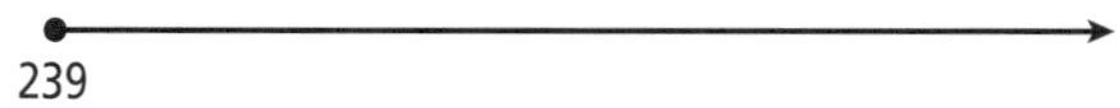

12. 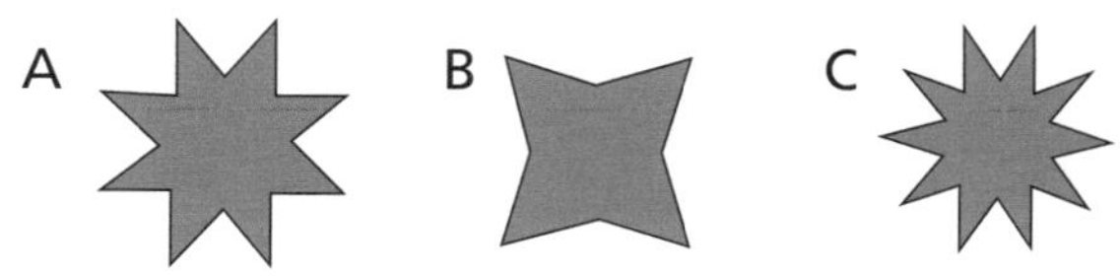

    - **a** Do all of these designs have rotational symmetry? ______
    - **b** Which has rotational symmetry of order 10? ______
13. 'pm' means ______
14.

1–10	IIII		
11–20	𝍸	𝍸	II
21–30	𝍸	𝍸	III

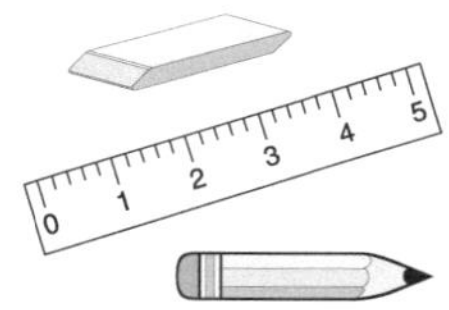

- **a** How many students scored 11–20 marks? ______
- **b** Do we know how many students scored 30? ______
- **c** How many scored over 10? ______

Area and perimeter (challenge)

The area of this shape is $100m^2$.

What is the perimeter?

______

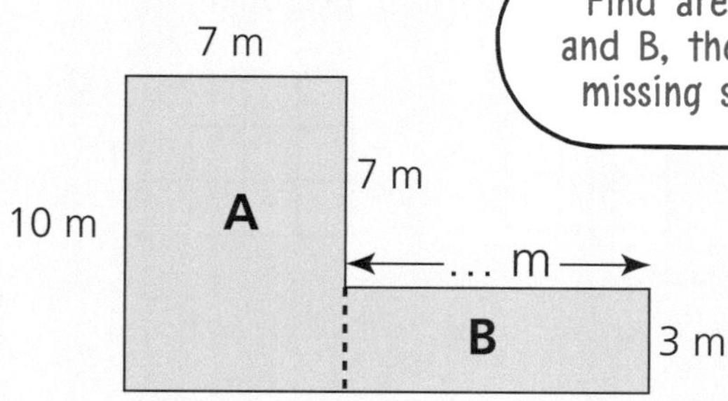

 • *AUSTRALIAN SIGNPOST MATHS 5 MENTALS* • ISBN 978 1 4886 2189 5

22:3 — ☐ out of 12

1.

	H	T	U
	3	0	0
×			2

2.

	H	T	U
		5	0
×			3

3.

	H	T	U
	2	0	0
×			2

4. $3\overline{)993}$

5. $2\overline{)862}$

6. $5\overline{)655}$

7. What is the volume of a box that is 4 cm wide, 5 cm long and 4 cm high? ________

8. This graph shows the response of 24 students. How many chose the category 'bird'? ________

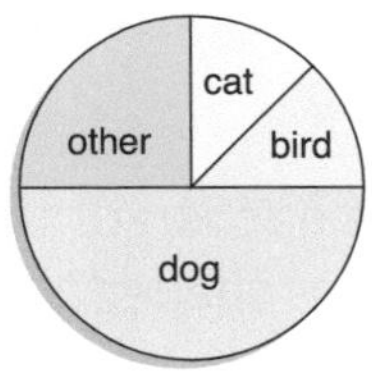

9. a Draw an obtuse angle.

   b Estimate your angle's size. ________

10. $\frac{3}{8} + \frac{2}{8}$ ________

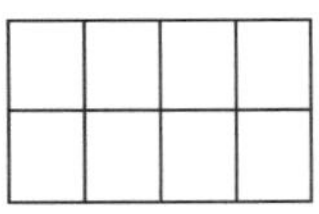

11. What is the time 2 hours after:

   a 10 am ________ b 7 pm ________

   c 11 pm ________ d 1 am ________

12. a The number before 7214. ________

   b The number 3 after 2919. ________

22:4 — Extension — ☐ out of 5

1. Six equal angles make up a straight angle. How big is each angle? ________

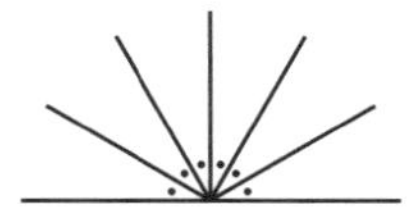

2. Sue-lin, Kai-lin, Naomi and Heather sent each other birthday cards.

   How many cards were sent? ________

3.

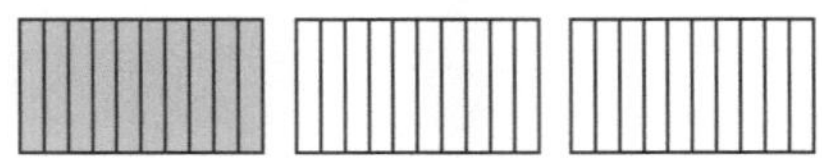

   a $1 \div 2$ ________ b $3 \div 2$ ________

4. This figure has squares of different sizes. How many squares altogether? ________

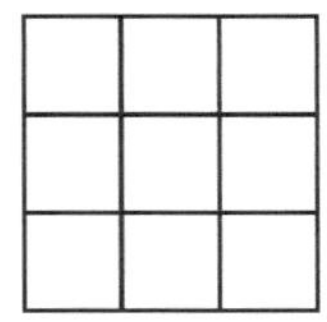

5. I fed 10 dogs either 6 or 7 biscuits each. I used 63 biscuits. How many dogs were given 7 biscuits? ________

Challenge

Write number sentences for addition of fractions, with a denominator of 8, eg $\frac{1}{8} + \frac{4}{8} + \frac{5}{8}$.

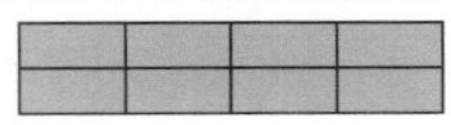

Turn to ID Card C on page 8.
Give the answers for these numbers.

(1) ________ **(2)** ________

(3) ________ **(5)** ________

(6) ________ **(8)** ________

(9) ________ **(10)** ________

(11) ________ **(12)** ________

Make a study card:
Put questions on one side
and answers on the other.

23:1   ☐ out of 18

1. 6×3 ______
2. $43 - 5$ ______
3. 27×10 ______
4. $21 \div 7$ ______
5. $\begin{array}{r} 445 \\ +653 \\ \hline \end{array}$
6. $10 - 10 + 8$ ______
7. $13 + 8$ ______
8. Half of 32. ______
9. 4 rows of 9. ______
10. $\begin{array}{r} 1253 \\ -\ 201 \\ \hline \end{array}$
11. Write 6:00 pm in 24-hour time. ______ : ______
12. True (T) or false (F)?
    a $\frac{5}{10} > \frac{1}{10}$ ______ **b** $\frac{6}{8} < \frac{4}{8}$ ______
13. **a** Is 376 closer to 300 or 400? ______
    b How many \$50 notes make \$300? ______
14. How many days in May? ______
15. **a** Months in a decade. ______
    b Months in a century. ______
16. **a** This is a ______ note.
    b The value of 3 of these notes. ______

(yellow)

17. 10, 13, 16, ______, ______, ______, ______
18. Use 0, 3, 9 and 6 to make the largest possible four-digit number. ______

23:2   ☐ out of 17

1. $14 \div 2$ ______
2. $96 - 8$ ______
3. $28 + 7$ ______
4. 13×10 ______
5. $\begin{array}{r} 738 \\ +235 \\ \hline \end{array}$
6. $20 - 5$ ______
7. 9×6 ______
8. 24 tens. ______
9. 8 more than 11. ______
10. $\begin{array}{r} 430 \\ -\ 90 \\ \hline \end{array}$
11. The time:
    a 6 hours after noon ______
    b 3 hours before midnight ______
12. 6000 + 400 + 20 + 9 ______
13. How many hours till 3:00 pm? ______

14. **a** What fraction of this shape is shaded? ______

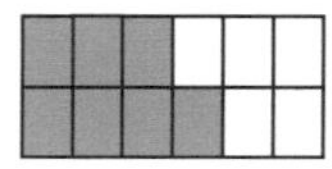

    b $\frac{7}{12} - \frac{2}{12}$ ______
15. A B C

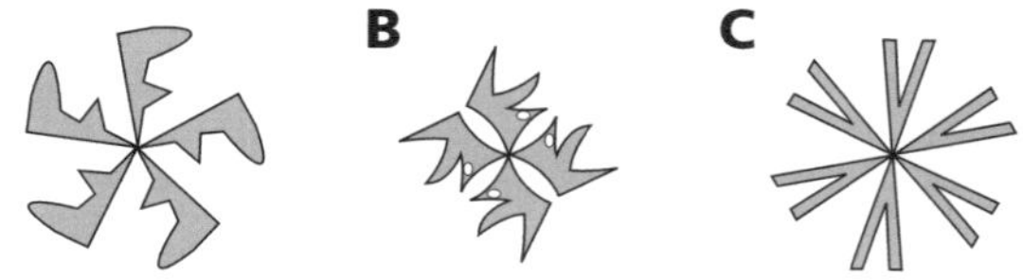

    a Which of these designs does not have rotational symmetry? ______
    b Which has rotational symmetry of order 5? ______
16. Write 7031 in words.
    ____
    ____
17. $\frac{7}{10} + \frac{2}{10}$ ______

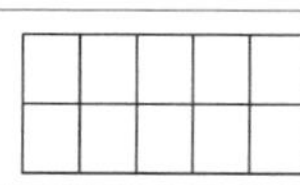

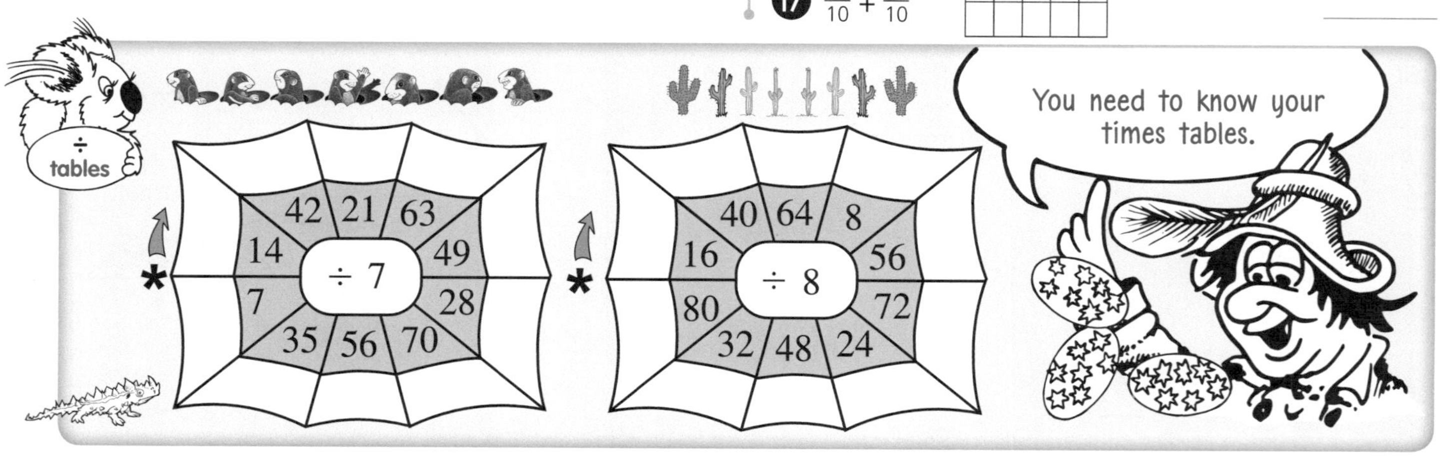

© PEARSON AUSTRALIA 2018 • *AUSTRALIAN SIGNPOST MATHS 5 MENTALS* • ISBN 978 1 4886 2189 5

23:3 — out of 12

1.
H	T	U
	4	0
×		3

2.
H	T	U
1	0	0
×		7

3.
H	T	U
	7	0
×		3

4. 10)200

5. 10)340

6. 10)703 r

7. Use am or pm to write:
   a 20:00 ______ b 07:00 ______

8. a Shade $\frac{3}{6}$ of this shape.

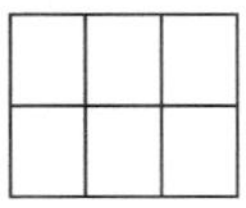

   b $\frac{3}{6} - \frac{2}{6}$ ______

9. There are 24 melons in 1 case. How many melons are in 10 cases? ______

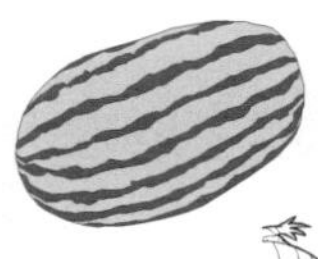

10.

Which of these fractions would:

a have the larger denominator? ______

b be the smaller fraction? ______

11. Complete the label for each clock.

12. $\frac{2}{3} + \frac{1}{3}$ ______

23:4 — Extension — out of 6

1. a 30 minutes after 5:48. ______
   b 15 minutes before 12:05. ______

2. (6 × 9) + (6 × 9) ______

3. a 440 ÷ 4 ______
   b 440 ÷ 10 ______

4. I opened a book. The product of the two page numbers I saw was 110. What were the numbers? ______

5. I spent half of my money on Thursday and one quarter of it on Friday. I had $2.50 left. How much did I start with? ______

6. a 201 more than 4 122. ______
   b 403 more than 5 121. ______

Challenge

Complete a design using rotational symmetry.

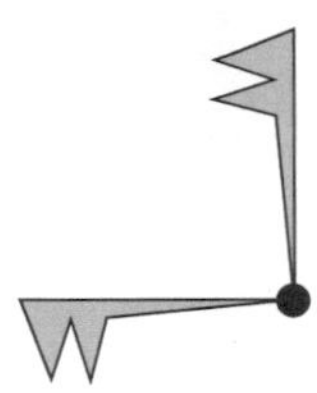

Roman numerals

1	I	one finger	
5	V	one hand	
10	X	two Vs	
50	L	half of a C	
100	C	centum = 100	

Write our numeral for:

a VIII ______ b XV ______ c LX ______

d CXX ______ e LXV ______ f CLX ______

Write the Roman numeral for:

g 22 ______ h 105 ______ i 212 ______

j 63 ______ k 75 ______ l 351 ______

24:1 out of 17

1. 23 + 6 ______
2. 70 − 9 ______
3. 2 × 14 ______
4. 14 − 7 ______
5. 1632 + 1066 ______
6. 8 × 100 ______
7. 30 ÷ 5 ______
8. Double 11. ______
9. 44 tens. ______
10. 279 − 254 ______
11. Round off 219 correct to the nearest hundred. ______
12. Write $6.50 in words. ______
13. How many sides has an octagon? ______
14. Which months have only 30 days? ______
15.

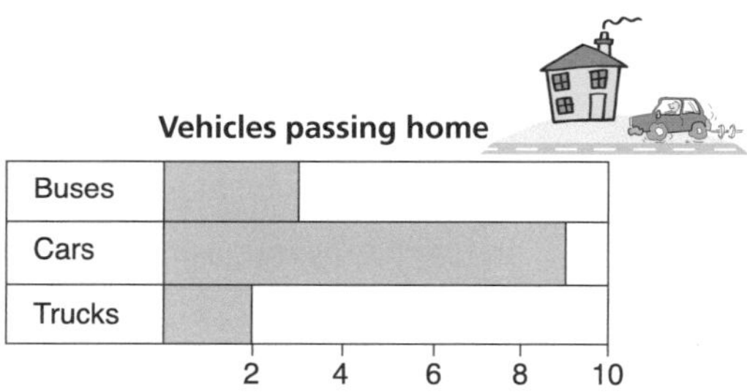

How many vehicles passed my home altogether? ______

16. List the factors of 6. ______
17. True (T) or false (F)?

a $\frac{2}{8} > \frac{6}{8}$ ______ b $\frac{3}{4} < \frac{2}{4}$ ______

24:2 out of 21

1. 16 ÷ 2 ______
2. 21 − 8 ______
3. 53 ×10 ______
4. 10 + 14 ______
5. $3.20 + $2.80 ______
6. 13 × 3 ______
7. $60 × 3 ______
8. 8 times 6. ______
9. Add 6 to 9. ______
10. $3.95 − $2.15 ______
11. The change from $3 if Seth spent $2.35. ______
12. a ______ × 8 = 24 b 24 ÷ 8 = ______
13. 56, 66, 76, ______, ______, ______
14. Shade $\frac{2}{12}$ of this shape.

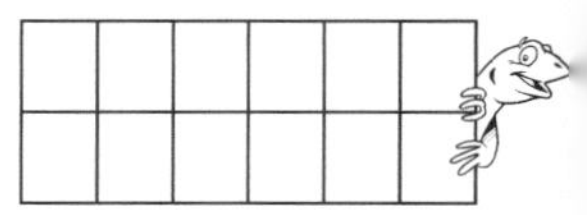

15. 3, 6, 9, ______, ______, ______, ______
16. How many groups of 8 fish in 32? ______
17. How many 20 cent coins have the same value as 1.40? ______
18. Which month has only 28 or 29 days? ______
19. The average of 11 and 25. ______
20.  What is the order of rotational symmetry on this shape? ______
21. $\frac{1}{4} + \frac{1}{4} + \frac{1}{4} + \frac{1}{4}$ 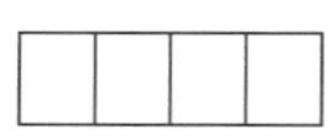 ______

 ISBN 978 1 4886 2189 5

24:3 [ ] out of 14

1. $10\overline{)520}$
2. $10\overline{)417}$ r
3. $10\overline{)341}$ r

4.
```
  89203
- 27432
```

5.
```
  67241
- 25473
```

6. a What fraction of this shape is shaded? ______

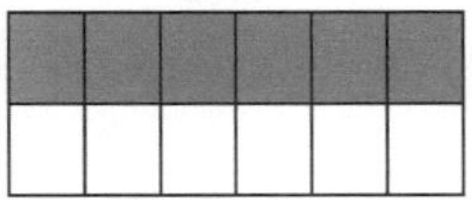

   b $\frac{6}{12} - \frac{3}{12}$ ______

7. Circle the numbers divisible by 2.

   37 16 8 13 1 4

8. Rhiannon scored 7 runs, Tiegan 5, Tran 9, Logan 11 and Pauline 8. What is their average number of runs? ______

9. True (T) or false (F)?
   a A cube has six faces. ______
   b A decagon has ten sides. ______

10. Alana is 27 years older than Flynn. How old will Alana be when Flynn is 5? ______

11. 49 ÷ 7 ______

12. Luke turns 15 in 2 years time. How old is he now? ______

13. The Roman numeral for 8. ______

14. $\frac{1}{4} + \frac{3}{4}$ ______

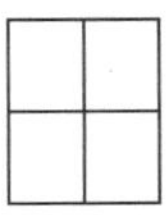

Extension

24:4 [ ] out of 4

1. a The Roman numeral for 26. ______
   b The Roman numeral for 52. ______

2. 12 apples and 4 oranges cost $3.20. How much will 3 apples and 1 orange cost? ______

3. 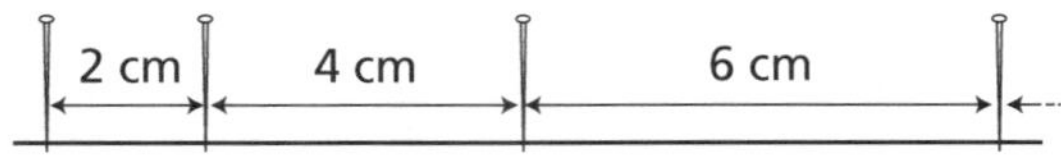

   Pins were stuck onto a board using the pattern shown above. What was the distance between:
   a the 5th and 6th pins? ______
   b the 1st and 6th pins? ______

4. If 67 × 14 = 938,
   a 938 ÷ 14 = ______
   b 938 ÷ 67 = ______

Challenge

Draw a design that has rotational symmetry.

	÷ 7	÷ 35	÷ 5
35			

	÷ 2	÷ 4	÷ 10
40			

	÷ 6	÷ 24	÷ 8
48			

	÷ 6	÷ 2	÷ 1
36			

25:1 ___ out of 18

1. 14 – 6 ______
2. 6 × 3 ______
3. 8 + 5 ______
4. 24 ÷ 4 ______
5.
```
  1648
+  341
```
6. 12 + 3 ______
7. 18 ÷ 6 ______
8. 74 tens. ______
9. 12 minus 7. ______
10.
```
  1374
–  230
```

11. List the first six multiples of 3.

    ______, ______, ______, ______, ______, ______

12. Alexa has 16 books on her desk and 8 in her bag. How many does she have altogether?

    ______

13. 6 + 9 + 4 + 1 ______
14. 75, 80, 85, ______, ______, ______
15. How many cubes do we need to make this shape?

    ______

16. The average of 6 and 10. ______
17. Write all the factors of 14.

    ______

18. True (T) or false (F)?

    a $\frac{3}{8} > \frac{1}{8}$ ______   b $\frac{5}{10} < \frac{3}{10}$ ______

25:2 ___ out of 16

1. 4 × 3 ______
2. 27 + 6 ______
3. 46 – 5 ______
4. 3 × 60 ______
5.
```
  558
+ 280
```
6. 20 ÷ 4 ______
7. 71 – 5 ______
8. 12 plus 99. ______
9. $70 × 2 ______
10.
```
  660
+ 340
```

11. Use the short form to write 5 cubic metres. ______
12. Ten less than thirty. ______
13.

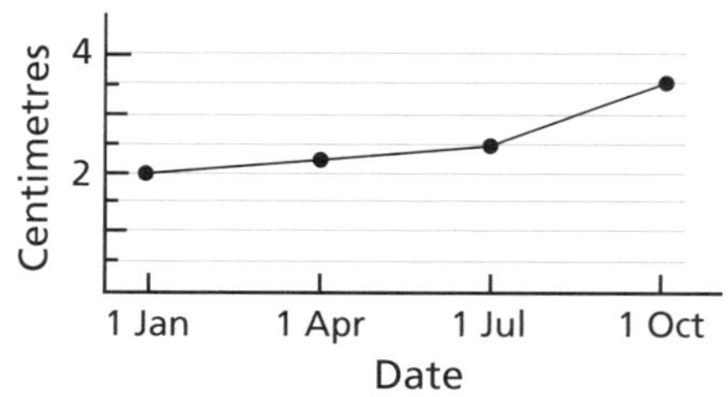

    a When was my goldfish 3·5 cm long? ______

    b How long was the fish on 1st July? ______

14. Sue wants to save $80 in 10 weeks. How much will she need to save each week? ______
15. Circle the numbers divisible by 3.

    12 3 8 6 4 15 7

16.

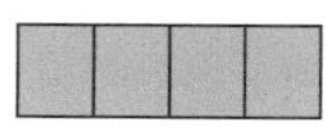

    a $\frac{3}{4} - \frac{2}{4}$ ______   b $\frac{2}{4} - \frac{1}{4}$ ______

 ISBN 978 1 4886 2189 5

25:3 ☐ out of 13

1. $5\overline{)505}$
2. $3\overline{)927}$
3. $4\overline{)424}$

4. $\begin{array}{r} 627 \\ +\,184 \\ \hline \end{array}$
5. $\begin{array}{r} 597 \\ +\,234 \\ \hline \end{array}$
6. $\begin{array}{r} 569 \\ +\,173 \\ \hline \end{array}$

7. The Roman numeral for 19. ______

8. 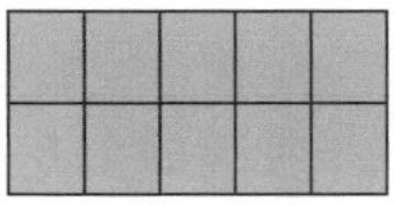

   a $\frac{2}{10} + \frac{5}{10} =$ ______ b $\frac{4}{10} + \frac{4}{10} =$ ______

   c $\frac{3}{10} + \frac{7}{10} =$ ______ d $\frac{2}{10} + \frac{6}{10} =$ ______

9. Circle the numbers divisible by 5.
   30 44 76 50 75

10. Use the short form to write 14 cubic centimetres. ______

11. Which is the most suitable unit (cm^3 or m^3) to measure the volume of a lunch box?

______

12. What was the average time taken to run a race if Annette took 13 seconds, Micah took 13 seconds, and Kwan took 10 seconds? ______

13. $\frac{3}{10} + \frac{3}{10} + \frac{2}{10} =$ ______

25:4 Extension ☐ out of 6

1. Write our numeral for:

   a CXVI ______ b CCLX ______

2. Which of the numbers 68, 198, 315 and 455 are divisible by:

   a 2 and 3? ______

   b 5 and 9? ______

3. $(10 \times 10) + (9 \times 9) + 19$ ______

4. Copy the drawing on the left.

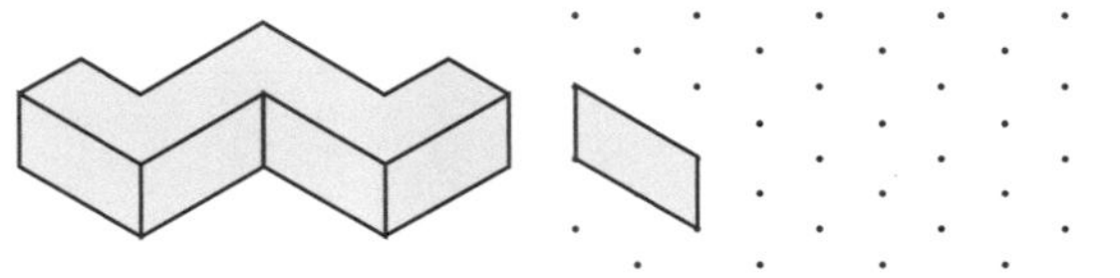

5. 23 + 20 + 11 + 30 ______

6. 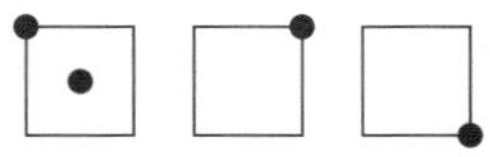 represents 623.

   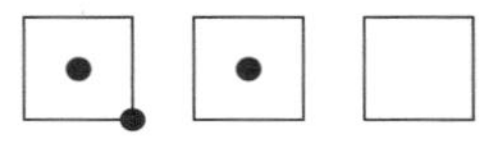 represents 850.

   What number is represented by

    ? ______

Challenge

List volumes that would be measured in:

cm^3	m^3

1 How many triangles are in this grid that have a side length of:

a 1 unit? ______ **b** 2 units? ______ **c** 4 units? ______

Some triangles will point down.

2 What is the greatest number of small triangles that can be shaded if no two shaded triangles share:

a a side? ______ **b** a corner? ______

 • *AUSTRALIAN SIGNPOST MATHS 5 MENTALS* • ISBN 978 1 4886 2189 5

26:1 ☐ out of 17

1. 6 + 5 _____
2. 17 tens. _____
3. 8 × 6 _____
4. 30 ÷ 3 _____
5. $\begin{array}{r} 178 \\ -\ 64 \\ \hline \end{array}$
6. 14 – 8 _____
7. 18 ÷ 3 _____
8. 7 times 9. _____
9. 22 × 10 _____
10. $\begin{array}{r} 294 \\ +702 \\ \hline \end{array}$
11. 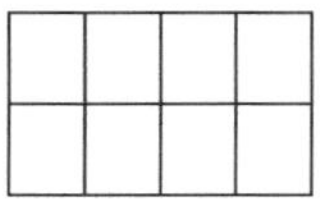

    a $\frac{5}{8} - \frac{3}{8} =$ _____ **b** $\frac{7}{8} - \frac{2}{8} =$ _____

    c $\frac{8}{8} - \frac{1}{8} =$ _____ **d** $\frac{6}{8} - \frac{5}{8} =$ _____
12. The sum of 17 and 9. _____
13. 25, 20, 15, _____, _____, _____
14. This is the net of which shape? _____

15. Write 13 cubic centimetres in short form. _____
16. List all the factors of 32.

    _____
17. **a** $1 - \frac{1}{6}$ _____ 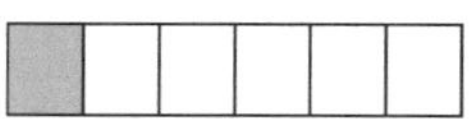

    b $1 - \frac{1}{4}$ _____ 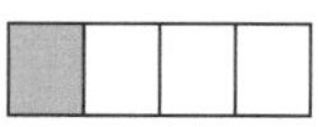

26:2 ☐ out of 15

1. 33 – 24 _____
2. 27 + 23 _____
3. 7 × 80 _____
4. 15 ÷ 3 _____
5. $\begin{array}{r} 670 \\ +350 \\ \hline \end{array}$
6. 8 × 90 _____
7. 15 – 6 _____
8. Half of 26. _____
9. 14 subtract 9. _____
10. $\begin{array}{r} 328 \\ -253 \\ \hline \end{array}$
11. List the first six multiples of 7.

    _____, _____, _____, _____, _____, _____
12. 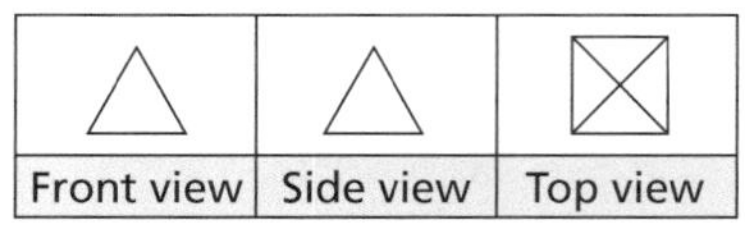

    This shape is a _____.
13. 2 × 24 = (2 × 20) + (2 × 4) = _____
14. **a** 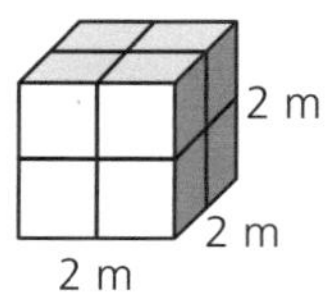

    Volume = _____

    b 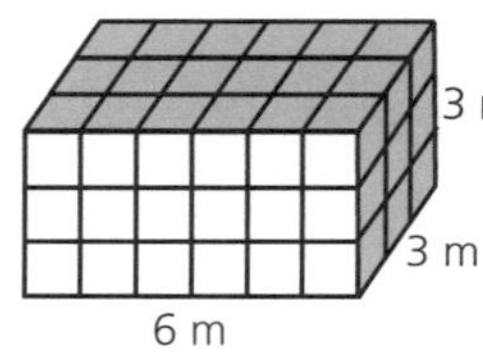

    Volume = _____
15. 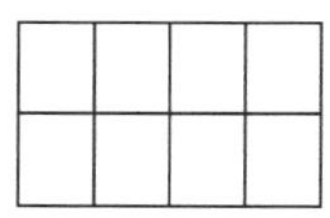

    a $\frac{2}{8} - \frac{3}{8} =$ _____ **b** $\frac{4}{8} - \frac{2}{8} =$ _____

    c $\frac{6}{8} - \frac{1}{8} =$ _____ **d** $\frac{2}{8} - \frac{5}{8} =$ _____

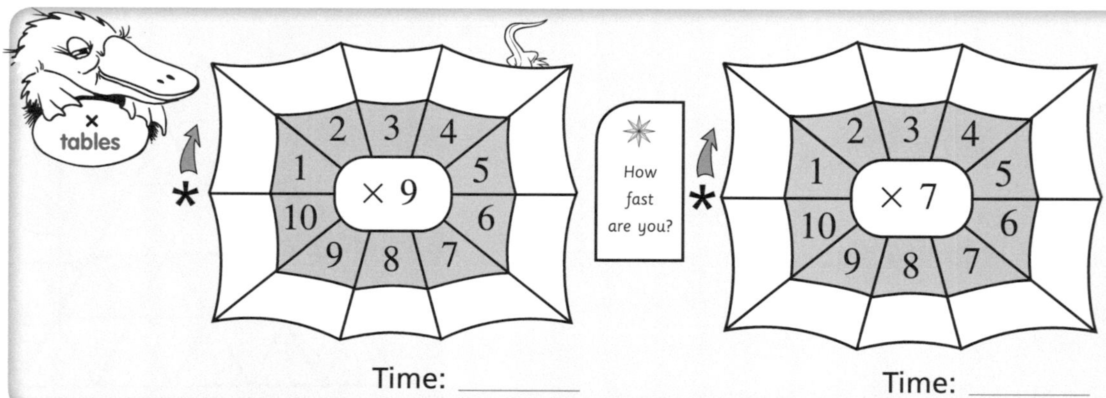

AUSTRALIAN SIGNPOST MATHS 5 MENTALS • ISBN 978 1 4886 2189 5

26:3 ☐ out of 10

1. 18 × 4
   = ______ × 2 × 4
   = ______

2. 32 × 25
   = ______ × 4 × 25
   = ______

3. 9)81 ______

4. 7)56 ______

5. 7)72 ______ r

6. The Roman numeral for 7. ______

7. a $1 - \frac{7}{10} =$ ______
   b $1 - \frac{3}{5} =$ ______

8. Use the short form to write 25 cubic metres. ______

9. 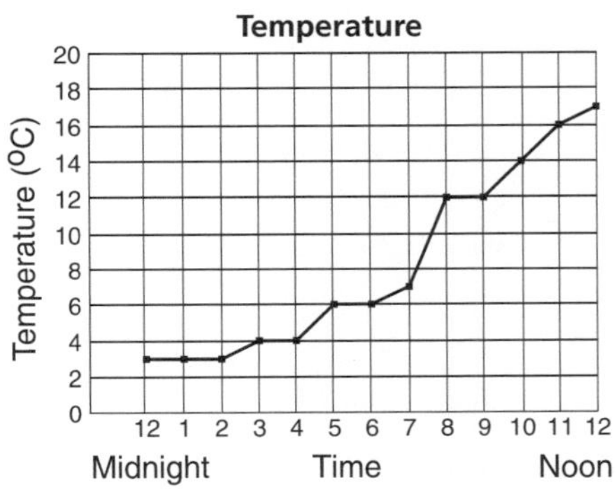

   a What was the temperature at 5 am? ______
   b At what time was it 14°C? ______

10. Would cm^3 or m^3 be the unit used to measure the volume of a truckload of soil? ______

26:4 Extension ☐ out of 6

1. The Roman numeral for:
   a 95 ______ b 150 ______

2. Our numeral for:
   a CCLX ______ b XCVIII ______

3. Which of the numbers 34, 95, 276 and 135 is divisible by both:
   a 2 and 3? ______ b 5 and 9? ______

4. a Is 0·7 equal to 0·70? ______
   b 0·70 ÷ 2 ______
   c 0·7 ÷ 2 ______
   d 0·1 ÷ 2 ______

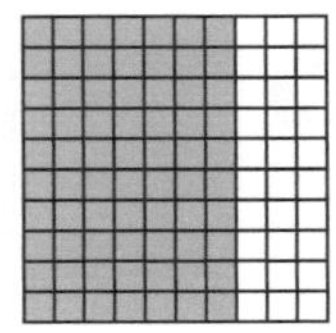

5. a (3 × 2) + (6 × 2) ______
   b (4 × 2) + (2 × 2) ______
   c (3 × 3) + (6 × 2) ______

6. Write the first 4 multiples of 13.
   ______

Challenge

Choose a household object.
Draw and label the top, side and front view below.

In each case, use the digits 3, 4, 5, 7, 8 and 9 to write one digit in each circle so that the numbers in each line have the same total.

a

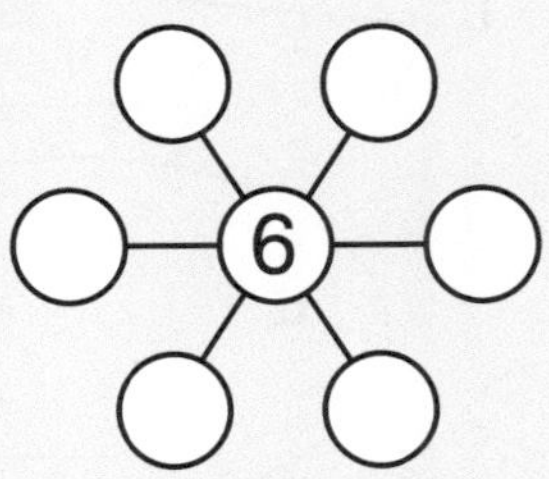

b

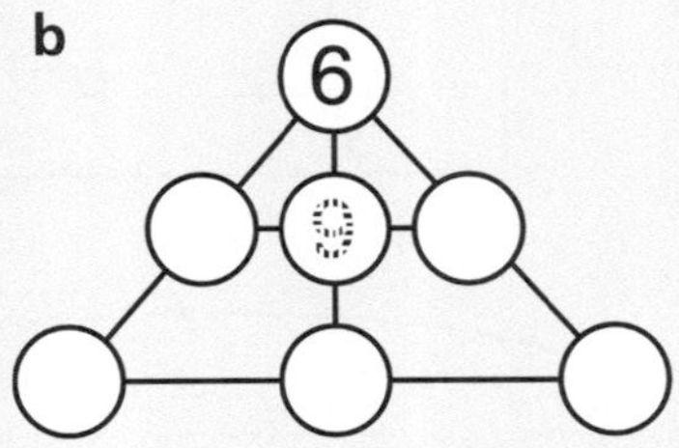

27:1 ☐ out of 17

1. 25 − 2 ______
2. 12 × 10 ______
3. 24 ÷ 3 ______
4. 8 × 6 ______
5. 459 − 454 ______
6. 14 ÷ 7 ______
7. 11 + 5 ______
8. 14 take away 5. ______
9. Add 10 and 12. ______
10. 246 + 747 ______

11. 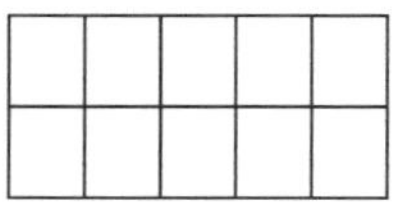

 a $\frac{8}{10} - \frac{4}{10} =$ ______ b $\frac{9}{10} - \frac{7}{10} =$ ______

12. Millimetres in 1 centimetre. ______
13. Arrange these from smallest to largest.
 186 94 261 172
 ____
14. The distance around a shape is called the
 p ______________.
 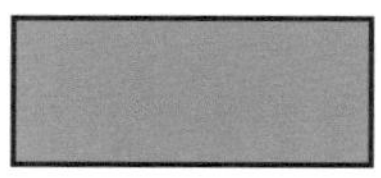
15. Plot this set of points and join them in order.
 1A, 1B, 0B, 1D,
 2D, 3B, 2B, 2A, 1A.
 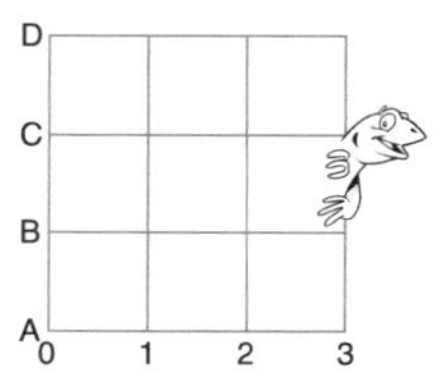

16. 4, 8, 12, 16, ______, ______, ______
17. a $\frac{3}{4}$ plus $\frac{1}{4}$. ☐☐☐☐ ______
 b 1 minus $\frac{1}{4}$. ______

27:2 ☐ out of 18

1. 7 × 20 ______
2. 50 ÷ 10 ______
3. 22 − 10 ______
4. 6 + 13 ______
5. 274 + 320 ______
6. 32 ÷ 4 ______
7. 10 + 28 ______
8. 19 take away 6. ______
9. Triple 8. ______
10. 1048 − 214 ______

11. a $1 - \frac{2}{3}$ ______ b $1 - \frac{6}{10}$ ______
12. Draw the front, side and top elevation.
 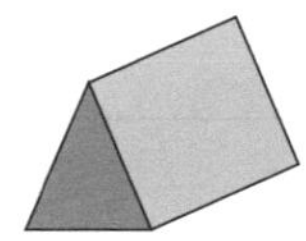
 Front Side Top
13. Which is bigger, 1·62 or 0·98? ______
14. Perimeter of a square of side length:
 a 8 m ______ b 4·5 m ______
15. Write 3 cm 6 mm as millimetres. ______
16. Complete this pattern.

1st number	5	6	7	8
2nd number	15	18	21	

17. Write a rule for the pattern above. ☐ top by ☐.
18. Choose the most suitable measure (cm^3 or m^3) for each of these volumes:
 a a swimming pool ______
 b a pencil case ______

Each block is 1 cm long.

Find the perimeter of each shape to the nearest cm.

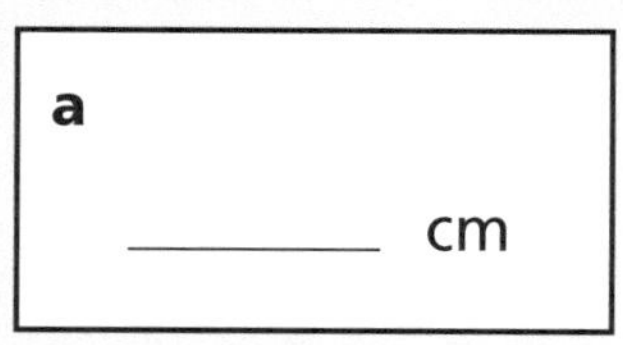

a ______ cm

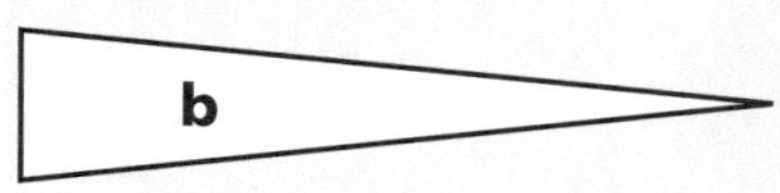

b ______ cm

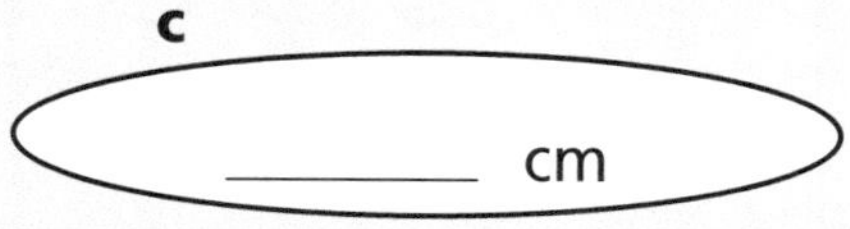

c ______ cm

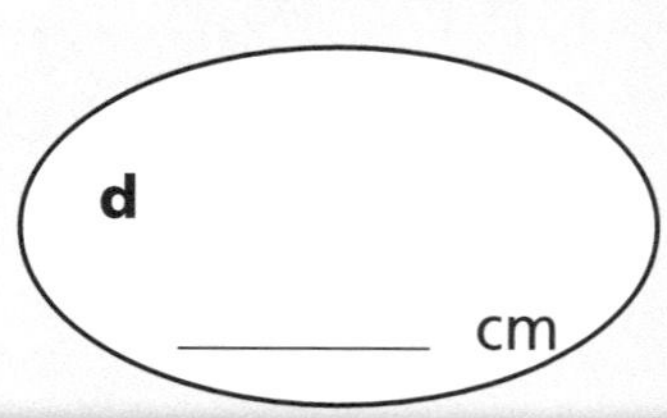

d ______ cm

 • *AUSTRALIAN SIGNPOST MATHS 5 MENTALS* • ISBN 978 1 4886 2189 5

27:3 out of 13

1 16 × 5
= ______ × 2 × 5
= ______

2 16 × 25
= ______ × 4 × 25
= ______

3 $2\overline{)814}$ **4** $2\overline{)806}$ **5** $4\overline{)416}$

6 4 × 17 = (4 × 10) + (4 × 7)
= ______

7 Estimate then measure the length of this bar, correct to the nearest millimetre.

Estimate = ______ Measure = ______

8 Which is smaller, 2·71 or 2·37? ______

9 Which prism has this net?

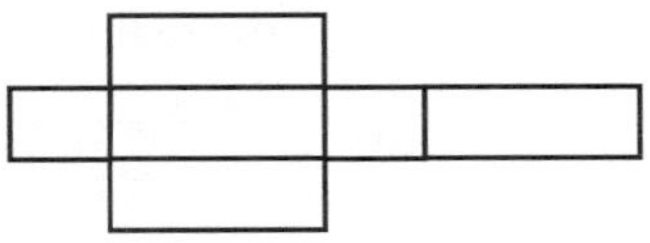

______

10 Use the short form to write 31 cubic metres. ______

11 **a** $8 - \frac{1}{2}$ ______ **b** $3 - \frac{1}{2}$ ______

12 Write the improper fraction for the shaded part.

a 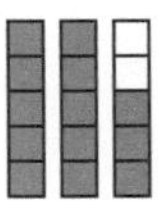 ______ **b** 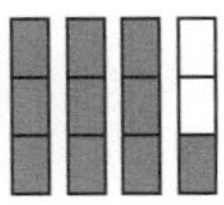 ______

13 The Roman numeral for:

a ten ______ **b** nineteen ______

27:4 Extension out of 6

1 Write our numeral for:

a XXIII ______

b LXXIX ______

2 What is the perimeter of a square of area 4 cm^3? ______

3 Our cricket team needed 260 runs to win the match. We scored only 123. How far short were we? ______

4 Write as centimetres:

a 5·85 m ______ **b** 14·6 m ______

5

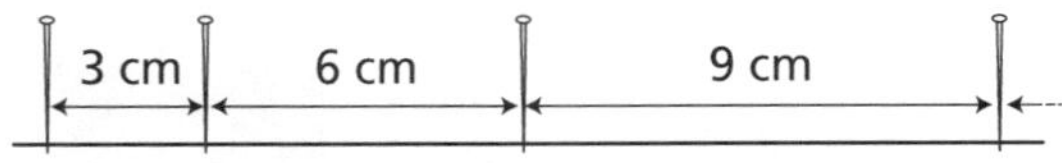

Pins were stuck onto a board using the pattern shown above.
What was the distance between:

a the 5th and 6th pins? ______

b the 1st and 6th pins? ______

6 118 + 11 + 9 + 22 ______

Challenge

Write your own number patterns and the rule for each.

______

______

______

______

Turn to ID Card A on page 6.
Give the answers for these numbers.

(20) 20 ______ 5 **(21)** 42 ______ 6

(22) ______ numbers **(23)** ______ numbers

(24) ______ numbers **(25)** ______ numbers

(26) ______ **(28)** ______

28:1 ☐ out of 16

1. 9 × 5 ______
2. 27 ÷ 9 ______
3. 24 – 13 ______
4. 17 + 4 ______
5. $\begin{array}{r} 274 \\ +327 \\ \hline \end{array}$
6. 36 – 24 ______
7. 20 ÷ 4 ______
8. 8 times 5. ______
9. Add 18 and 6. ______
10. $\begin{array}{r} 892 \\ -605 \\ \hline \end{array}$

11. Circle the measure correctly written.

    A 3 cms **B** 3 cm **C** 3 CM **D** 3 Cm

12. The perimeter of the black rectangle is

    ________ centimetres.

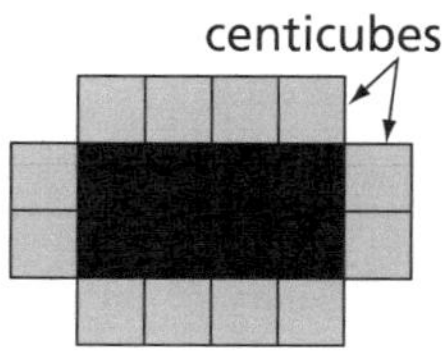

13. Write the time that is 5 minutes after 5 past 8. ________
14. 87 – 84 ________
15. Joshua has 6 budgerigars and Farida has 23. How many birds altogether?

____

16. **a** The perimeter of this shape. ________

    b The area of this shape. ________

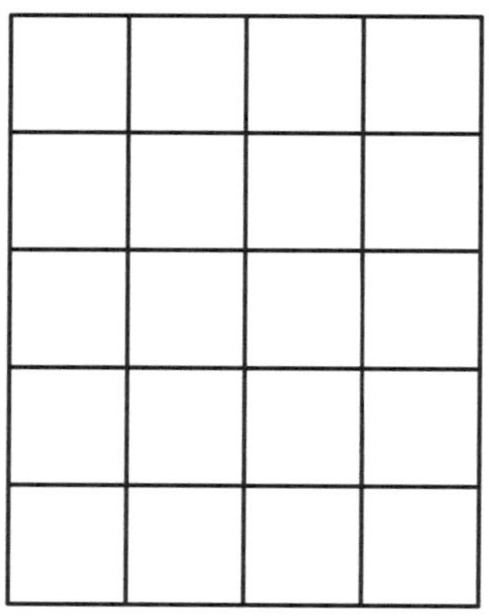

28:2 ☐ out of 16

1. 15 ÷ 5 ______
2. 92 – 4 ______
3. 12 + 16 ______
4. 36 ÷ 6 ______
5. $\begin{array}{r} 827 \\ -643 \\ \hline \end{array}$
6. 4 × 3 ______
7. 61 – 17 ______
8. Halve 18. ______
9. 3 times 8. ______
10. $\begin{array}{r} 653 \\ +721 \\ \hline \end{array}$

11. 3 × 63

    = (3 × 60) + (3 × 3)

    = ________

12. 6 × 37

    = (6 × 30) + (6 × 7)

    = ________

13. Estimate then measure the length of this bar in millimetres.

    Estimate = ______ mm Measure = ______ mm

14. 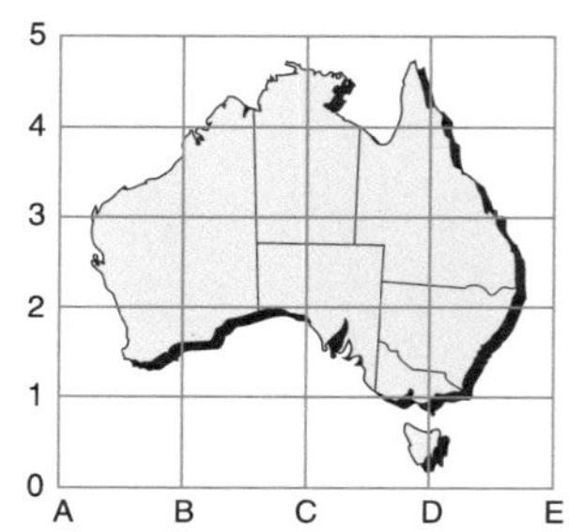

One grid reference for Queensland is D4.
Give the best possible reference for:

a Qld ________ **b** NSW ________

c SA ________ **d** Vic ________

15. Millimetres in 7 cm 9 mm. ________
16. **a** $1 - \frac{4}{5}$ ________ **b** $\frac{4}{5} - \frac{2}{5}$ ________

Find the perimeter of each shape.

a Perimeter = ______________ cm

b Perimeter = ______________ cm

4 + 4 + 4 + 4 = 16
So perimeter = 16 cm

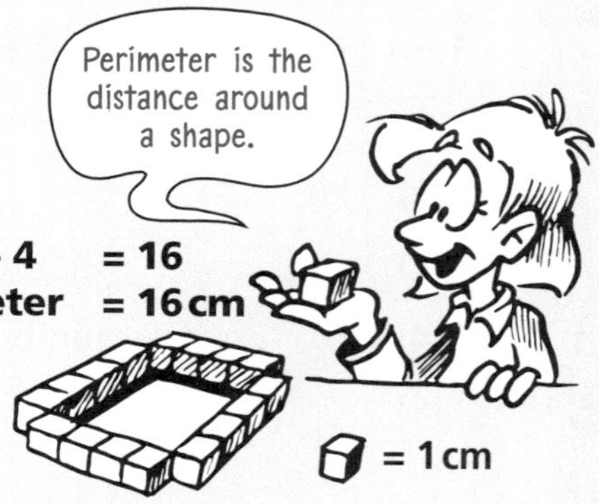

out of 14

1.
$$\begin{array}{r} 321 \\ 403 \\ +\ 142 \\ \hline \end{array}$$

2.
$$\begin{array}{r} 600 \\ -397 \\ \hline \end{array}$$

3.
$$\begin{array}{r} 892 \\ -294 \\ \hline \end{array}$$

4. 7)30 r ____

5. 4)23 r ____

6. Which is larger, 29·34 or 29·31? ________

7. 6 millimetres plus 7 millimetres.

________ millimetres

8. a Find the perimeter.

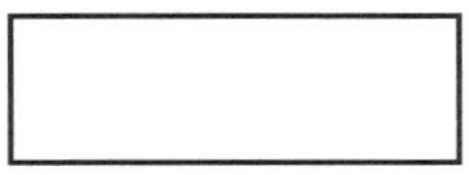

____

b Find the area.

____

9. Write the fraction that has 5 out of 8 equal parts. ________

10. Find the perimeter of a rectangle with side lengths 3 cm and 9 cm. ________

11. a Write 32 mm as centimetres and millimetres. ________

b How many millimetres in 2 cm 6 mm? ________

12. Complete this pattern:

Pentagons	1	2	3	4	5
Sides	5				

13. 12, 18, 24, ______, ______, ______

14. The Roman numeral for fifty-five. ________

out of 6

1. Write the Roman numeral for:

a 54 ________

b 99 ________

c 376 ________

2. a $2\frac{1}{2}$ m = ______ cm b $2\frac{1}{2}$ cm = ______ mm

3. The distance around each square is 16 metres. How far is it around the rectangle?

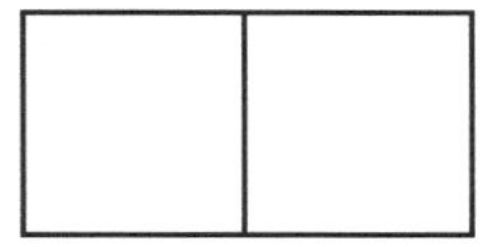

____

4. What will the time on this watch be in 11 hours and 40 minutes?

____

5. Svetla hit 13 runs. Evan hit 3 times as many. How many runs did they hit altogether?

____

6. (20 × 2) + (20 × 2) = ________

Challenge

Draw and label different types of lines.

In each case finish the given pattern.

a Add 4.

23					

b Multiply by 2.

2					

c Subtract 9.

82					

d Add 11.

88					

e Multiply by 2 and add 1.

3					

f × 3 and then – 30.

16					

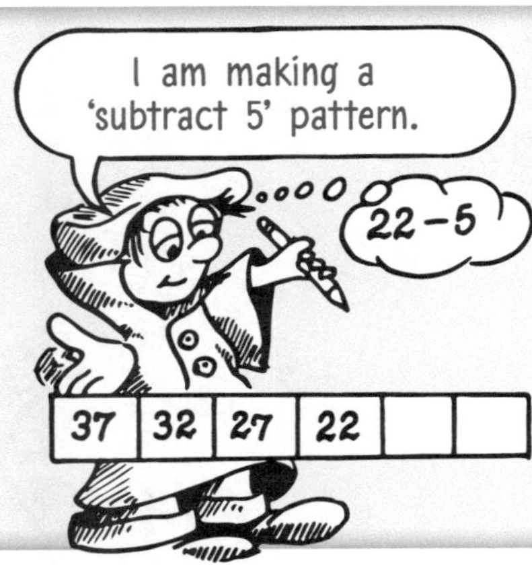

29:1 ☐ out of 18

1. 8 + 14 ______
2. 6 × 40 ______
3. 14 − 4 ______
4. 24 ÷ 2 ______
5. $\begin{array}{r} 137 \\ -\ 48 \\ \hline \end{array}$
6. 24 × 10 ______
7. 12 + 8 ______
8. 14 take away 5. ______
9. Double 11. ______
10. $\begin{array}{r} 876 \\ +315 \\ \hline \end{array}$
11. Continue this pattern.

    0·7, 0·8, 0·9, ______, ______, ______

12. Daniel has three beach balls, five toy boats and two toy aeroplanes.

    a How many beach balls and toy boats does Daniel have? ______

    b How many toys altogether? ______

13. Centimetres in 1 m 72 cm. ______ cm
14. Which months make up spring? ______

    ______

15. 6 + 6 + 6 + 6 ______
16. How many groups of 5 fish in 20? ______

17. Hours from 9 am till noon. ______
18.

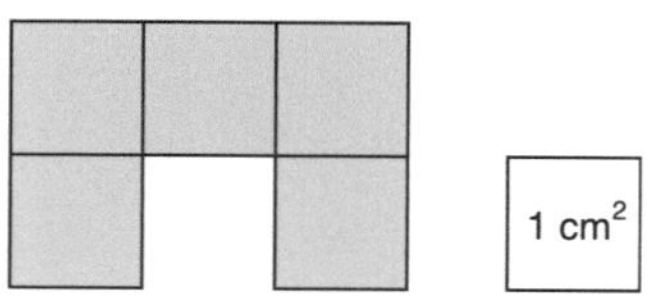

    a What is the area? ______

    b What is the perimeter? ______

29:2 ☐ out of 18

1. 15 × 2 ______
2. 99 ÷ 3 ______
3. 28 + 15 ______
4. 18 − 4 ______
5. $\begin{array}{r} 572 \\ +146 \\ \hline \end{array}$
6. 45 ÷ 9 ______
7. 92 − 3 ______
8. 2 times 81. ______
9. Halve 144. ______
10. $\begin{array}{r} 246 \\ -184 \\ \hline \end{array}$
11. a

______ past

    b

______ past

12. a Months in $2\frac{1}{2}$ years. ______

    b The months of summer. ______

    ______

13. Write in short form, 17 shared by 3. ______
14. How many quarters in 3 apples? ______
15. 10 less than 100. ______
16. How many 30c apples can I buy for $1.80? ______
17. a Complete this pattern.

    $\frac{22}{100}$, $\frac{21}{100}$, $\frac{20}{100}$, ______, ______, ______

    b The rule is ______

18. a $\begin{array}{r} 7\cdot 3 \\ -\ 2\cdot 1 \\ \hline \end{array}$ b $\begin{array}{r} 6\cdot 5 \\ -\ 3\cdot 2 \\ \hline \end{array}$

Find the perimeter of each curved shape.

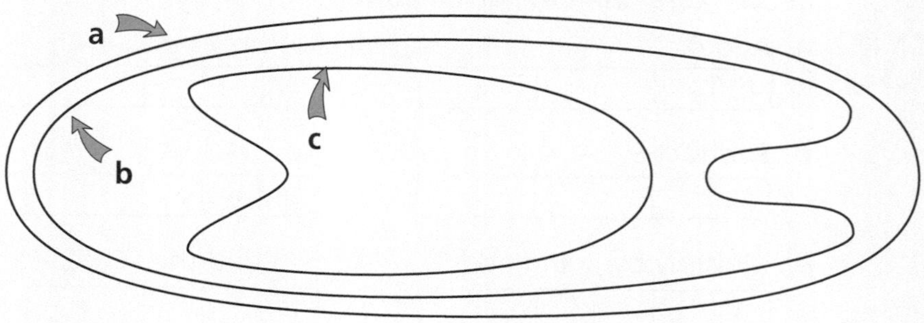

a ______ cm b ______ cm c ______ cm

29:3 — out of 8

1. 5 × 28
   = (5 × 20) + (5 × 8)
   = ______

2. 4 × 42
   = (4 × 40) + (4 × 2)
   = ______

3.

	H	T	U
		5	7
×			4

4.

	H	T	U
		3	4
×			6

5. 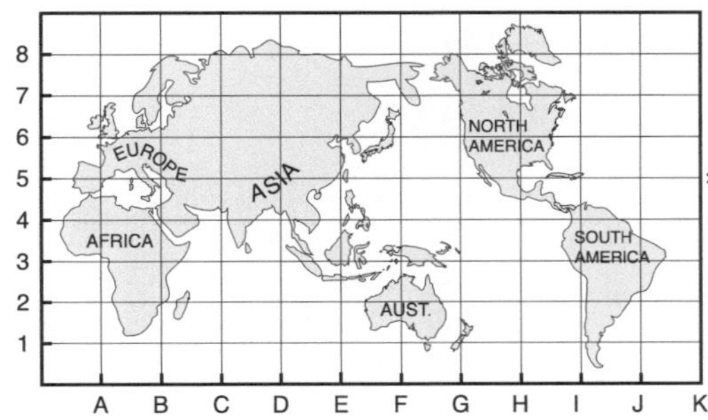

a What continent is north-west of Australia? ______

What continent has coordinates

b A4? ______

c J3? ______

d What coordinates could be used to locate Australia? ______

6. 0·5, 2·5, 4·5, ______, ______

7. Find the perimeter of a rectangle with side lengths 4 cm and 3 cm. ______

8. Millimetres in 2·7 cm. ______

29:4 — Extension — out of 5

1. a Write 160 in Roman numerals. ______
   b Our numeral for CXCIV. ______

2. What is the perimeter of a square that has an area of 16 cm^3? ______

3. 9 o'clock, quarter past 12, half past 9, 3 o'clock.
   At which of the above times are the hour and minute hands at right angles?
   ______

4. There are 8 petals on each flower.

   a How many petals altogether? ______
   b How many flowers would make 200 petals? ______

5. a 157 ÷ 3 ______ r ______
   b 157 ÷ 5 ______ r ______

Challenge

Write your own number patterns using fractions and decimals and the rule for each.

______

______

______

______

30:1 [ ] out of 14

1. 22 − 3 ______
2. 7 + 20 ______
3. 4 + 16 ______
4. 15 − 3 ______
5. $\begin{array}{r} 2476 \\ -1320 \\ \hline \end{array}$
6. 27 ÷ 3 ______
7. 59 + 7 ______
8. 34 × 10 ______
9. 8 groups of 4. ______
10. $\begin{array}{r} 1684 \\ -\ 746 \\ \hline \end{array}$

11. Write the digital time using am or pm.

______ : ______ ______

Morning

12. 5 red and 4 green marbles are in a bowl. Which colour is more likely to be chosen at random? ______

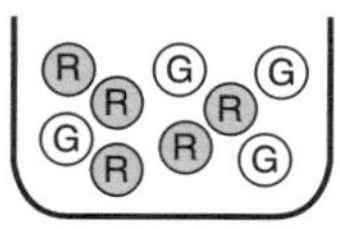

13. Continue this pattern.

0·72, 0·73, ______, ______, ______

14.

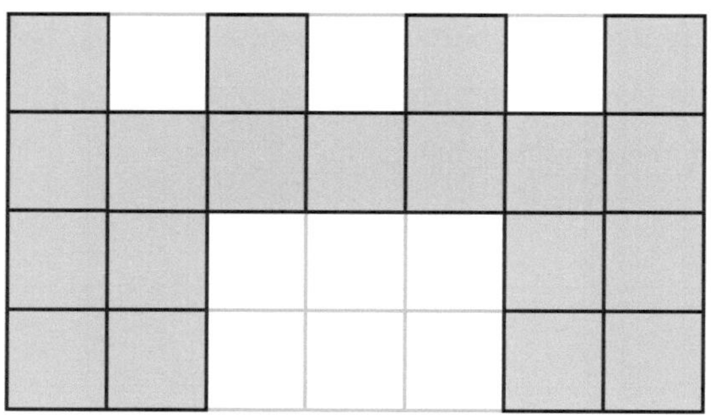

a What is the area in cm^2 of the shaded castle? ______

b What is the perimeter? ______

30:2 [ ] out of 16

1. 6 + 7 ______
2. 13 − 7 ______
3. 8 × 6 ______
4. 24 ÷ 4 ______
5. $\begin{array}{r} 1281 \\ -\ 623 \\ \hline \end{array}$
6. 70 − 21 ______
7. 8 + 9 ______
8. 4 lots of $1\frac{1}{2}$. ______
9. Triple 11. ______
10. $\begin{array}{r} 284 \\ +134 \\ \hline \end{array}$

11. Complete this pattern.

0·42, 0·41, 0·4, ______, ______, ______

12. Days in April. ______

13. How much more is needed to make 150?

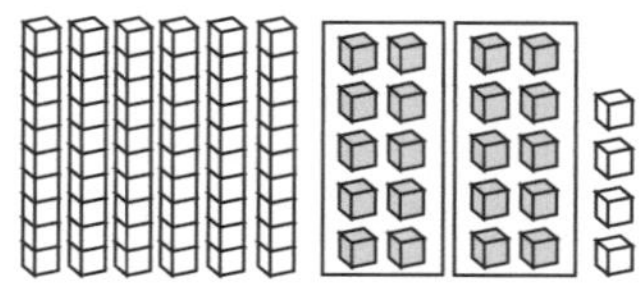

______

14. What's the time when it's 1 minute after 5 to 12? ______

15. What is the time $2\frac{1}{2}$ hours after 5 am? ______

16.

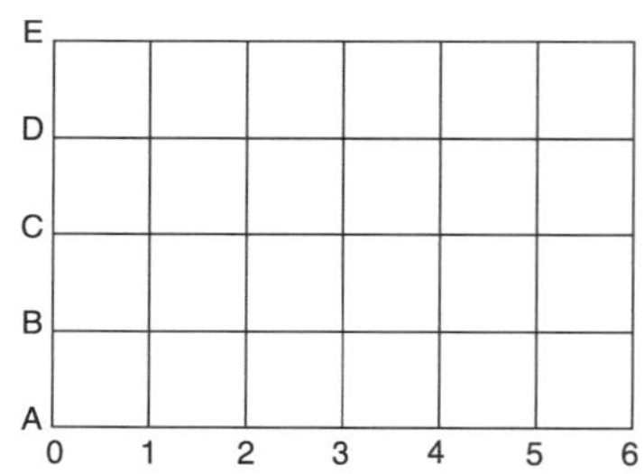

a Plot this set of points on the grid and join them in order.
1B, 2D, 3D, 4D, 5B, 4B, 3B, 2B, 1B

b What shape is formed? ______

Chance

Is this game fair?

Two coins are tossed.

Toss two coins 50 times. Keep a tally of your results in the table below.

H and H	
T and T	
H and T	

 • *AUSTRALIAN SIGNPOST MATHS 5 MENTALS* • ISBN 978 1 4886 2189 5

30:3 ☐ out of 13

1

	H	T	U
	2	6	9
×			2

2

	H	T	U
	1	6	1
×			4

3 $7\overline{)917}$

4 $5\overline{)785}$

5 $6\overline{)728}$ r

6 Order from smallest to largest:

$\frac{15}{100}$, $\frac{21}{100}$, $\frac{11}{100}$ ______, ______, ______

7 Is 42 × 7 less than 42 × 6? ______

8 50 socks, 30 shoes. How many more socks than shoes? ______

9 How many 10c coins could I exchange for 74 five-cent coins? ______

10 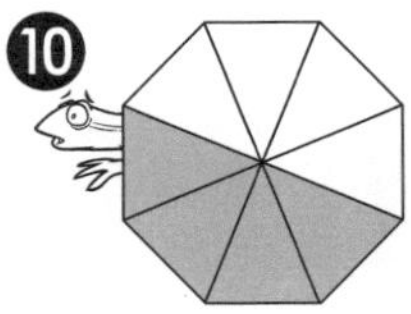
What is the chance, as a fraction, that the spinner will land on grey? ______

11 Use am or pm to write the time one hour before:

a 16:32 ______ **b** 19:09 ______

c 09:23 ______ **d** 05:58 ______

12
$$\begin{array}{r} 4\cdot3 \\ +\ 5\cdot3 \\ \hline \end{array}$$

13
$$\begin{array}{r} 6\cdot1 \\ +\ 3\cdot6 \\ \hline \end{array}$$

30:4 ☐ out of 6

Extension

1 Write our numeral for:

a CXXVII ______ **b** CCCIX ______

2 The coordinates of the 4th corner if:

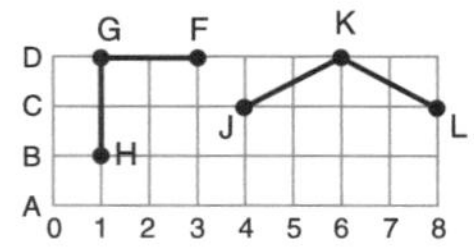

a F, G, H is to be a square. ______

b J, K, L is to be a rhombus. ______

3 **a** 16 minutes before 1:05. ______

b 23 minutes after 10 to 7. ______

4 50 – 12 – 25 + 8 ______

5 What is:

a one third of half an hour? ______

b two thirds of half an hour? ______

6 After losing \$20 and finding only \$7, I had \$78. How much did I start with? ______

Challenge

Write facts about the number 603 730.

______

______

______

______

______

______

Turn to ID Card D on page 9.
Give the answers for these numbers.

(1) ______ (2) ______ or ______

(3) ______ (11) ______

(15) net of a ______ (20) ______

(21) ______ (22) ______

(23) ______ will not roll. (26) ______

31:1 [ ] out of 17

1. 8×2 ______
2. $26 + 16$ ______
3. $28 \div 7$ ______
4. 8×5 ______
5. $1624 + 585$

$$\begin{array}{r} 1624 \\ +\ 585 \\ \hline \end{array}$$

6. $15 - 7$ ______
7. $20 \div 5$ ______
8. 6 more than 19. ______
9. 38 take away 35. ______
10. $6573 - 2483$

$$\begin{array}{r} 6573 \\ -2483 \\ \hline \end{array}$$

11. Write the numeral for one thousand, three hundred and eight. ______
12. $6 + 6 + 6 + 6$ ______
13. Write in centimetres:
   a 1 m 49 cm ______
   b 2 m 5 cm ______
14. Complete this number sentence.

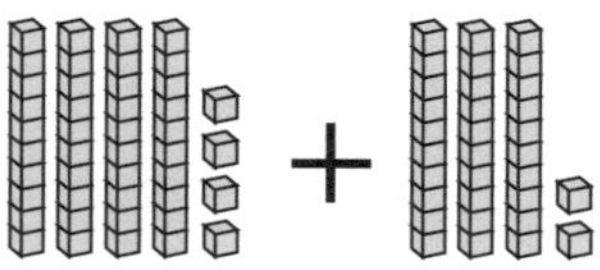

______ + ______ = ______

15. How many tens in 382? ______
16. The numeral for 200 + 50 + 6. ______
17. Write a digital label for each time.

a

morning
[:]

b

evening
[:]

31:2 [ ] out of 16

1. $20 \div 5$ ______
2. 9×3 ______
3. $12 + 22$ ______
4. 10×55 ______
5. $739 + 282$

$$\begin{array}{r} 739 \\ +282 \\ \hline \end{array}$$

6. $18 - 6$ ______
7. 68×10 ______
8. 19 take away 4. ______
9. Half of 24. ______
10. $1276 - 839$

$$\begin{array}{r} 1276 \\ -\ 839 \\ \hline \end{array}$$

11. We write 'post meridiem' as ______
12. What is the time 3 hours after 2:30 pm? ______
13.

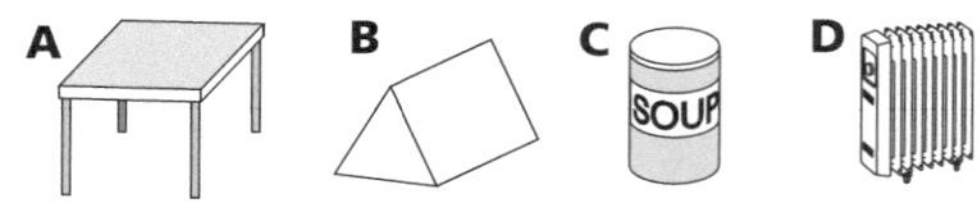

   a Which of the objects has a top view that is a circle? ______
   b Which of the objects has a top view that is a square? ______
14. $2 \times 3 \times 6$ ______
15. $\frac{1}{4}$ of one litre. ______
16.

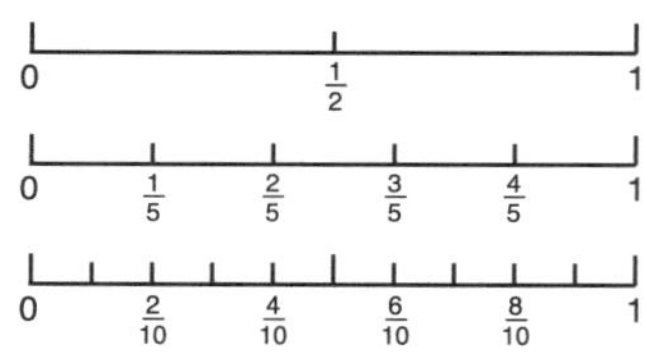

a $\frac{1}{2} = \frac{\square}{10}$ $\square$ = ______

b $\frac{8}{10} = \frac{\square}{5}$ $\square$ = ______

c $\frac{2}{5} = \frac{\square}{10}$ $\square$ = ______

d $1 = \frac{\square}{5}$ $\square$ = ______

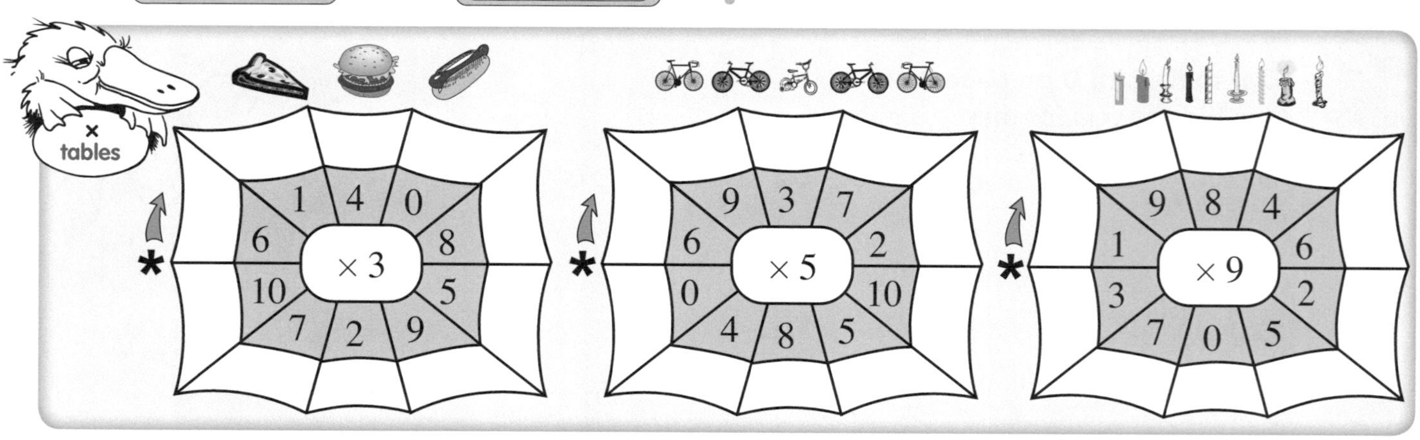

 • *AUSTRALIAN SIGNPOST MATHS 5 MENTALS* • ISBN 978 1 4886 2189 5

31:3 ☐ out of 11

1

H	T	U
	3	1
		6

2

	H	T	U
		9	7
×			2

3

	H	T	U
	1	4	1
×			3

4 **a** Estimate 145 + 68.

E = ______ + ______

= ______

b Estimate 614 – 293.

E = ______ – ______

= ______

5 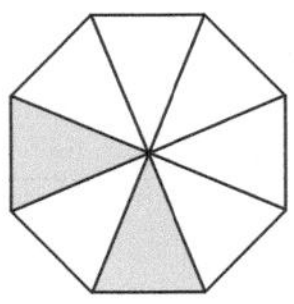 What is the chance, as a fraction, that the spinner will land on grey? ______

6 The Roman numeral for:

a 55 ______ **b** 109 ______

7 How many wheels on 15 cars? ______

8 Months in 3 years. ______

9 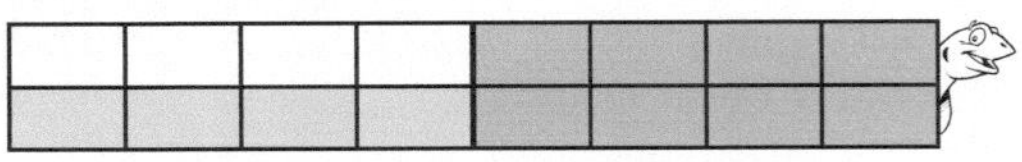

a $\frac{4}{16} = \frac{\square}{4}$ **b** $\frac{8}{16} = \frac{\square}{2}$

c $\frac{6}{16} = \frac{\square}{8}$ **d** $1 = \frac{\square}{16}$

10 Use 24-hour time to write the time:

a one hour after 4 pm ______

b 12 hours before 4 pm ______

11 Is 68 × 8 less than 69 × 11? ______

31:4 ☐ out of 6

Extension

1 Complete each pattern.

a 0·34, 0·36, 0·38, ______, ______, ______

b 0·62, 0·66, 0·7, ______, ______, ______

2 Our numeral for CCLXIV. ______

3 **a** 8 minutes before 12:05 pm. ______

b 20 minutes after 11:55 am. ______

4 (2 × 3) + (3 × 3) ______

5 Which part is the: $\frac{7}{10}$

a numerator? ______

b denominator? ______

c Which of the fractions shaded would have the smaller denominator? ______

6 I must choose an item from each square. How many groups are possible? ______

Challenge

Write equivalent fractions for:

a $\frac{1}{2}$ *b* $\frac{1}{3}$ *c* $\frac{1}{4}$

Codes

Use this code to write *true* or *false* for each code statement.

A	B	C	D	E	F	G	H	I	J	K	L	M	N	O	P	Q	R	S	T	U	V	
4	9	6	?	/	2	$	+	5	<	&	0	>	7	#	1	=	8	3	*	(	)	•

a *+8//•>#8/•*+47•757/•53•/=(40•*#•*+58*//7. ______

b 641*457 •6##& •64>/•28#> •/7$047? •0#7$ •4$#. ______

c 400 •6#(7*57$ •7(>9/83 •+4)/ •#7/ •43 •4 •246*#8. ______

32:1 ☐ out of 18

❶ 0 × 17 _____

❷ 17 + 27 _____

❸ 18 − 6 _____

❹ 14 − 9 _____

❺ $\begin{array}{r} 186 \\ +\ 38 \\ \hline \end{array}$

❻ 10 × 50 _____

❼ 100 + 14 _____

❽ Take 3 from 37. _____

❾ Triple 12. _____

❿ $\begin{array}{r} 417 \\ -136 \\ \hline \end{array}$

⓫ Would you use millilitres or litres to measure the water in a bathtub?

____

⓬ How many \$10 notes have the same value as \$40? _____

⓭ Is 529 closer to 500 or 600? _____

⓮ \$3.20 = _____ cents.

⓯ In a 100 m race, I fell after running 85 m. How far was I from the finish?

_____

⓰ Centimetres in 3 metres. _____

⓱ What year would be 9 years after 2013? _____

⓲

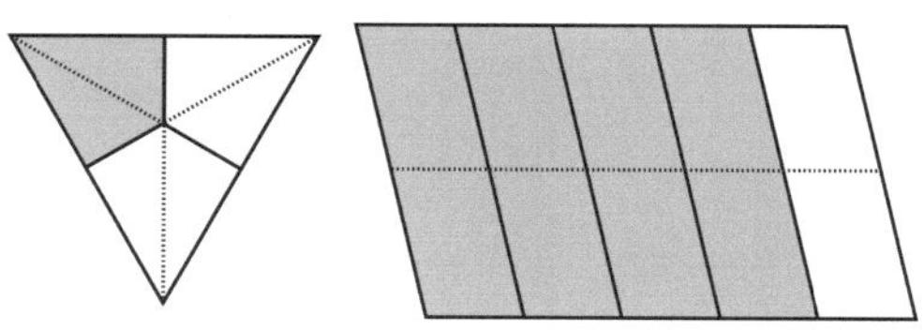

a $\frac{2}{6} = \frac{\square}{3}$ b $\frac{8}{10} = \frac{\square}{5}$

32:2 ☐ out of 18

❶ 24 + 50 _____

❷ 8 + 13 _____

❸ 22 − 12 _____

❹ 31 − 2 _____

❺ $\begin{array}{r} 612 \\ +\ 97 \\ \hline \end{array}$

❻ 10 × 74 _____

❼ 9 × 6 _____

❽ 82 × 10 _____

❾ \$21 + \$11 + \$5 _____

❿ $\begin{array}{r} \$227 \\ -\$188 \\ \hline \end{array}$

⓫ The abbreviation for 'litre'. _____

⓬ Write 3:27 as analogue time. __________

⓭ One table is 2 m long. What is the total length of 4 tables? _____

⓮ Sam has 20 books and Gino has 3 times as many. How many books do the boys have altogether?

_____

⓯ An exercise book costs \$2.40. Circle the best estimate for the cost of 9 books.

\$10   \$20   \$30   \$50

⓰ An angle larger than a straight angle is called a

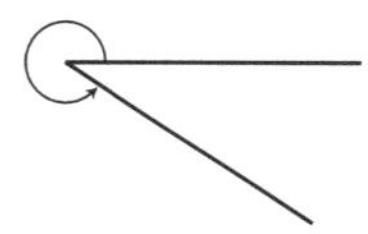

__________ angle.

⓱ 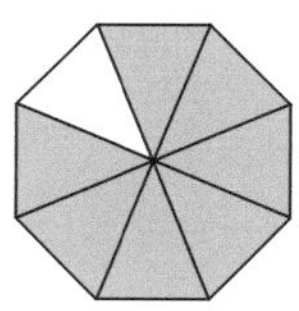

What is the chance, as a fraction, that the spinner will land on:

a white? _____

b grey? _____

⓲ Use am or pm to write 13:43. _____

 ISBN 978 1 4886 2189 5

32:3 ☐ out of 12

❶
```
  243
×   4
```

❷
```
  1305
×    8
```

❸
```
  1135
×    6
```

❹ Estimate 439 + 35.

E = _____ + _____

= _____

❺ Estimate 475 – 233.

E = _____ – _____

= _____

❻ 15 mL  60 mL 

How many caps of water are needed to fill the eggcup? _____

❼ An obtuse angle is between 90° and 180°. What is a reflex angle between?

_____

❽ How many nails in three packets of 32? _____

❾ Is each angle acute or obtuse?

a 78° _____ **b** 96° _____

❿ Share 27 pens among 3 girls.

One share = _____

⓫ **a** 142 more than 18. _____

b 142 more than 318. _____

c 142 more than 5318. _____

⓬ 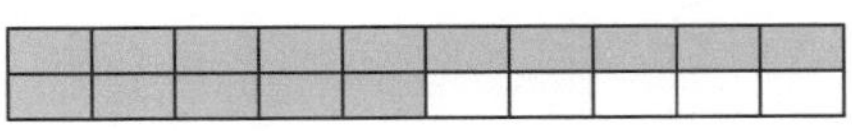

a $\frac{3}{4} = \frac{\square}{20}$ **b** $\frac{1}{2} = \frac{\square}{20}$

c $\frac{2}{20} = \frac{\square}{10}$ **d** $\frac{1}{20} = \frac{\square}{10}$

32:4 ☐ out of 7 Extension

❶ The Roman numeral for 329. _____

❷ **a** 2·5, 3·5, 4·5, _____, _____, _____

b 0·8, 1·0, 1·2, _____, _____, _____

❸ How many minutes are there from 9:35 am until 11:14 am? _____

❹ What fraction of this shape is shaded? 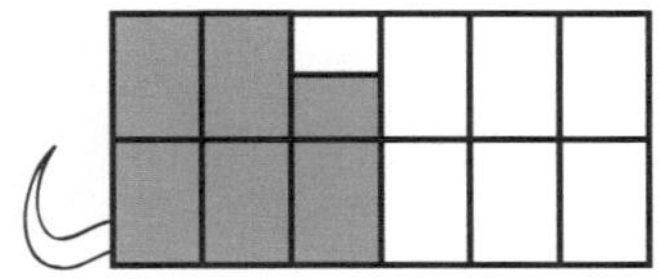

_____

❺ **a** 2·5 L = _____ mL **b** 800 mL = _____ L

❻ How many axes of symmetry has:

a a regular heptagon? (This has 7 sides.) _____

b a regular nonagon? (This has 9 sides.) _____

❼ How many diagonals has a:

a pentagon? _____ **b** hexagon? _____

Challenge

Draw and label different types of angles.

In a magic square, the sum of each row, column and diagonal is the same.

11	6	7
4	8	12
9	10	5

Here, all lines add up to 24.

Complete these magic squares.

a

8	3	4
	5	9
6		

b

9		5
2		10
7		3

c

8		
9	7	
		6

33:1 | out of 15

1. 1 × 77 ______
2. 40 – 6 ______
3. 14 ÷ 2 ______
4. 10 + 99 ______
5. $\begin{array}{r} 6238 \\ +\ \ 280 \\ \hline \end{array}$
6. 18 ÷ 3 ______
7. 102 – 10 ______
8. 74 take away 10. ______
9. 9 lots of 4. ______
10. $\begin{array}{r} 5050 \\ +\ \ 860 \\ \hline \end{array}$

11. Round these numbers to the nearest hundred.
    a 754 ______ **b** 587 ______
12. What must we add to $16 to get $21? ______
13. 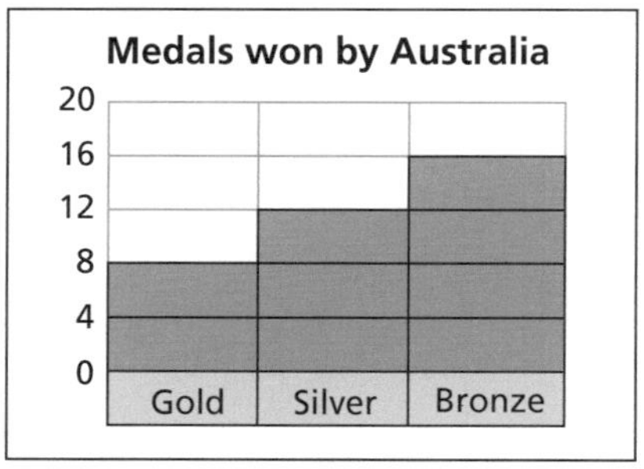

    a How many of each medal were won?
    G = ______ S = ______ B = ______
    b The type of medal won most. ______
    c How many more Bronze than Gold were won? ______
14. Which part is the: $\frac{3}{4}$
    a numerator? ______
    b denominator? ______
15. Metres in 1 kilometre. ______

332 | out of 16

1. 8 × 4 ______
2. 23 – 5 ______
3. 45 ÷ 5 ______
4. 36 + 14 ______
5. $\begin{array}{r} 6854 \\ -\ \ 861 \\ \hline \end{array}$
6. 80 – 8 ______
7. 59 × 10 ______
8. Halve 178. ______
9. Add 99 and 11. ______
10. $\begin{array}{r} 6000 \\ -5882 \\ \hline \end{array}$
11. Write an equivalent fraction for:
    a $\frac{1}{3}\frac{(\times 2)}{(\times 2)} =$ ______ **b** $\frac{4}{5}\frac{(\times 3)}{(\times 3)} =$ ______
12. What is the total quantity held by these bottles? ______

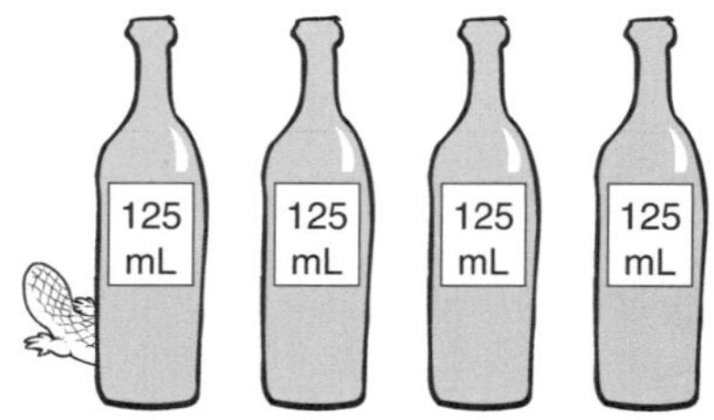

13. Millilitres in $5\frac{1}{2}$ L. ______
14. **a** $\frac{1}{2} = \frac{\square}{12}$
    b $\frac{1}{4} = \frac{\square}{12}$

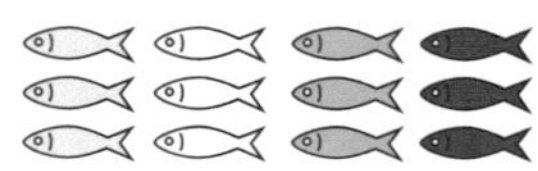

15. I scored 83 out of 100 in a test. How many more marks did I need to score 100? ______
16. **a** 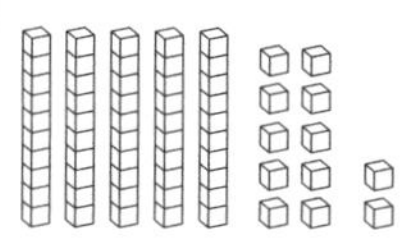
    62 – 34 = ______
    b 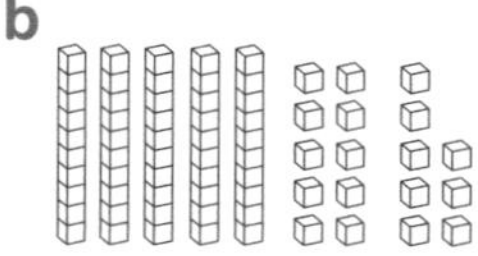
    68 – 29 = ______

Turn to ID Card B on page 7.
Give the answers for these numbers.

(9) ______ line
(10) ______ line
(12) ______ of an angle
(14) ______ angle
(15) ______ angle
(16) ______ angle
(17) ______ angle
(18) ______
(24) ______ of ______
(26) ______

333 | out of 12

1 106 × 8

2 203 × 4

3 1014 × 3

4 Estimate 27 × 12.

E = ______ + ______

= ______

5 Estimate 35 × 253.

E = ______ + ______

= ______

6 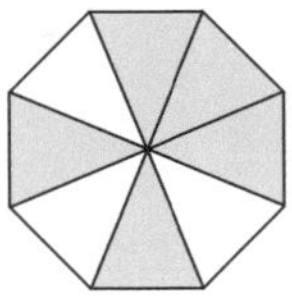

What is the chance, as a fraction, that the spinner will land on:

a white? ______

b grey? ______

7 300 mL of milk is left in a 2 L milk container. How much has been used?

______

8 How many 250 mL glasses can I fill with 3 L of water?

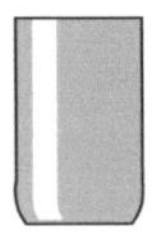

______

9 How many right angles are needed to make a revolution?

______

10 Grams in $4\frac{1}{2}$ kg. ______

11 **a** 121 more than 29. ______

b 121 more than 329. ______

c 121 more than 4 329. ______

12 **a** $\frac{1}{2} = \frac{\square}{12}$

b $\frac{1}{4} = \frac{\square}{12}$

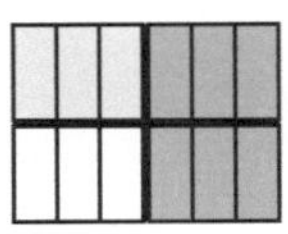

33:4 | Extension | out of 5

1 Is $\frac{3}{5}$ equal to $\frac{9}{10}$? ______

2 Round off 6 543 correct to the nearest hundred. ______

3 An octagon with the head of a tiger inside it, represents 80 tigers. What number is represented below:

______

4 The name of a polygon with:

a 7 sides ______

b 9 sides ______

5 How many axes-of-symmetry has:

a a regular decagon? ______

b a regular dodecagon? (This has 12 sides.) ______

Challenge

List events that have a chance of $\frac{1}{2}$.

______

______

______

______

______

______

Roman numerals

1	I	one finger
5	V	one hand
10	X	two Vs
50	L	half of a C
100	C	centum = 100
500	D	half of an ⊕
1000	M	mille = 1000

IX = 10 − 1 = 9 | XC = 100 − 10 | CD = 500 − 100

1 Write our numeral for:

a XXXIX ______ **b** XL ______

c CCCIV ______ **d** CD ______

e DCXXI ______ **f** MDLI ______

2 Write the Roman numeral for:

a 65 ______ **b** 240 ______

c 966 ______ **d** 2 500 ______

e 392 ______ **f** 1 999 ______

AUSTRALIAN SIGNPOST MATHS 5 MENTALS • ISBN 978 1 4886 2189 5

34:1

out of 15

1. 30 ÷ 10 ______
2. 4 × 5 ______
3. 16 – 2 ______
4. 19 + 6 ______
5. $\begin{array}{r} 859 \\ +533 \\ \hline \end{array}$
6. 15 – 5 ______
7. 26 ÷ 2 ______
8. Add 9 and 4. ______
9. 60 × 4 ______
10. $\begin{array}{r} 452 \\ +163 \\ \hline \end{array}$

11. a Centimetres in 1 m 17 cm. ______
    b Write 351 cm in metres and centimetres. ______
12. Morgan owes his father $90. If he pays $10 a week, for how many weeks will he have to pay? ______
13. Fifty grams in short form. ______
14. 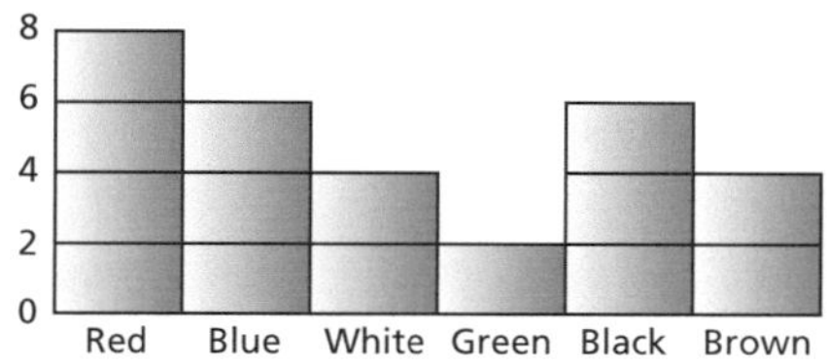

    a How many white cars? ______
    b What colour is least popular? ______
    c What colour is most popular? ______
    d How many blue, black and brown cars altogether? ______
    e How many cars altogether? ______
15. a Grams in a $\frac{1}{2}$ kilogram. ______
    b Grams in $1\frac{1}{2}$ kilograms. ______

34:2

out of 17

1. 6 × 4 ______
2. 79 – 10 ______
3. 62 ÷ 2 ______
4. 45 + 45 ______
5. $\begin{array}{r} 639 \\ +281 \\ \hline \end{array}$
6. 81 ÷ 9 ______
7. Halve 94. ______
8. 5 lots of 3. ______
9. 65 + 9 ______
10. $\begin{array}{r} 1000 \\ -\ \ 148 \\ \hline \end{array}$
11. Grams in 4 kilograms. ______
12. Use the short form to write 1 metre 17 centimetres. ______
13. Round off 1 296 to the nearest thousand. ______
14. Tonnes in 17 000 kg. ______
15. Multiply the numerator and denominator by 2 to find an equivalent fraction.
    a $\frac{1}{3}$ = ______ b $\frac{4}{5}$ = ______
16. The mass in kg of 16 elephants if each has a mass of 4 tonnes.

______

17. a 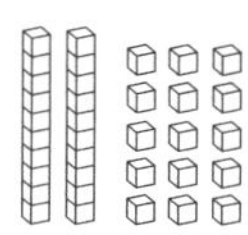
    35 − 17 = ______
    b 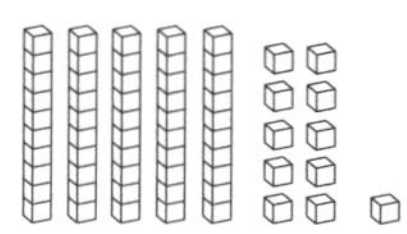
    61 − 39 = ______

Which total is easiest to throw using two dice?

a Which total would you choose? ______

b Toss two dice 50 times. Keep a tally of these results in the table below.

Number	1	2	3	4	5	6	7	8	9	10	11	12
Tally												

c Which total occurred most often? ______

34:3 ☐ out of 12

1
$$\begin{array}{r} \$83.42 \\ \$12.21 \\ +\$\ \ 1.13 \\ \hline \end{array}$$

2
$$\begin{array}{r} 400 \\ \times\ \ \ 8 \\ \hline \end{array}$$

3
$$\begin{array}{r} 4620 \\ \times\ \ \ \ 3 \\ \hline \end{array}$$

4 Estimate 42 × 12.

E = _____ + _____

= __________

5 Estimate 536 × 34.

E = _____ + _____

= __________

6 6 m 80 cm = ________ centimetres.

7 Grams in 4 kg. ________

8 Round off 56 761 to the nearest thousand. ________

9 What change do I get from $50 if buy 3 bears? ________

10 Write the equivalent fraction for:

a $\frac{3}{4}\ \frac{(\times 2)}{(\times 2)} =$ _____ **b** $\frac{2}{3}\ \frac{(\times 4)}{(\times 4)} =$ _____

11

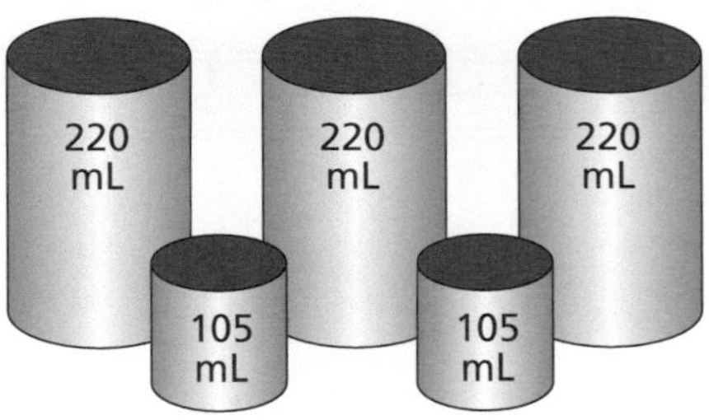

Find the total capacity. ________

12 **a** 247 more than 32. ________

b 247 more than 332. ________

c 247 more than 4 332. ________

34:4 ☐ out of 4

Extension

1 I make rings that have a mass of 25 g, 58 g, 73 g or 99 g. I weighed four of the rings. Their total mass was 318 g. Which rings were weighed?

____

2 I bought at least one of each of these items. The total cost was $3.25. How many oranges did I buy?

$1.10

35c

____

3 A truck can carry 10 tonnes. How many trips would be needed to carry 125 tonnes?

____

4 An astronaut can orbit a planet four times in a month. How many times could he orbit it in 8 years?

____

Challenge

List objects that would be measured in:

g	kg	t

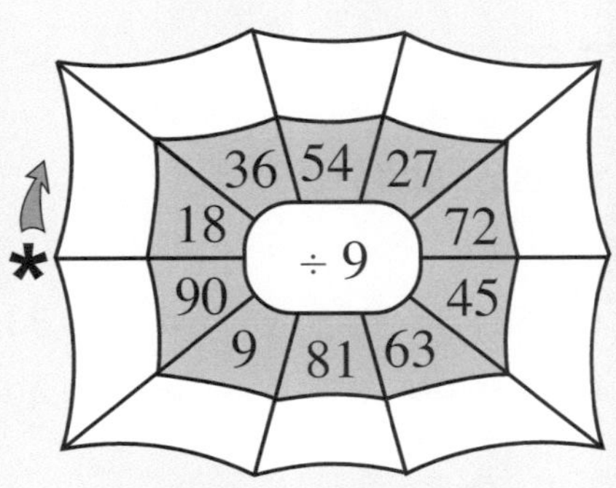

9 × 7 = 63
63 ÷ 9 = 7

35:1 ☐ out of 20

❶ 18 − 17 ____

❷ 19 + 4 ____

❸ 64 ÷ 2 ____

❹ 7 × 5 ____

❺
```
  625
+200
```

❻ 40 × 4 ____

❼ 28 − 16 ____

❽ Divide 40 by 5. ____

❾ Half of 22. ____

❿
```
 62
× 3
```

⓫ Does 100 cm equal 1 metre? ____

⓬ Centimetres in 3 metres. ____

⓭ 14, 21, 28 are multiples of ____.

⓮ Charlotte's change from $5 if she bought an ice-cream for $1.50?

____

⓯ Use the short form to write:

a two hundred grams ____

b thirty-seven kilograms ____

⓰ Mark has $3.20. Bananas cost 60 cents each. How many can he buy? ____

⓱ Enlarge this drawing.

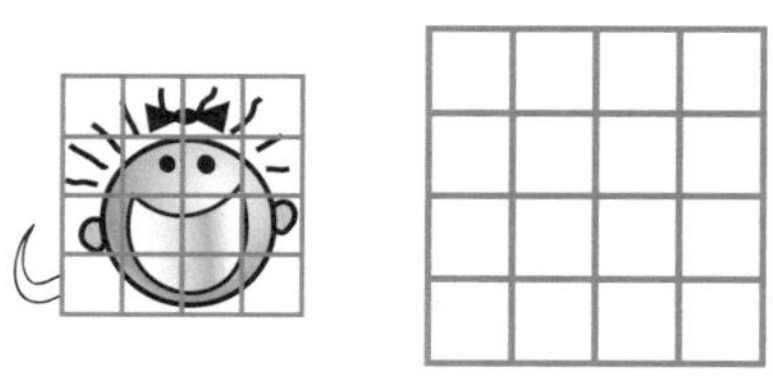

⓲ 150 cm − 80 cm ____

⓳ Centimetres in 1 metre. ____

⓴ Grams in 2 kg. ____

35:2 ☐ out of 16

❶ 9 + 8 ____

❷ 6 × 9 ____

❸ 32 − 4 ____

❹ 21 − 2 ____

❺
```
 613
+ 97
```

❻ 100 × 6 ____

❼ 17 + 16 ____

❽ 33 ÷ 3. ____

❾ $12 + $5 + $1 ____

❿
```
 3000
− 452
```

⓫ I have 3 pieces of string. Their lengths are 1 m 30 cm, 1 m 42 cm, and 2 m 15 cm.

What is the total length? ____

⓬ A kite costs $12.30. How much will Megan have to pay for 3 kites?

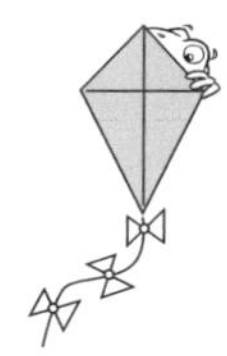

____

⓭ Grams in 3 kg 270 g. ____

⓮ Write the temperature shown.

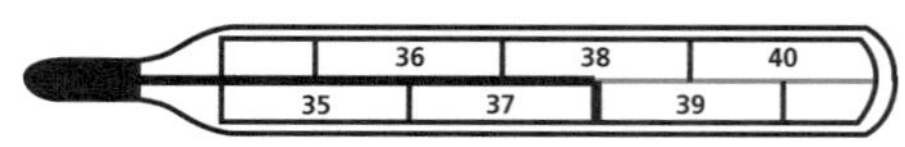

☐ °C

____

⓯ Tonnes in 3 000 kg. ____

⓰ Jacob had $26. He bought these items.

$2.60

$3

$15

Total amount spent: ____

Amount left: ____

Concept

To round to the nearest 5 cents, give the closest answer that ends in 5 or 0.

Cash registers round off correct to the nearest 5 cents if you pay with cash.

a Is $19.98 closer to $19.95 or $20? ____

Round off each of these to the nearest 5 cents.

b $17.68 ____ **c** $21.01 ____ **d** $33.33 ____

e $18.97 ____ **f** $46.96 ____ **g** $52.49 ____

 ISBN 978 1 4886 2189 5

35:3 out of 10

1. $ 23.2 + $ 60.8

2. $ 43.25 + $ 10.73 + $ 21.68

3. $ 14.64 + $ 23.21 + $ 17.56

4. $5\overline{)845}$ r

5. $6\overline{)872}$ r

6. Write 2 m 44 cm in centimetres. ______

7. Is the length of a bed about 2 m, 4 m or 1 m? ______

8. Tiffany had $40. She spent:
   - on food $14.50
   - at the movie $ 7.00
   - on stamps $ 2.25

   Tiffany's total: ______

   Amount of money left: ______

9. Kilograms in 5 t. ______

10. 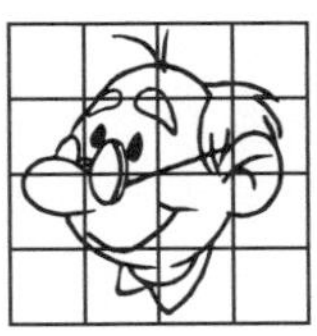

    Draw Mr Dunn, copying one square at a time.

    Is the enlargement factor $\frac{1}{2}$, 2 or 4? ______

35:4 out of 4

Extension

1. 

   How many small Vikings are needed to balance the large one? ______

2. What is the least number of matchsticks needed to make:

   a 2 hexagons? ______

   b 7 hexagons? ______

3. a What fraction of these results are odd? ______

Even	𝍸 𝍸 𝍸 IIII
Odd	𝍸 𝍸 𝍸 I

   b On a die, is the chance of throwing an odd or even number the same? ______

4. 63 – 10 – 5 – 12 ______

Challenge

Draw a picture in the first grid.
Draw it again in the second grid with an enlargement factor of 2.

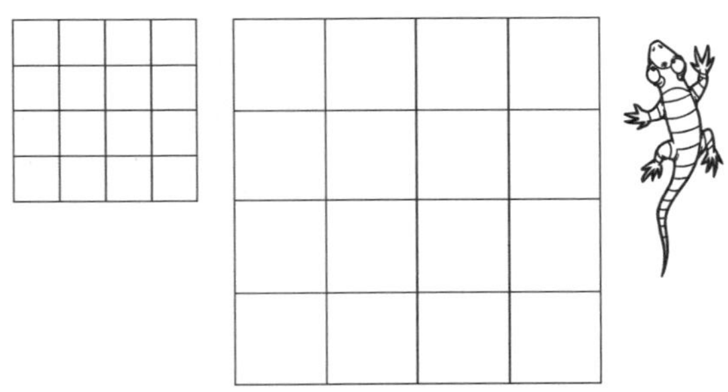

Can you balance this 25 kg mass using only the masses shown below?

Use the columns in the table to show as many answers as you can.

$(2 \times 10) + (1 \times 5) = 25$

10 kg	2								
5 kg	1								
2 kg	0								
1 kg	0								

36:1

Score: ____ out of 21

1. 7 × 4 ____
2. 19 – 17 ____
3. 36 ÷ 6 ____
4. 18 + 8 ____
5. $\begin{array}{r} 1423 \\ \times \quad 3 \\ \hline \end{array}$
6. 10 + 11 ____
7. 8 lots of 1. ____
8. Divide 40 by 8. ____
9. 21 take away 5. ____
10. $\begin{array}{r} 2396 \\ + \ 231 \\ \hline \end{array}$
11. The abbreviation for 'metres'. ____
12. Centimetres in a metre. ____
13.

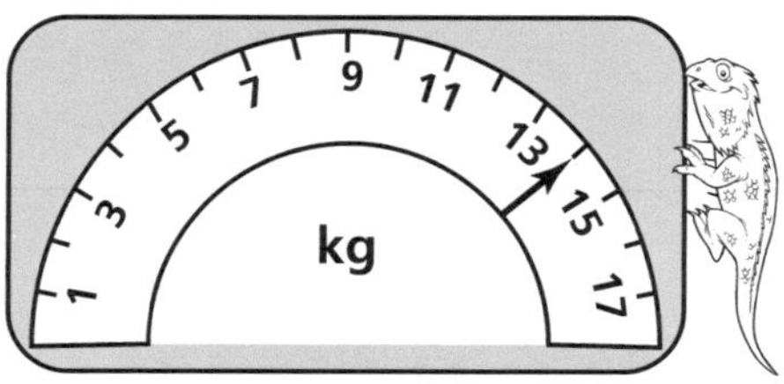

The measure is ____ kg.

14. Write 2 metres and 39 centimetres as centimetres. ____ cm
15. $\frac{5}{8}$ means ____ out of ____.
16. Litres in 5 000 mL. ____
17. How many grams in 4 kg 600 g? ____
18. Michael earned $50 but spent $10.50 on fares and $6.50 on food. How much does he have left? ____
19. Will a cup hold more than 1 litre? ____
20. Milk is measured in ____.
21. Centimetres in 2 metres. ____

36:2

Score: ____ out of 12

1. 15 – 4 ____
2. 42 ÷ 6 ____
3. 9 × 10 ____
4. 70 ÷ 7 ____
5. $\begin{array}{r} 9801 \\ + \ 835 \\ \hline \end{array}$
6. 22 – 11 ____
7. 8 × 8 ____
8. 8 times 11. ____
9. Add 38 and 42. ____
10. $\begin{array}{r} 3209 \\ + \quad 19 \\ \hline \end{array}$
11. Enlarge this shape by a factor of 2.

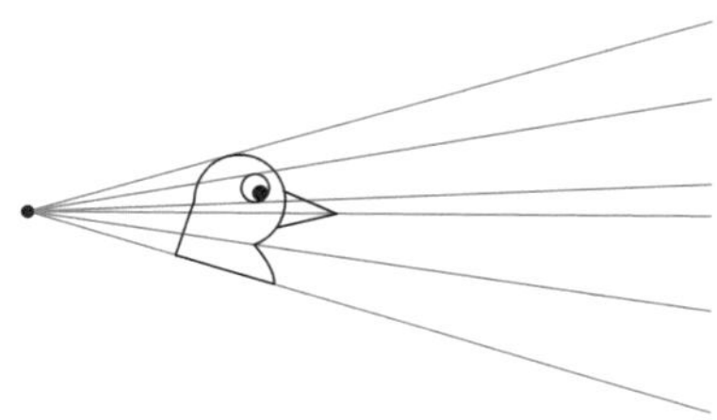

12.

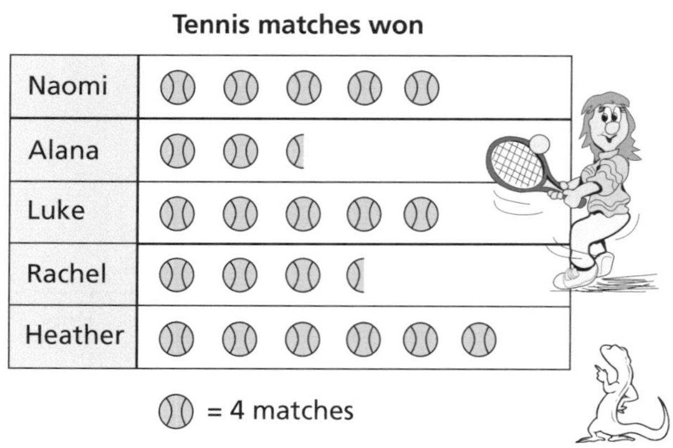

a How many matches were won by Alana? ____

b Which player won 14 matches? ____

c Which player won more than 20 matches? ____

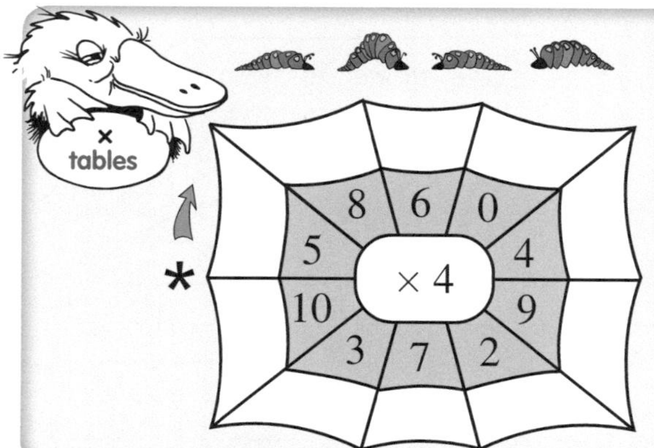

36:3 ☐ out of 12

❶
```
  $ 24.31
  $  7.20
+ $ 10.14
```

❷
```
  $ 83.20
  $ 21.60
+ $ 16.10
```

❸
```
  $ 18.71
  $ 24.38
+ $ 19.06
```

❹ $3\overline{)750}$

❺ $10\overline{)460}$

❻ $10\overline{)273}$ r

❼ What is the probability, as a fraction, of tossing a 3 on a regular dice? ______

❽ **a** This is a ______ note.

(green)

b The value of three of these. ______

❾

$ 2.40	$ 6.35	$ 7.95

a What is the total cost of the star, the car and the drum? ______

b How much change would you get from $10 if you buy the star and the car? ______

❿ Use the decimal form to write 93 mm as centimetres. ______

⓫ Grams in 1 kilogram. ______

⓬ 3 metres can also be written as: ______

36:4 ☐ out of 5

Extension

❶ The masses of four boxes are 3 kg, 580 g, 1 kg 56 g and 2 300 g.

What is the total mass? ______

❷ This figure has hexagons of different size and shape. How many hexagons are there altogether? ______

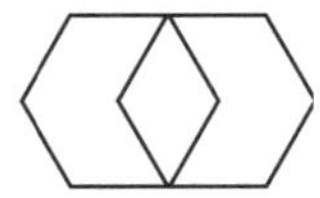

❸ What is the smallest number of matchsticks needed to make:

a 2 small triangles? ______

b 5 small triangles? ______

❹ In how many different ways can you make 45 cents using only 5c, 10c and 20c coins? ______

❺ How many diagonals on 25 hexagons?

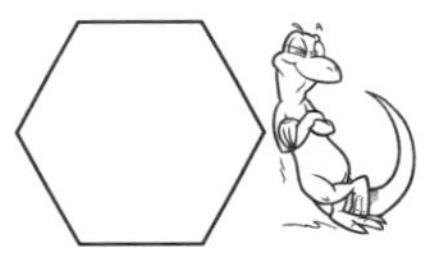

______

Challenge

Draw a picture in the first grid.
Draw it again in the second grid with an enlargement factor of $\frac{1}{2}$.

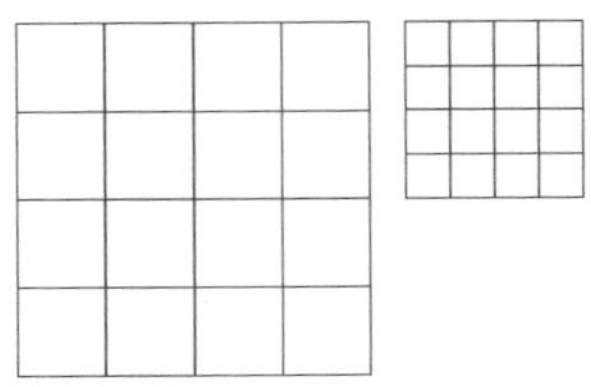

a How many stakes are needed for a fence 30 m long if the stakes are 5 m apart? ______

b The sum of two numbers is 11 and their product is 24. What are the numbers? ______

c The average of two numbers is 9. If one number is 4, what is the other? ______

37:1 ☐ out of 20

1. 99 − 5 ____
2. 18 + 60 ____
3. 9 × 9 ____
4. 42 ÷ 7 ____
5. $\begin{array}{r} 2750 \\ \times \quad 3 \\ \hline \end{array}$
6. 40 − 8 ____
7. 600 ÷ 6 ____
8. 8 lots of 6. ____
9. 7 times 8. ____
10. $\begin{array}{r} 1458 \\ \times \quad 2 \\ \hline \end{array}$

11. The abbreviation for 'centimetres'. ____
12. 68% means ____ out of ____.
13. Which month comes two months after August? ____
14. Halves in $7\frac{1}{2}$. ____

15. What year is it 4 years after 2017? ____
16. Days in 3 weeks. ____
17. The product of 5 and 8. ____
18. The change from $2 if Andrew spent 75c. ____
19. **a** Dad's hat cost $18.20. What was the change from $30? ____

    b How many of these hats can be bought with $80? ____
20. Colour 46% of this hundred square.

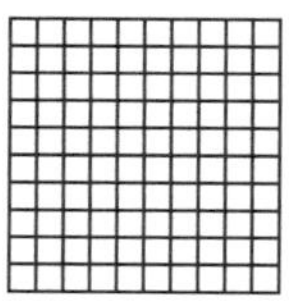

37:2 ☐ out of 15

1. 7 × 9 ____
2. 20 − 11 ____
3. 36 ÷ 9 ____
4. 8 × 8 ____
5. $\begin{array}{r} 6{\cdot}54 \\ +1{\cdot}07 \\ \hline \end{array}$
6. 35 ÷ 7 ____
7. 9 × 8 ____
8. Take 15 from 80. ____
9. Add 77 and 9. ____
10. $\begin{array}{r} 7{\cdot}50 \\ -3{\cdot}24 \\ \hline \end{array}$
11. Write the missing fraction and decimal.

34%	——	0·____

12. What type of angle is between 0° and 90°? ____
13. Arrange from smallest to largest.
    6307, 6370, 6730
    ____
14. Rewrite 2·73 m as metres and centimetres.
    ____
15. 

    a How many has Rajiv won? ____
    b How many more has Mark won than Kari? ____
    c How many have Rajiv and Kari won altogether? ____

Turn to ID Card C on page 8.
Give the answers for these numbers.

(19) 3 out of ____
(20) $\frac{\square}{10}$ shaded
(21) $\frac{\square}{10}$ shaded
(22) $\frac{\square}{10}$ shaded
(23) 0·____ shaded
(24) 0·____ shaded
(26) 19 out of ____
(27) ____ % shaded
(28) ____ · ____
(30) $0{\cdot}3 = \frac{\square}{10}$, $0{\cdot}30 = \frac{\square}{10}$

© PEARSON AUSTRALIA 2018 • *AUSTRALIAN SIGNPOST MATHS 5 MENTALS* • ISBN 978 1 4886 2189 5

37:3

[ ] out of 14

1.
```
 5631
  209
+1434
```

2.
```
 $ 2.99
 $21.63
+$13.05
```

3.
```
 $22.31
 $40.62
+$18.07
```

4. $3\overline{)201}$

5. $2\overline{)830}$

6. $6\overline{)456}$

7. Is 354 closer to 300 or 400? ______

8. Complete the following.

a

$\frac{37}{100}$	0•	%

b

$\frac{96}{100}$	0•	%

9. If lengths on a drawing are 5 times larger than the real thing, what is the scale? ______

10. I bought a dress for $8.50, a hat for $12 and socks for $7.80. What is the change from $50? ______

11. I read 18 pages of my book each night for one week. How many pages did I read? ______

12. 23 × 31
= (20 × 30) + (20 × 1) + (3 × 30) + (3 × 1)
= ______

13. 0·43 = ______ out of ______ = ______%.

14. **a** 9·37 m = ______ m and ______ cm
b 5 m 23 cm = ______ m

37:4

Extension

[ ] out of 7

1. I spent $7.40 on four items like these. What did I buy?

______

2. **a** 0·7 ÷ 7 ______
b 0·7 ÷ 10 ______
c 0·7 ÷ 2 ______
d 0·7 ÷ 5 ______

0·7 = 0·70

3. A plane ticket to Armidale costs $174. What is the cost of:

a 5 tickets? ______
b 6 tickets? ______

4. (6 × 3) + 7 – 9 ______

5. Minutes in $3\frac{3}{4}$ hours. ______

6. 49 – 21 – 13 – 8 ______

7. What must we add to $83.29 to make $100? ______

Challenge

Complete this table.

Fraction	Decimal	Percentage
$\frac{20}{100}$	0·20	20%
	0·41	
		86%

Fill out this table about yourself, a relative or a friend.

Name: ______ **Date:** ______

Age:	______	Mass:	______ kg	Shoe size:	______
Height:	______ cm	Waist:	______ cm	Neck size:	______ cm

How have these measurements changed since Unit 1 was done?

______

Examples of Measurements

1
- The **width of your finger** is about **1 cm**.
- The **length of a place-value tens block** is **10 cm**.

2
- The **height of the girl** is a little more than **1 m**.

3
- The **container of milk** holds **2 L**.
- The **can of Fizz** holds **375 mL**.
- The **teaspoon** holds **5 mL**.

4
- The **boy** has a mass of **40 kg**.
- The **margarine** has a mass of **500 g**.

5
- **A double page of the newspaper** has an area of **half of 1 m²**.
- The **top of a place-value ones block** has an area of **1 cm²**.

6
- **30°C** is a **hot** day.
- **3°C** is a very **cold** day.

Use the pictures above to estimate the answers to these questions.

1 a How high is the glass?
b How wide is the table?

2 a How wide would the clothes line be?
b How tall is the mother?

3 a How much will the bucket hold?
b How much will the cup hold?

4 a What is the mass of the dog?
b What is the mass of 2 L of milk?

5 a What is the area of the window?
b What is the area of the top of the matchbox?

6 a What is the temperature on a very hot day?
b What is the temperature on a cool day?